College Reading Skills

Stimulating Selections
for Indifferent Readers

Topics for the Restless

Books in this Series:
The Olive Book
The Brown Book
The Purple Book

Editor: Edward Spargo

Jamestown Publishers
Providence, Rhode Island

Topics for the Restless

COLLEGE READING SKILLS SERIES

Selections from the Black

   701 - The Olive Book, ISBN 0-89061-000-2

   702 - The Brown Book, ISBN 0-89061-001-0

   703 - The Purple Book, ISBN 0-89061-002-9

Voices from the Bottom

   721 - The Olive Book, ISBN 0-89061-003-7

   722 - The Brown Book, ISBN 0-89061-004-5

   723 - The Purple Book, ISBN 0-89061-005-3

Topics for the Restless

   741 - The Olive Book, ISBN 0-89061-006-1

   742 - The Brown Book, ISBN 0-89061-007-X

   743 - The Purple Book, ISBN 0-89061-008-8

Cover and Text Design by Stephen R. Anthony

Layout and Illustrations by Mary M. Macdonald

Cover Photograph by Bob Emerson

Printed in the United States
80 81 82 83 9 8 7 6 5 4 3

Readability
Selections 2-10: Level L
Selections 11-20: Level M
Selections 21-30: Level M

Preface

Topics for the Restless, as the name implies, seeks to fill a need which exists in reading improvement instruction—that of relevant, timely and stimulating reading selections; selections which will appeal to indifferent readers.

While many anthologies are available today which do offer relevant reading matter, none of these contain the systematic presentation of questions, exercises and instruction needed by older students who are poor readers.

The opportunity for continuous diagnosis through the comprehension question labels, coupled with the use of adult literature exclusively, makes *Topics for the Restless* a unique three-book program.

As part of the nine-book College Reading Skills series, *Topics for the Restless* complements *Selections from the Black* and *Voices from the Bottom.* Collectively, these nine texts provide a complete, graded, organized and relevant program of reading improvement for older students and adults of all backgrounds and all interests.

As with any text, no editor works alone, and the efforts of many are represented here.

I am grateful most of all to my wife for her encouragement, her search for suitable materials, and her efforts to obtain reprint permissions. I am grateful also to Mary M. Macdonald for the illustrations and James and Livia Giroux for the comprehension questions and vocabulary exercises. The customary fine service and excellent cooperation of the Providence Public Library personnel is also appreciated.

E.S.

Contents

Part Three: Selections 21—30

Answer Key

Part One
Introductory Selection
Selections 2-10

Topics for the Restless

Introductory Selection

Explains How the Text Is Organized and How to Use It to Maximum Advantage

(Before you begin reading this selection, turn to page 13 and record the hours and minutes on the line labeled *Starting Time* in the box at the bottom of the second column. If you are using this text in class and your instructor has made provisions for timing, you need not stop now; read on.)

You are using this text for two purposes: (1) to improve your reading skills, and (2) to read articles and selections designed to make you think. Not every selection will be so demanding, however; many articles were chosen just for pure reading pleasure and enjoyment.

An effort was made to find and include writings which show the real world, the world we all have to face daily.

These selections span the range of human experience. On these pages you will read and learn about current problems facing our society: the use and abuse of alcohol and drugs, the struggle of women for recognition as free and independent beings, the seemingly unsolvable problem of disposing of garbage and other wastes of industrial production.

Many selections deal with the quality of our environment and possible new life styles we may be forced to adopt in the future unless we deal now with air and water pollution, population growth, supplying food needs, caring for the homeless and aged with dignity and respect.

However, many selections treat of some of the more pleasant concerns of today's older and mature student. And, finally, some selections just make for enjoyable reading.

Do not expect every selection to be equally interesting to you. In such a wide distribution of subject matter there are bound to be stories which will turn you on, but turn others off. Selections which may bore you, and therefore be hard to read and understand, may very well spark the interest of another reader.

Such a situation cannot be avoided. The book which appeals exclusively to you has never been written. But, be not discouraged. Many situations you encounter in the everyday world require you to read and master material which you consider dull and uninteresting.

A serious student, therefore, will approach each selection in this text with equal enthusiasm and a determination to succeed. This is the kind of attitude to develop toward reading—an attitude which will serve you well for the rest of your life.

The other purpose for using this text, that of reading and study improvement, recognizes reality, too: the reality of today. This text will help you to develop skills and techniques necessary for efficiency in our society.

Today's reader must be flexible, must choose from a repertory of skills those suitable for the reading task at hand. The skilled reader has learned that there is no one best way to read everything, that each kind of reading matter demands a corresponding kind of reading technique. As you complete the selections and exercises in this book, you will find yourself growing in technique.

USING THE TEXT

The thirty selections are designed to be read in numerical order, starting with the Introductory Selection and ending with Selection 30. Because the selections increase in difficulty as you progress through the book, the earlier ones prepare you to handle successfully the upcoming ones.

Here are the procedures to follow when reading each selection.

1. **Preview before Reading.** Previewing acquaints you with the overall content and structure of the selection before you actually read. It is like consulting a road map before taking a trip: planning the route gives you more confidence as you proceed and, perhaps, helps you avoid any unnecessary delays. Previewing should take about a minute or two and is done in this way:

a) Read the Title. Learn the writer's subject and, possibly, his point of view on it.

b) Read the Opening and Closing Paragraphs. These contain the introductory and concluding remarks. Important information is frequently presented in these key paragraphs.

c) Skim Through. Try to discover the author's approach to his subject. Does he use many examples? Is his purpose to sell you his ideas? What else can you learn now to help you when you read?

2. **Read the Selection.** Do not try to race through. Read well and carefully enough so that you can answer the comprehension questions which follow.

Keep track of your reading time by noting when you start and finish. A table on page 173 converts your reading time to a words-per-minute rate. Select the time from the table which is closest to your reading time. Record these figures in the box at the end of the selection. There is no one ideal reading speed for everything. The efficient reader varies his speed as the selection requires.

Many selections include a brief biography and perhaps a photograph of the author. Do not include this reading in your time. It is there to introduce you to the writer. Many of the selections have been reprinted from full-length books and novels. Complete information is contained in a bibliography (list of books) on page 170. If you find a particular selection interesting, you may enjoy reading the entire book.

3. **Answer Vocabulary and Comprehension Questions.** Immediately following each selection is a vocabulary exercise for you to complete. The vocabulary exercises are designed to help you improve your ability to use context (the surrounding words) as an aid to understanding words. The efficient use of context is a valuable vocabulary tool.

Each exercise contains five words from the selection, reprinted in context to help you recall how the words were used. Also given is the location of each word in the selection so that, if necessary, you can find it again and read the adjoining sentences to understand it better. The exercise asks you to select the best of the four meanings accompanying each word.

As you complete the exercises, keep in mind that the precise meaning of a word depends largely on how it is used. Because dictionaries normally list several meanings for a single word, two or three of the choices in a vocabulary exercise may be "dictionary correct," but only one is the *best* meaning for the word as used in this context.

After you complete the vocabulary exercise, turn the page to find the comprehension questions. These have been included to test your understanding of what you have read. The questions are diagnostic, too. Because the comprehension skill being measured is identified, you can detect your areas of weakness.

Read each question carefully and, without looking back, select one of the four choices given which

answers that question most accurately or most completely. Frequently all four choices, or options, given for a question are *correct*, but one is the *best* answer. For this reason the comprehension questions are highly challenging and require you to be highly discriminating. You may, from time to time, disagree with the choice given in the Answer Key. When this happens, you have an opportunity to sharpen your powers of discrimination. Study the question again and seek to discover why the listed answer may be best. When you disagree with the text, you are thinking; when you objectively analyze and recognize your errors, you are learning.

The Answer Key begins on page 165. Find the answers for your selection and correct your comprehension and vocabulary work. When you discover a wrong answer, circle it and check the correct one.

The box following each selection contains space for your comprehension and vocabulary scores. Each correct vocabulary item is worth twenty points and each correct comprehension answer is credited with ten points.

Pages 174 and 175 contain graphs to be used for plotting your scores and tallying your incorrect responses. On page 174 record your comprehension score at the appropriate intersection of lines, using an X. Use a circle, or some other mark, on the same graph to record your vocabulary results. Some students prefer to use different color inks, or pencil and ink, to distinguish between comprehension and vocabulary plottings.

On page 175 fill in the squares to indicate the comprehension questions you have failed. By referring to the Skills Profile as you progress through the text, you and your instructor will be able to tell which kinds of questions give you the most trouble. As soon as you detect a specific weakness in comprehension, consult with your instructor to see what supplementary materials he can provide or suggest.

A profitable habit for you to acquire is the practice of analyzing the questions you have answered incorrectly. If time permits, return to the selection to find and underline the passages containing the correct answers. This helps you to see what you missed the first time. Some interpretive and generalization type questions are not answered specifically in the text. In these cases bracket that part of the selection which alludes to the correct answer. Your instructor may recommend that you complete this step outside of class as homework.

4. **Complete the Accompanying Exercises.** The page preceding the comprehension questions contains exercises designed to improve your word analysis and word meaning skills. The important

areas of phonics, spelling and syllabication, dictionary skills, contextual aids, prefixes, suffixes and roots, and expectancy clues are all covered.

Each exercise contains the directions you need and many of them provide sample items to help you get started. The same answer key you have been using gives the correct responses for these exercises.

If class time is at a premium, your instructor may prefer that you complete these exercises outside of class.

The following selections in this text are structured just like this introductory one. Having completed this selection and its exercises, you will then be prepared to proceed to Selection 2.

Starting Time: _____	Finishing Time: _____
Reading Time: _____	Reading Rate: _____
Comprehension: _____	Vocabulary: _____

VOCABULARY: The following words have been taken from the selection you have just read. Put an *X* in the box before the best meaning or synonym for the word as used in the selection.

1. **seemingly**, page 11, column 1, paragraph 4
   "...the seemingly unsolvable problem of disposing of garbage and other wastes..."
   ☐ a. apparently
   ☐ b. actually
   ☐ c. probably
   ☐ d. totally

2. **distribution**, page 11, column 1, paragraph 7
   "In such a wide distribution of..."
   ☐ a. dispensing
   ☐ b. classification
   ☐ c. spread
   ☐ d. similarity

3. **repertory**, page 11, column 2, paragraph 3
   "...must chose from a repertory of skills..."
   ☐ a. stock
   ☐ b. reputation
   ☐ c. theater
   ☐ d. cast

4. **corresponding**, page 11, column 2, paragraph 3
   "...demands a corresponding kind of reading technique."
   ☐ a. written
   ☐ b. matching
   ☐ c. different
   ☐ d. reporting

5. **efficient**, page 12, column 1, paragraph 5
   "The efficient use of context is a valuable vocabulary tool."
   ☐ a. economical
   ☐ b. active
   ☐ c. knowledgeable
   ☐ d. effective

CONTEXTUAL AIDS: OBJECT OF PREPOSITION

Studies of good readers show that they are aware of the context of what they are reading. This means that they are anticipating what is coming next by what has gone before.

Context refers to the words surrounding those you are reading. These surrounding words create the total situation from which we get meaning. Using the context as an aid to rapid understanding is a valuable tool to the reader.

The many ways in which context functions to help the reader recognize words are called contextual aids.

Contextual Aid. Words can be understood as objects of prepositions. A clue to the meaning of an unknown word is sometimes revealed by the preposition preceding it in a phrase. In the sentence, **He washed up at the ____,** the preposition **at** clues the reader that the missing word is probably **sink**. The preposition **in** would have probably clued the reader to **tub**.

In the following sentences, examples of this type of contextual aid have been used, followed by nonsense words. Underline the nonsense word and write the correct word on the line following each sentence. The first one has been done for you.

1. So that he would not be seen, he traveled by slint.

   _____

2. The circus performer slipped from the wire but landed in the tul.

   _____

3. We've no time to lose; do it at ponb.

   _____

4. He is not home; he is busy at remok.

   _____

5. You cannot tell me it was an accident; he did it on bontage.

   _____

6. The speech was broadcast over the salipar but was not televised.

   _____

7. The prisoners hid until dark and then climbed over the mose.

   _____

8. The pitcher, who was weakening, threw a curve to the klomp.

   _____

9. He looked at the manp to tell the time.

   _____

10. The huskies pulled the sled through the knell.

   _____

PREVIEWING

Students frequently ask, "What can I do to improve my reading?" Believe it or not, there is a one-word answer to this question: preview.

The single most important technique which you can acquire in any reading course is the habit of previewing.

Most students (and everyone else, too) jump in with the first word and meet the author's words and ideas head-on. This is a poor approach because it is inefficient.

What do athletic coaches do before upcoming games? They scout the opponents. Why? To see how they play and to form a game plan for the team to follow.

To be efficient in reading you must do this same thing—scout the author to see how he writes and to discover the best way to read him.

What do you do before assembling a jig-saw puzzle? You study the picture to see what the puzzle looks like when the pieces are all in the right places.

Do this too in reading: see the whole picture before you begin putting the words and ideas together. See where the author is going, what he plans to do or say, what concepts or examples he uses to present his ideas. If you can discover the author's main point and his arguments supporting it, you can begin to organize and interpret his ideas right from the start—you can read intelligently—and see how everything fits.

Don't read at a disadvantage. Preview first to get the picture. There are no educational guarantees in life but this is as close as you can come to ensuring better reading and comprehension in less time.

Pregame warm-ups improve performance on the field. Preview to improve your performance on the page.

On the following pages you will learn how to preview and the steps to follow when previewing a selection.

COMPREHENSION: For each of the following statements and questions, select the option containing the most complete or most accurate answer.

1. Reading skills
(f)
   - ☐ a. improve with age and maturity.
   - ☐ b. can be improved through instruction and practice.
   - ☐ c. require a detailed understanding of phonics.
   - ☐ d. are dependent on native intelligence and opportunity.

2. The introductory selection
(g)
   - ☐ a. eliminates the need for oral instruction.
   - ☐ b. explains in detail the proper use of the text.
   - ☐ c. permits the student to learn by doing.
   - ☐ d. allows for variety and interest.

3. *Topics for the Restless* is based on which of
(e) the following premises?
   - ☐ a. All students are restless.
   - ☐ b. Some students learn best when they are restless.
   - ☐ c. Writings dealing with real problems and situations should interest many students.
   - ☐ d. All of the selections in this text should interest all students.

4. The introductory selection suggests that
(h)
   - ☐ a. most readers are not flexible.
   - ☐ b. students will discover their own best way to read.
   - ☐ c. students today read better than students of the past.
   - ☐ d. thirty selections is an ideal number for a reading improvement text.

5. The author considers previewing
(g)
   - ☐ a. essential for efficient reading.
   - ☐ b. more useful for nonfiction than fiction.
   - ☐ c. a student rather than an adult reading technique.
   - ☐ d. important and useful.

6. The editor explains that he expects that some
(b) of the answers given in the key will
   - ☐ a. be completely acceptable.
   - ☐ b. provoke discussion.
   - ☐ c. be incorrect.
   - ☐ d. be easy to understand.

7. The selection stresses the modern reader's
(b) need for
   - ☐ a. a repertory of skills.
   - ☐ b. rapid reading skills.
   - ☐ c. an extensive reading background.
   - ☐ d. comprehension skills.

8. How does he writer feel about reading speed
(f) (rate)?
   - ☐ a. It is a minimal aspect of the total reading situation.
   - ☐ b. It ranks second (following comprehension) in the priority of skills.
   - ☐ c. It is interrelated with comprehension.
   - ☐ d. It should be developed at an early age.

9. How much time should be devoted to pre-
(b) viewing a selection?
   - ☐ a. Time will vary with each selection.
   - ☐ b. About one minute.
   - ☐ c. No specified time is suggested.
   - ☐ d. None; the instructor times the selection.

10. The way the vocabulary exercises are con-
(c) structed suggests that
   - ☐ a. the meaning of a word depends on how it is used.
   - ☐ b. the final authority for word meaning is the dictionary.
   - ☐ c. words have precise and permanent meanings.
   - ☐ d. certain words will be difficult to understand.

> Comprehension Skills: a—isolating details; b—recalling specific facts; c—retaining concepts; d—organizing facts; e—understanding the main idea; f—drawing a conclusion; g—making a judgment; h—making an inference; i—recognizing tone; j—understanding characters; k—appreciation of literary forms.

Are You Really Ready for the Highways?

Before a Long, High-Speed Trip, Check Your Car—and Yourself

Norman Richards

My grandfather never drove on a modern interstate superhighway, and he probably would have been scared to death if he had. He would have considered it foolhardy to drive at the dizzying speed of 70 miles an hour with other traffic on the road, and unwise to risk a mechanical breakdown on a bleak highway, miles from help. Yet in the past 25 years, due to the greatest road building effort in world history, most Americans have become accustomed to at least an occasional high-speed trip on a freeway, turnpike, or expressway.

What's more, the gloomy predictions of wholesale highway slaughter by a few early critics have been refuted by national statistics. Superhighways have proved to be safer than ordinary streets and roads. The federal plan for the present network of interstate highways centered on safety as well as speed. The concept of limited access, elimination of traffic lights, division of lanes and improved grading has eliminated some of the more persistent causes of accidents. But one of the keys to this superior safety record has been driver adaptation to the greater speed and other special conditions of traveling on superhighways.

Superhighway driving *is* different, of course, from the kind of short-haul, in-town driving that most of us do on a daily basis. The average motorist puts a very small percentage of his annual mileage on the high-speed thoroughfares. When he does venture onto them for a vacation trip or other special journey, he's faced with a different set of conditions. How well he adapts to them determines his degree of safe—and pleasurable—traveling.

What are the most common difficulties in adjusting to superhighway driving? What advice do authorities give motorists for better traveling on the high-speed thoroughfares? In seeking the answers to these questions, I talked to state police officers, driver education authorities, members of state highway safety commissions, and officials of the American Automobile Association and the Automobile Legal Association. I also sought advice in the literature available to the motoring public.

Unfortunately, there is a dearth of printed advice on superhighway driving. Automotive magazines, driving school text material, and the literature

of many state highway commissions rarely differentiate between the techniques for safe short-haul driving and those required for the expressways and turnpikes. But the authorities with whom I talked were unanimous in their concern that drivers should approach superhighway driving alert to the special demands they impose on driving skills.

"One of the main causes of expressway accidents is slow reflexes," an Illinois state policeman told me. "People just seem to forget they're traveling at much greater speeds on these roads. A driver takes his eyes off the road to light a cigarette or glance at a road map. He looks up again and he's on top of the car in front of him. This is what causes so many tailgate collisions."

Rear-end collisions often occur on highway entrance ramps, too. Have you ever been the second driver on a ramp, waiting to enter the stream of traffic, when the car ahead of you starts to move forward toward the lane of traffic, then stops short? If you had assumed the driver in front of you was going to continue ahead and were looking to your left at the oncoming traffic, you would have hit him.

Plan your trip in advance, say safety authorities. You can save yourself a lot of anxiety and risk if you check a road map before you get on an expressway. Know the number of your exit and the number of miles to it, and have a passenger watch for the exit signs, too. And, of course, if you miss your exit, don't back up, but continue on to the next one and double back.

Most of us are aware of the coordination required to change lanes and pass another car at high speed, but too many drivers neglect to use their directional signals when doing it. Those signals help drivers several car-lengths behind to assess the situation. AAA officials recommend scanning the traffic ahead as far as you can see, rather than keeping your eyes only on the car in front of you. This technique helps drivers avoid getting trapped behind slow-moving vehicles, and it gives them warning of drivers to watch out for: cars that are weaving from lane to lane and ones that straddle the line dividing the lanes.

"Another dangerous, but all-too-common practice," says an Indiana state policeman, "is traveling in the 'blind spot' to the left and behind another car. If the other car changes lanes, there's likely to be an accident. Drivers should get in and out of that blind spot in a hurry when passing."

State highway safety commissions rate fatigue and drowsiness among the most important causes of superhighway accidents. Superhighways have a hypnotic quality and dull the senses during long trips. It's always better to drive in daylight hours when visibility is good, and you're not likely to be tired. Physicians point out that eyestrain is a big factor, too: The glare of oncoming headlights and the limited visibility at night can strain a driver's eyes.

If you're taking any kind of medicine or drugs before an expressway or turnpike trip, you'd do well to check their side effects with your doctor or read the label for warnings. Even such over-the-counter remedies as decongestants and certain cough syrups should be avoided, as well as prolonged use of aspirin. Other obvious medicines to avoid are pep pills and tranquilizers.

Doctors and safety officials warn against eating heavy meals before or during a lengthy trip. They point out that too much food—especially hard-to-digest fried foods like hamburgers and french fries—relaxes, dulls the senses, and causes drowsiness. Soup and frequent light snacks have a better effect and provide all the energy a driver needs. Coffee breaks relieve drowsiness, of course, and one driver training instructor told me he always chews gum on a long trip—it requires him to move his jaws and facial muscles enough to keep him alert. Another important consideration is the frequent circulation of fresh air in the car, even in winter when it may be temporarily uncomfortable.

What about the business of having a breakdown, miles from the nearest service station? Police and highway commissioners are aware of these problems and can even predict the approximate number of breakdowns per year on various highways. "The obvious way to avoid breakdowns is to check the car before starting a trip," says a Missouri state

trooper. "Tires are most important. So are brakes, steering, windshield wipers."

Suppose you have checked to be certain your car is in good working order, and you still have a breakdown. There's nothing bleaker than the feeling of being abandoned on a lonely stretch of road with no help in sight. But there's really little cause for alarm. Most highways are well patrolled by police cars and emergency vehicles. Their schedules are arranged so that no stretch of the highway goes unnoticed for a long time.

Police say the important thing to do when a car breaks down is to get it completely off the pavement, even if it means driving on a flat tire for a distance. The standard distress signals in all states, of course, are emergency flasher lights and a raised hood. Drivers without flasher lights should display a white handkerchief on the left side of the car and turn off all lights at night. Safety officials say many a parked car has been hit when an oncoming motorist followed a pair of taillights in the dark without realizing they weren't moving.

On long trips, driver fatigue may loom as one of the greatest dangers. Set realistic mileage goals in advance—300 to 400 miles a day is considered a safe figure. Monotony may not be as great a safety meance as fatigue, but if it affects children on a family trip, it can result in frayed nerves and distraction for the driver. To break the monotony, it's good to keep the children's interest alive with games and such.

Although pressure by the federal government has spurred the introduction of automotive safety equipment in recent years, the government has failed in one important safety area: the establishment of uniform national traffic laws. Superhighway drivers should be aware that such practices as passing on the right are legal in some states but not in others. At present, 44 states allow passing on the right on multi-lane highways, but few of them have made it mandatory for cars to be equipped with mirrors on the right side, which most safety experts consider essential.

Some authorities condemn laws that allow passing on the right as a danger to motorists. Philip C.

Wallwork, public relations director of the Automobile Legal Association, is one of a growing group who recommends abolishing them.

"We've seen an increasing number of turnpike and expressway accidents where a car bolts across the center strip out of control because the driver was startled by a car suddenly overtaking him on the right," he says. "If the police would make a greater effort to discourage the slow drivers who block the left lanes, there would be no need to allow passing on the right."

Efforts are being made to establish a uniform national system of highway traffic laws, but until this is achieved, the best advice to the motorist is to keep in mind the inconsistencies among state traffic laws and to check the legal regulations before he takes to the superhighways.

Starting Time: _____	Finishing Time: _____
Reading Time: _____	Reading Rate: _____
Comprehension: _____	Vocabulary: _____

VOCABULARY: The following words have been taken from the selection you have just read. Put an X in the box before the best meaning or synonym for the word as used in the selection.

1. **refuted**, page 16, column 1, paragraph 2
"...the gloomy predictions of wholesale highway slaughter by a few early critics have been refuted by national statistics."
☐ a. disproved
☐ b. proven
☐ c. refused
☐ d. reflected

2. **bleaker**, page 17, column 2, paragraph 2
"There's nothing bleaker than the feeling of being abandoned on a lonely stretch of road..."
☐ a. more confusing
☐ b. more dangerous
☐ c. more exciting
☐ d. more depressing

3. **monotony**, page 17, column 2, paragraph 4
"To break the monotony, it's good to keep the children's interest alive with games and such."
☐ a. sound
☐ b. boredom
☐ c. exhaustion
☐ d. silence

4. **spurred**, page 17, column 2, paragraph 5
"Although pressure by the federal government has spurred the introduction of automotive safety equipment..."
☐ a. forced
☐ b. stimulated
☐ c. halted
☐ d. increased

5. **mandatory**, page 17, column 2, paragraph 5
"...few of them have made it mandatory for cars to be equipped with mirrors on the right side, ..."
☐ a. optional
☐ b. legal
☐ c. important
☐ d. obligatory

TOPICS FOR THE RESTLESS

PREFIXES

Many English words consist of a base or root word to which prefixes (beginnings) and suffixes (endings) have been added. To the root word **agree** (a verb) we can add both a prefix and a suffix to get **disagreeable** (an adjective) which has an opposite meaning.

A prefix is added to the beginning of a word and causes a change in the meaning of that word. We have just seen how the prefix **dis** reverses the meaning of **agree**.

Two Prefixes

1. **mis-** is an Old English prefix which means **badly** or **wrong**. To behave badly is to **misbehave**.

2. **ex-** is a Latin prefix which means **out**. An **exit** provides the way out.

In the following sentences the words in bold print need prefixes. Add one of these two prefixes to each word and write your word on the line following the sentence.

1. Cutting too many classes will cause you to be **pelled**.

   _____

2. The senator was accused by his colleagues of **conduct**.

   _____

3. You may **cerpt** a passage from this book and quote it.

   _____

4. Actually, it's a minor offense, a **demeanor**.

   _____

5. We no longer **clude** lawyers from membership.

   _____

6. It wasn't a quarrel or disagreement; it was merely a **understanding**.

   _____

7. Automobile fumes, given out as **haust**, contribute substantially to air pollution.

   _____

8. Because of an error in the proceedings, the judge declared a **trial**.

   _____

9. He knew he had done wrong and he admitted his **take**.

   _____

10. The body will be **humed** and an autopsy performed.

    _____

HOW TO PREVIEW, I

Previewing is known by many names. It is called surveying and prereading too.

1. Read the Title. You would do this anyway before reading a selection, but in previewing we want you to be aware of what you can *learn* from the title. Not only can you learn the author's subject, you can also frequently learn how he *feels* toward his subject. Lester David once wrote an article entitled *The Natural Inferiority of Women*. From the title you can tell the author's feeling on the subject, and you would expect to find in the article arguments supporting his position and illustrations demonstrating his case. With just this little bit of information, the reader can approach this selection intelligently, knowing what to expect.

Another article by Mark Clifton was entitled *The Dread Tomato Addiction*. You would expect to find humor or satire in the author's account.

Headlines and titles are considered quite influential by authors and editors. Many magazines survive on the appeal or shock value of the titles of their articles.

2. Read the Subhead. In textbooks especially, and in many popular magazines as well, subheads are used following the title to give the reader even more information on the subject. In textbooks this is frequently a one-line digest of the chapter—"Here's what we are going to cover." In magazines teaser-type statements follow the title to further spark the reader's curiosity. Look for a subhead when previewing.

3. Read the Illustration. If a picture or illustration accompanies the article, don't just look at it, *read* it. Interpret it to learn what you can about the content of the article. The Chinese have said that a picture is worth ten thousand words. Good illustrations are much more than pretty pictures. See what you can learn visually before reading.

COMPREHENSION: For each of the following statements and questions, select the option containing the most complete or most accurate answer.

1. Superhighways are safer than ordinary streets
(c) and roads because they are
- □ a. faster.
- □ b. well designed.
- □ c. well traveled.
- □ d. patrolled.

2. Whenever the average motorist takes to the
(c) open highways, he must
- □ a. adjust to new conditions.
- □ b. prepare for the worst.
- □ c. check weather conditions.
- □ d. take proper medication.

3. One of the main causes of highway acci-
(b) dents is
- □ a. high speeds.
- □ b. poor lighting.
- □ c. tailgating.
- □ d. slow reflexes.

4. Safety authorities stress the importance of
(b) advance knowledge of
- □ a. exit number.
- □ b. exit speed.
- □ c. traffic conditions.
- □ d. rest areas.

5. The advice given by AAA officials urges all
(c) motorists
- □ a. to concentrate on the car ahead of them.
- □ b. to travel to the left and behind another car.
- □ c. to analyze the total situation.
- □ d. to keep an eye on the following traffic.

6. It can be inferred from the selection that
(h) highway travel
- □ a. should not be taken lightly.
- □ b. should not be attempted by young, inexperienced drivers.
- □ c. requires highly trained motorists.
- □ d. should be avoided whenever possible.

7. The tone of the selection is
(i)
- □ a. frightening.
- □ b. factual.
- □ c. threatening.
- □ d. negative.

8. It can be inferred that the hypnotic effect of
(h) highway driving may be related to
- □ a. the large numbers of cars on the highway.
- □ b. slow reflexes and poor coordination.
- □ c. long, straight stretches of road.
- □ d. the poor demarcation between driving lanes.

9. One of the greatest dangers drivers should
(a) guard against is
- □ a. fatigue.
- □ b. heavy food.
- □ c. monotony.
- □ d. abandoned cars.

10. Traffic laws governing highway travel should be
(c)
- □ a. adapted to local conditions.
- □ b. relaxed whenever conditions permit.
- □ c. standardized across the country.
- □ d. reviewed to meet international standards.

Comprehension Skills: a—isolating details; b—recalling specific facts; c—retaining concepts; d—organizing facts; e—understanding the main idea; f—drawing a conclusion; g—making a judgment; h—making an inference; i—recognizing tone; j—understanding characters; k—appreciation of literary forms.

The 1972 World Chess Tournament

While Spassky Can Say that "Chess Is Like Life," Fischer Charges that, "Chess Is Life."

Carolyn McCoy

The old Russian proverb "check and mate and the game is finished" was never more true than on September 1, 1972, when Russian Boris Spassky resigned to American Bobby Fischer, ending the 1972 World Championship chess tournament.

The finish of 24 straight years of Russian domination of world chess, the loss shamed a political system that culls champions from its four million registered chess players in a manner which resembles the training of thoroughbred horses. To the Russian, winning at chess is as important as leading the world in the art of ballet. To have Boris Spassky defeated by Bobby Fischer is tantamount to harming the Russian national image. Moreover, Bobby Fischer reigns as king to the 60 million chess players in the world, and has forever secured his position of admiration in Russia along with pianist Van Cliburn. To give Spassky some understanding in his loss, he had the weight of the entire Soviet system to cope with as well as individualist, intransigent, uncommunicative, uncooperative American Bobby Fischer, who, through his demands and irascible behavior made the chess tournament an international incident.

He did this through his brilliant playing which has been likened to carrying a set of premises to a thrilling and unexpected conclusion in the same manner as did Mozart and Einstein. And he became notorious for being a pouty nonconformist who has stated, "If there is one thing I ask for and I don't get, then I don't play."

Fischer had confrontations not only with Spassky, but with the governing body of world chess, the Federation Internationale des Echecs [FIDE], with the Russians, television and film crews, and with the Icelandic Chess Federation. At one point, Presidential adviser Henry Kissinger felt compelled to intervene "for the good of the country" to make peace in Reykjavik, Iceland, for the battle was more than between two chess champions: it became a matter of prestige and honor between East and West in games played before a worldwide audience.

It is ironic that the 21-game confrontation in which Spassky resigned with a final score of Fischer 12½ and Spassky 8½ took place in peaceful Iceland, a country that seems to have let the rest of the world go by since the Vikings settled there 1000 years ago. The size of Ohio, with a population of some 210,000, Iceland has no armed forces, no unemployment, no smog and no crime. Few people outside its own shores thought much about Iceland until the most famous confrontation in 1300 years of chess history left its ravages on the consciousness of the world much like Iceland's still active volcanoes burst through the ice to send millions of tons of sand and rocks to obliterate well-known landmarks.

Bobby Fischer has been a legend since he won the U.S. Junior Open Tournament when he was thirteen and the U.S. Championship one year later. At fifteen, he became the youngest grandmaster in history. A solitary individual who dropped out of high school at the age of sixteen, he has insulted a number of individuals from his teachers on up to the Russians, whom he accused in 1964 of having fixed world chess so that none but a Russian player could win. He has walked out on a number of tournaments and refused to play on international competitive levels until the FIDE changed rules which Fischer felt favored the Soviet players.

Fischer's confrontations and demands have become his trademark, and they rarely fail to bring results. What some called the tantrum that resounded round the world brought millions of new chess enthusiasts to the game. During the championship matches, department stores in major U.S. cities were selling chess sets so rapidly they began promoting them with full-page newspaper ads. Enthralled crowds gathered on the streets to watch television reports of the match, the U.S. Chess Federation reported a tremendous increase in membership applications, and public libraries found it difficult to keep chess books on their shelves. The world of chess, which previously was of minor, or no interest to most Americans, had suddenly become a subject of major preoccupation. There are few adults today who do not have at least a fundamental grasp of the power of chess pieces and game procedure, and who do not marvel at the game expertise of Bobby Fischer, and who are not amazed at the trail of rash behavior he blazed at the championship match.

And what were Bobby Fischer's actions that prompted the Soviet press to call him uncultured, a "temperamental child" whose "endless whims" and "absurd accusations" create a "spirit of ill will and suspicion in the noble sports competition"? That caused FIDE President Dr. Euwe to condemn his behavior? That prompted millions to watch with keen interest?

From the very start, negotiations were strained. Yugoslavia, which offered a $152,000 stake to host the tournament, dropped out of game site negotiations after Fischer demanded a part of the profits from the tournament and refused to put up a $35,000 cash guarantee which would be forfeited if he did not appear. Iceland then offered to host the entire match at their original offer of $125,000 and the FIDE, already exasperated over negotiations, accepted, giving Bobby a deadline to accept the offer. Under protest, Bobby agreed, but accused the Russian government of defending a title by "chicanery instead of skill," and expressed the fear that Iceland had a lack of technical facilities that would hamper TV coverage. Yet the meeting place for the world championship was settled with the first game scheduled Sunday, July 2.

A seemingly confident, relaxed Spassky arrived with the Russian entourage nearly two weeks before the match was to begin, but no one knew where Bobby was. In the U.S., he had gone into hiding and through a spokesman demanded a bigger piece of the profits. While Spassky appeared amiable and friendly at news conferences, American newsmen could not even find Fischer, who, the day before the scheduled start of the tournament, asked for a postponement. It was granted and Fischer finally arrived in Iceland, but only after a British millionaire offered $125,000 to double the already high game stakes.

To add insult to insult, Fischer slept in his hotel room, sending a second to meet with Spassky to draw lots for who had the right to play White in the first game. Now Spassky stalked out of the room, countering with a demand for Fischer to apologize for his delaying tactics. Fischer complied, admitting he was "carried away by my petty dispute over money," but further insulted the Soviet delegation by sending a messenger carrying an unsigned mimeographed note. By now, Russian ire was at its peak. Fischer's behavior was condemned by Dr. Euwe, and the match got underway on July 6 after Fischer delivered a handwritten and signed apology to Spassky.

But that was not the end of discordant confrontations. Spassky showed up on time to draw lots, but Fischer was twenty minutes late. This tardiness, typical of Fischer, was to continue throughout the games. Onlookers noticed that when one player walked on stage to find his opponent's chair empty, he would often walk off again to show up later, after the other player appeared. The first move of most games was not with a chess piece, but who would show up first.

Other difficulties moved Fischer to action. He refused to use chairs provided by the Icelandic Chess Federation and had a special chair flown in from New York. He nearly walked out again over a television and film dispute. He insisted that lighting be readjusted and the distance between the players and the audience be increased. After losing the first game, he forfeited the second by staying in his hotel room, insisting he would not continue to play until all TV and movie cameras were removed.

Fischer's behavior had its ramifications. Some thought he had gone out of his mind, others that he was afraid to meet Spassky. Many deplored his "disgraceful" behavior and a number of Americans attending the tournament apologized to Icelanders. It appeared that the comment made by veteran chess analyst Hans Kmoch might be correct after all: "Finally the U.S.A. produces its greatest chess genius and he turns out to be just a stubborn boy." And in many ways it did appear that Fischer was less intent on winning the World Championship than he was on money, playing conditions and other side benefits such as the private swimming pool, a new automobile, a wider choice of restaurants in which to dine, an indoor tennis court, pocket money to be paid in advance, and a broader selection of current reading material.

Fischer's actions were having their effect on Spassky. He appeared to be a changed man after the sixth game, behind by a full point. As games continued he looked more restless, nervous and haggard and sought a postponement on medical grounds from the ninth game. In the previous six games, he had been able to gain only one point and he now trailed 5 to 3. When the ninth game was played, it was a draw and twelve games later Spassky, who had clashed with Fischer over chess five times with three victories and two draws, had lost the World Championship.

Bobby Fischer had not only beat Spassky, but he had brought chess to national significance. It has been said that as Fischer goes, so goes American chess. With only 35,000 registered chess players in the United States, chess has a meagre following. Most U.S. players feel lucky if they win $500 plus expenses for winning a major event. The highest rated player in the history of chess with an international rating of some 2,800, Fischer's sole income rests on his chess earnings. One of perhaps six professional chess players in the U.S., he earned an average of $20,000 a year from prematch income. In one of his best-paying matches, he netted the $7,500 winner's share of a $10,000 purse when he defeated Petrosian in Buenos Aires. Fischer has long wanted to impress the world with the fact that chess players, like other sports heroes, are entitled to maximum compensation for their time and effort, and he did just that with the World Championship tournament.

Starting Time: _____ Finishing Time: _____

Reading Time: _____ Reading Rate: _____

Comprehension: _____ Vocabulary: _____

VOCABULARY: The following words have been taken from the selection you have just read. Put an X in the box before the best meaning or synonym for the word as used in the selection.

1. **culls**, page 21, column 1, paragraph 2
   "...a political system that culls champions from its four million registered chess players..."
   □ a. sculls
   □ b. selects
   □ c. rejects
   □ d. collects

2. **irascible**, page 21, column 1, paragraph 2
   "...through his demands and irascible behavior made the chess tournament an international incident."
   □ a. irritable
   □ b. diplomatic
   □ c. calm
   □ d. annoying

3. **intervene**, page 21, column 1, paragraph 4
   "...Henry Kissinger felt compelled to intervene..."
   □ a. argue
   □ b. take sides
   □ c. encourage
   □ d. come between

4. **strained**, page 22, column 1, paragraph 3
   "From the very start, negotiations were strained."
   □ a. tense
   □ b. pulled
   □ c. filtered
   □ d. important

5. **ire**, page 22, column 1, paragraph 5
   "By now, Russian ire was at its peak."
   □ a. dissatisfaction
   □ b. delight
   □ c. anger
   □ d. concern

EXPECTANCY CLUES

The most important aids to word recognition and, therefore, fluency in reading are meaning clues. Good readers use these clues effectively and automatically. Meaning clues permit the reader to anticipate words before actually reading them.

Expectancy clues are one type of meaning clue. These refer to the sorts of words and concepts one might expect to encounter in a given subject. For example, in a story about big city life, the reader should expect to meet words like *subway, traffic congestion, urban renewal, ghetto, high-rise apartments,* and so on. Anticipating or expecting these words enables the reader to move along the printed lines rapidly, with understanding.

Here are two exercises to help you develop your skill in using expectancy clues.

The following words, except two, all appeared in a story about taxes. Think first about the kinds of words you would find in such a story and then examine the words below. Underline the two words you would *not* expect to find in this story.

1. homeowner	5. income	9. computed
2. toothache	6. base rate	10. forestry
3. burden	7. assessment	11. property
4. percentage	8. government	12. income

Which of the following phrases would you expect to read in a newspaper account of a school committee meeting? Put an *X* in the box before them.

☐ 1. problems of bussing	☐ 11. books and supplies
☐ 2. library improvements	☐ 12. balmy spring weather
☐ 3. increasing maintenance costs	☐ 13. construction of new classrooms
☐ 4. birds flying overhead	☐ 14. behind closed doors
☐ 5. statement to be released	☐ 15. new appointments
☐ 6. colored in bright red	☐ 16. at the firehouse door
☐ 7. a pastoral setting	☐ 17. curriculum revisions
☐ 8. merit ratings	☐ 18. in annual increments
☐ 9. based on years of service	☐ 19. teacher salaries
☐ 10. without justification	☐ 20. loss of tenure

HOW TO PREVIEW, II

We have seen how previewing is necessary for intelligent reading. The first three steps to previewing are 1) Read the Title, 2) Read the Subhead, and 3) Read the Illustration. Here are the last three steps:

4. Read the Opening Paragraph. The first paragraph is the author's opening, his first opportunity to address the reader. This paragraph is also called the introductory paragraph because it is precisely that—an introduction to the article or chapter. Opening paragraphs are used in different ways. Some authors announce what they plan to do in the following paragraphs. Other authors tell us why they are writing this article or chapter or why this is important for us to learn. Still other authors will do what speakers do—start with a story or anecdote to set the stage. This provides the setting or mood they need to present their material.

5. Read the Closing Paragraph. The next step in previewing: go to the end and read the last paragraph. This is the author's last chance to address the reader. If he has any closing remarks or final thoughts, here's where they'll come. If the author wishes to reemphasize or restate his principal thoughts or arguments, he'll do it here. Because this is the concluding paragraph, you'll find here the concluding or summarizing thoughts. This is where you'll see what the writer considers important—in his closing paragraph.

6. Skim Through. Finally, before completing your preview, skim quickly through the article or chapter to see what else you can learn. Be on the watch for headings and numbers, indicating important divisions in the author's presentation. You may learn that this material is divided into four or five major aspects, which will be helpful to know when reading.

COMPREHENSION: For each of the following statements and questions, select the option containing the most complete or most accurate answer.

1. The attitude of Russians toward chess is
(c)
- [ ] a. calm.
- [ ] b. passionate.
- [ ] c. strange.
- [ ] d. vicious.

2. Compared to Bobby Fischer, Boris Spassky
(f) had to cope with
- [ ] a. less sleep.
- [ ] b. more pressures.
- [ ] c. unfamiliar customs.
- [ ] d. international criticism.

3. Fischer's chess style and personal behavior
(g) ranged from
- [ ] a. the sublime to the ridiculous.
- [ ] b. daring to conservative.
- [ ] c. the unexpected to the ordinary.
- [ ] d. average to considerate.

4. The purpose of Kissinger's intervention in
(f) Reykjavik was
- [ ] a. resented.
- [ ] b. personal.
- [ ] c. patriotic.
- [ ] d. diplomatic.

5. The choice of Iceland for the Fischer/Spassky
(h) confrontation was
- [ ] a. most probably a wise decision.
- [ ] b. a cause of international friction.
- [ ] c. most probably made by Spassky.
- [ ] d. an honor for the chess capital of the world.

6. Bobby Fischer seems
(j)
- [ ] a. to overlook the value of money.
- [ ] b. to yield easily to pressure.
- [ ] c. to thrive on confrontation.
- [ ] d. to enjoy public attention.

7. In 1972, the World Championship chess
(c) tournament
- [ ] a. strengthened U.S. relations with Russia.
- [ ] b. renewed public interest in the game.
- [ ] c. weakened the prestige of grandmasters.
- [ ] d. weakened the determination of Russian players.

8. The accusations made by the Soviet press
(g) against Fischer were
- [ ] a. easily dismissed.
- [ ] b. totally unnecessary.
- [ ] c. highly prejudiced.
- [ ] d. not groundless.

9. Spassky is to Fischer as
(j)
- [ ] a. slow-witted is to brilliant.
- [ ] b. reserved is to shy.
- [ ] c. friendly is to companionable.
- [ ] d. sociable is to eccentric.

10. An important part of Fischer's game and pre-
(h) game strategy was to publicize
- [ ] a. the need for chess schools in America.
- [ ] b. the superiority of American chess players.
- [ ] c. the financial discrimination suffered by professional chess players.
- [ ] d. the lack of sportsmanship in a game which enjoyed a high reputation.

Comprehension Skills: a—isolating details; b—recalling specific facts; c—retaining concepts; d—organizing facts; e—understanding the main idea; f—drawing a conclusion; g—making a judgment; h—making an inference; i—recognizing tone; j—understanding characters; k—appreciation of literary forms.

Toward Understanding, I

A Three-day Rap Session between Students and Businessmen Mostly about Philosophies and Goals

Jan Smith

Violence over civil rights in the 1960s, moratoriums, marches, new sexual freedom, drugs, campus takeovers, Kent State, Chicago, Earth Day, apathy—these phenomena of the recent past represent an unprecedented social upheaval, a massive protest, mostly on the part of the young, against a society that fails to cope with its most crucial problems. Young people, especially, lay much of the blame on the business system. It's unresponsive and uncaring, they say.

Naturally, businessmen deny this charge. They're proud of what the free enterprise system has accomplished. They suspect that many dissenters don't grasp economic realities.

It's a standoff. That's why it was significant, I thought, that these two groups were meeting at all. Yet, here they were, students and businessmen from all over the country, jammed together in the lobby of Washington's Park-Sheraton Hotel, waiting to register for "Business Tomorrow," a three-day conference in which they would talk informally, get to know one another, and learn something about the differences in life-style and philosophy that so sharply divide them.

The idea for the conference had originated with a group of students at Princeton University, who had formed an organization called the Foundation for Student Communication. The Foundation's aim: to "foster better relations between students and businessmen." These young people, unlike some of their peers, don't think that all business is all bad. But they do think business should take more initiative and make better use of its resources in order to achieve a closer balance between profit and poverty in this country. This is the theme that runs through the Foundation's magazine, "Business Today," a professional-looking quarterly that goes to over 200,000 students.

These Foundation members and other politically moderate students like them are the ones most likely to enter the business world when they graduate, and they're concerned about what their roles might be. They recognize, as business does, a need for the two groups to communicate, to understand each other. That's why they held the conference.

In the beginning, when the conference was still in blueprint form, the students set about enlisting industry's support. Letters and printed materials were sent to presidents of corporations, then Foundation members went calling. They spent the summer selling their idea to corporations. One thousand visits and 100,000 miles later, nearly a hundred companies had agreed to participate; and, to cover expenses, the students had garnered pledges of $2,500 each from fifty corporations: AT&T to Marathon to Xerox.

Students from over 160 universities were chosen by fellow students and university presidents to participate in the meeting—some from schools of business, many from liberal arts colleges. This was to make a definite difference in the tone of the conference because, generally, students of the humanities tend to emphasize the value of the individual, making them especially critical of conformity in the corporation.

The two groups were a study in contrasts as they stood in long lines that snaked around haphazard piles of luggage in front of the registration desk. Bell bottom corduroys, turtle necks, beards and mustaches accentuated the crisp white shirts, ties, and dark suits of the cleanshaven businessmen, and spoke volumes about their differences.

Late that afternoon students and businessmen met in the Cotillion Room for the opening reception. There was little of the usual cocktail party small talk. Students were ready to wrestle with the issues. A businessman, finding it difficult to make polite conversation, remarked to a tense, watchful student that he and some of the others seemed suspicious, even hostile. "It's a good way to be," the young man answered. "We've laid down too long. We've accepted so many of the values of business today, and we're in one hell of a mess right now—war, the environment, poverty. We've heard all the excuses. All we're interested in now is what you're going to do about it."

My initial impression that young people are often deliberately blunt was strengthened as the conference progressed. I sensed that they're blunt because they don't want their meaning or intent obscured by a lot of conventional Establishment niceties, and while they consider their direct manner to be truthful, many businessmen consider it rude. It's this language barrier—not what they say to each other, but how they say it—that often makes it so difficult for the two groups to communicate. As the conference progressed, though, both businessmen and students began to acquire the knack of concentrating on the problems, rather than the way in which the problems were presented—which is what everyone had hoped would happen.

Dinner was congenial, but there was one incident that pointed to still other basic differences that work to keep the generations apart. A businessman who had taken a martini to the table with him, was alternately ogling a pretty student hostess and talking loudly about money in general, his investments in particular. Then, nodding toward the hostess, he told the students with a wink that, if it weren't for girls like her, he might be a rich man today. He had invested in a company that makes the best bras in the country, he said, and then bras went out of style. The students just stared, and the one sitting beside me muttered "chauvinist pig" under his breath. Unfortunately, this is the stereotyped image some young people have of businessmen, just as many businessmen think the radical is representative of all youth.

Later in the evening, Clifford Hewitt, chairman of the Foundation for Student Communication, made the opening remarks. He said that students and business executives were more and more striving toward common social goals, but there was still disagreement on the means of achieving these goals. As a result, little collaborative activity was taking place. "Considering the increasing importance of young people in the affairs of this nation, it is important that students have an understanding of the men and corporations that are playing a significant part in the major issues of our day. And, in order that executives in corporations have the support of the young people, whose goals they so often share, it is important that these men understand and respond to the ideas of young people." He added that these potentially constructive groups cannot continue to work at cross purposes if the current problems of our society are to be solved.

Stewart Cort, chairman of Bethlehem Steel, and Charles Bluhdorn, chairman of Gulf and Western Industries, gave the keynote addresses. Mr. Cort stressed the fact that businessmen are taking a more active role in improving the environment, at least to an extent consistent with prudent management of corporate resources. He told the students that "Young people have historically pointed the way to healthy social change. Your generation is by no means unique in this regard. The quality that makes you exceptional is your determination to succeed where others have fallen short. Business needs the qualities you have to offer. Business is the best place to put these qualities to work, for your own benefit and for the benefit of society. In other words, business is the best place to do your own thing."

Mr. Bluhdorn, a European immigrant who first worked for $15 a week and attended college at night, said that many of the problems this country is facing now are a direct result of a lack of discipline—on the part of labor, of business, and the community at large. "We must find a way to develop a national sense of responsibility," he said.

Starting Time: _____	Finishing Time: _____
Reading Time: _____	Reading Rate: _____
Comprehension: _____	Vocabulary: _____

VOCABULARY: The following words have been taken from the selection you have just read. Put an *X* in the box before the best meaning or synonym for the word as used in the selection.

1. **foster**, page 26, column 1, paragraph 4
"...to 'foster better relations between students and businessmen.' "
☐ a. encourage
☐ b. support
☐ c. discourage
☐ d. demand

2. **garnered**, page 26, column 2, paragraph 1
"...the students had garnered pledges of $2,500 each..."
☐ a. hoarded
☐ b. made
☐ c. collected
☐ d. garnished

3. **accentuated**, page 26, column 2, paragraph 3
"...beards and mustaches accentuated the crisp white shirts, ..."
☐ a. revealed
☐ b. adorned
☐ c. emphasized
☐ d. accompanied

4. **intent**, page 26, column 2, last paragraph
"...they don't want their meaning or intent obscured..."
☐ a. plot
☐ b. purpose
☐ c. definition
☐ d. feelings

5. **congenial**, page 27, column 1, paragraph 2
"Dinner was congenial, but there was one incident that pointed to..."
☐ a. disagreeable
☐ b. congenital
☐ c. delicious
☐ d. pleasant

PREFIXES

Many English words consist of a base or root word to which prefixes (beginnings) and suffixes (endings) have been added. To the root word **agree** (a verb) we can add both a prefix and a suffix to get **disagreeable** (an adjective) which has an opposite meaning.

A prefix is added to the beginning of a word and causes a change in the meaning of that word. We have just seen how the prefix **dis** reverses the meaning of **agree**.

Two Prefixes

1. **in-** is a Latin prefix which has the meaning of **not** or **opposing**. An **insincere** person is not sincere.

2. **pre-** is also Latin and it means **before**. A **prefix** is added before the root word.

In the following sentences the words in bold print need prefixes. Add one of these two prefixes to each word and write your word on the line following the sentence.

1. Let's do what we can to **vent** disease.

   _____

2. He has become **active** since his retirement.

   _____

3. Proper **natal** care results in healthier children.

   _____

4. The judge ruled the evidence **admissible**.

   _____

5. **Judice** is based on opinions formed before the facts are known.

   _____

6. Certain **cautionary** measures should be taken.

   _____

7. The apprentice was not only **competent**; he also failed to show up for work.

   _____

8. There were obvious **equalities** in the way the two groups were treated.

   _____

9. Lawyers search for a **cedent** to serve as an example.

   _____

10. The defendant claimed that his arrest was an **justice** and a violation of his rights.

    _____

QUESTION THE AUTHOR

You've probably heard it said that you'll never learn if you don't ask questions.

Why is an inquisitiveness associated with learning? We speak of the student seeking knowledge, or of the inquiring mind, and both of these concepts imply asking or questioning.

This is because learning is not a passive process; it is something we do. Learning is an activity—it requires us to go after it, seek it out. This is why we say that questioning is part of learning.

A technique good students use is to question the author. We question following previewing by asking, "What can I expect to learn from this chapter or article? Based on my prereading what are some of the things to be covered or presented? What will the author tell me about this subject?" Questions like these "frame" the subject for us, give us an outline to fill in when reading.

Another thing we hope to discover from questioning is the author's method of presentation. There are many different methods the author can use in presenting his material. He may ask questions and answer them, adopting this technique to make his subject easier to learn. He may give details, or describe and illustrate, or he may use comparison and contrast. Whatever his method, discover it and put it to use when studying.

In many books the questions are already there waiting to be used. Check your textbooks. Are there questions following the chapters? If so, use them during previewing to instill the inquisitiveness so necessary to learning. These are special questions—these tell us what the author considers important in each chapter, what he really expects us to learn.

Develop the technique of questioning. Try whenever you study to create questions you expect to find answered.

COMPREHENSION: For each of the following statements and questions, select the option containing the most complete or most accurate answer.

1. The unrest of the 1960s would probably not
(h) have happened if
  - □ a. business had responded to the demands of youth.
  - □ b. the authorities had not met protest with force.
  - □ c. society had succeeded to respond to its needs.
  - □ d. young people had cooperated with government agencies.

2. Businessmen argue that many dissenters are
(c)
  - □ a. uneducated.
  - □ b. dishonestly motivated.
  - □ c. unrealistic.
  - □ d. being decieved.

3. The objective of "Business Tomorrow" was
(c)
  - □ a. to recruit promising young executives.
  - □ b. to establish lines of communication.
  - □ c. to expose the hypocrisy of the business world.
  - □ d. to establish goals for a new society.

4. The Foundation for Student Communication
(b) was organized
  - □ a. to encourage better relations between students and businessmen.
  - □ b. to publish the quarterly magazine "Business Today."
  - □ c. to involve the academic community of Princeton University.
  - □ d. to host the annual conference "Business Tomorrow."

5. The mentality of the Foundation members
(g) and other politically moderate students should
  - □ a. be an obstacle to a successful business career.
  - □ b. provoke suspicion in the business world.
  - □ c. be a warning to those who plan to oppose them.
  - □ d. improve the attitude of business in the future.

6. The presence at the conference of students
(f) from liberal arts colleges
  - □ a. guaranteed the success of the conference.
  - □ b. embarrassed the business delegates.
  - □ c. threatened the success of the conference.
  - □ d. influenced the spirit of the conference.

7. The mood of the student delegates at the
(i) opening reception was
  - □ a. aggressive.
  - □ b. casual.
  - □ c. violent.
  - □ d. friendly.

8. The communication problems experienced
(g) by the students and the business delegates resulted from
  - □ a. organized hostility.
  - □ b. financial problems.
  - □ c. different mentalities.
  - □ d. inadequate accommodations.

9. Clifford Hewitt's opening remarks stressed
(e) the need for
  - □ a. a clear definition of goals.
  - □ b. a meeting of the minds.
  - □ c. different points of view.
  - □ d. more and better conferences.

10. The keynote addresses delivered by Stewart
(c) Cort and Charles Bluhdorn stress the need for
  - □ a. corporate profit and power.
  - □ b. prudent management and self-discipline.
  - □ c. rapid change and education.
  - □ d. student power and government controls.

Comprehension Skills: a—isolating details; b—recalling specific facts; c—retaining concepts; d—organizing facts; e—understanding the main idea; f—drawing a conclusion; g—making a judgment; h—making an inference; i—recognizing tone; j—understanding characters; k—appreciation of literary forms.

Toward Understanding, II

And the Exchange of Ideas Proved Tonic to Both Sides, a Step Toward Mutual Understanding.

Jan Smith

In the remaining two days of the conference, guest speakers were paired off in forums. Here's how the discussions lined up:

Consumerism: Ralph Nader and H. Bruce Palmer, president of the Council on Better Business Bureaus.

Environment: William May, chairman of American Can; and Jerome Kretchmer, administrator of the Environmental Protection Agency of New York City.

Corporate social responsibility: Raymon Mulford, chairman of Owens-Illinois; and Alice Tepper, chairman of the Council on Economic Priorities.

Urban problems; Richard Lee, Yale professor and former Mayor of New Haven; and Richard Clark, president of Richard Clark Associates.

Following each set of speakers, businessmen and students locked horns in small workshops to try to batter through some of the obstacles blocking communication. Sixteen hours a day they talked, shouted, and listened. Their ideas ranged from conservative to liberal to radical. Some samples:

"The way I feel about it," a student from Berkeley said, "if you work for a company that's soaking the ocean and the beaches with oil, *you're* the one who's responsible. Don't pass the buck to your board of directors or somebody. Man, if you're workin' for 'em, you're guilty. It's the same deal if you work for a company that makes a profit off the war. *You're* the one that's killing us."

A businessman from Michigan urged the students to believe that most executives are deeply troubled with the problem of achieving a sound balance between traditional demands for maintaining high profit and newer demands for solving urgent social problems. "Corporate omnipotence is pure myth," he told them. "Remember, we have our stockholders to answer to. It's their money."

A lanky University of Houston student was asked if he thought young people could change the corporations that employed them. He answered, "No way. No way. We have to have a revolution. A social revolution, I mean, not a bloody one. Just not buying certain products, things like that. Fifty percent of the population is under 25, and that's a lot of power. Especially voting power. In two weeks we registered 10,000 voters at the University of Houston alone, and I would say 70 percent of these are committed to changing the system. They're going to vote for any man who's against big business."

"I know you're not going to agree with this," a man who works for a California conglomerate said, "but the customer is still king. If we fail to serve the customer, we're finished. If we just stand still, stop growing, as many seem to think we should, and don't keep moving to meet the changing needs in a changing America, we'll make no profit. We'll just die on the vine. Then, for one thing, who takes care of our employees?"

A young lady read a quote from Henry Ford: "Business and industry are first and foremost a public service. We are organized to do as much good as we can, everywhere, for everybody concerned. I do not believe we should make such an awful profit on our cars. A reasonable profit is right, but not too much. So it has been my policy to force the price of the car down as fast as production would permit and give the benefits to the users and laborers with resulting surprisingly enormous profits to ourselves."

"*Enlightened* self-interest is good business," Owens-Illinois chairman Raymon Mulford told the young people. "We embrace the moral and social reasons for participating in these programs (hiring and training minorities), but our prime consideration is a pragmatic one. An economy that offered full participation to our present underprivileged would dramatically increase our gross national product and substantially decrease negative forces, such as the cost of welfare, of crime, of social disturbances inherent in any national policy that discriminates against any segment of the population."

"Ralph Nader spoke on our campus, and I wasn't really impressed. He reminded me of George Wallace," drawled a soft-spoken University of Alabama student. "You'll have to admit, though, Nader makes you think" another student said. "Yeah. Well—so does Wallace," was Alabama's reply.

A University of Vermont student, who looked like Elliott Gould, was asked where he thought he'd be ten years from now, what he thought he'd

be doing. Before he could answer, a businessman replied, somewhat wistfully, "Probably not where you think you'll be." The student immediately answered: "I haven't even thought about it. Things change so fast it's hard to tell." Then he looked at the businessman and added, "But I'll be where I *should* be."

On the drawbacks of affluence: "When I was growing up we had the Depression, then World War II on top of that. Believe me, people who got through both of those were entitled to some financial security and a few luxuries for themselves and their families, and they worked damned hard to get them. I resent being expected to justify this to the very kids who've benefited by it, who take it all for granted. And I resent, too, the implication that my whole working life has been a farce. You can't have poets without power tools first."

On joining a corporation: "Don't sit there and tell me there's any tolerance of individuality in the corporation, when you *know* there just isn't—especially when it comes to dissent or dispute on public issues. What they really want is what they've got now. Thousands of Walter Mittys, some of whom might make the big move to middle management at 45 or 50—if they're obsequious enough—then again, maybe not. Thank you very much, but no thanks."

On the economic system: "Ours is a planned economy. Business and government control so much, and that control is so pervasive that you certainly can't call it free enterprise. If you think it is, you're living in a fantasy world."

On the social obligations of business: ". . . the first business of American business is to stay in business," a corporation president pointed out. "If a corporation so diverts its energies and resources as to go broke, there is nothing it can do—nothing at all—even if it claims to have a heart and conscience as big as the world."

But what did it all accomplish—this rap session between businessmen and youth? Surely few minds were changed. Yet most of the participants felt the conference had been a success. For one thing, the very fact that such a meeting had taken place was cause for optimism. And the exchange of ideas proved tonic to both sides, a step toward mutual understanding. It was a beginning. In fact, it was such a good beginning that they decided they should give it another try. Not on the same scale, of course, but in smaller groups after they had returned home.

With this idea in mind, students and businessmen from the same parts of the country met in separate workshops. They agreed to continue to meet in the months ahead to decide what they could do, together, to improve the quality of life where they lived.

Goodbyes were enthusiastic. At the regional meeting I attended, a student pretty well summed up the feelings of the group: "All I can say is, this is a great start. This is exactly what we're looking for."

Starting Time: _____	Finishing Time: _____
Reading Time: _____	Reading Rate: _____
Comprehension: _____	Vocabulary: _____

VOCABULARY: The following words have been taken from the selection you have just read. Put an *X* in the box before the best meaning or synonym for the word as used in the selection.

1. **pragmatic**, page 31, column 2, paragraph 4
" '...but our prime consideration is a pragmatic one.' "
☐ a. active
☐ b. meddlesome
☐ c. practical
☐ d. hostile

2. **farce**, page 32, column 1, paragraph 2
" 'And I resent, too, the implication that my whole working life has been a farce.' "
☐ a. mockery
☐ b. amusement
☐ c. tragedy
☐ d. fancy

3. **tolerance**, page 32, column 1, paragraph 3
" 'Don't sit there and tell me there's any tolerance of individuality in the corporation, ...' "
☐ a. indication
☐ b. permissiveness
☐ c. endurance
☐ d. open-mindedness

4. **obsequious**, page 32, column 1, paragraph 3
" '...some of whom might make the big move to middle management at 45 or 50—if they're obsequious enough—' "
☐ a. submissive
☐ b. observant
☐ c. arrogant
☐ d. talented

5. **pervasive**, page 32, column 1, paragraph 4
" 'Business and government control so much, and that control is so pervasive...' "
☐ a. perverse
☐ b. complete
☐ c. strict
☐ d. irresponsible

CONTEXTUAL AIDS: OBJECT OF PREPOSITION

Studies of good readers show that they are aware of the context of what they are reading. This means that they are anticipating what is coming next by what has gone before.

The many ways in which context functions to help the reader recognize words are called contextual aids.

Contextual Aid. Words can be understood as objects of prepositions. A clue to the meaning of an unknown word is sometimes revealed by the preposition preceding it in a phrase. In the sentence, **He washed up at the _____**, the preposition **at** clues the reader that the missing word is probably **sink**. The preposition **in** would have probably clued the reader to **tub**.

In the following sentences, examples of this type of contextual aid have been used, followed by nonsense words. Underline the nonsense word and write the correct word on the line following each sentence.

1. He cannot pay his bills; he is deeply in plast.

   _____

2. On election day the voters lined up at the sults.

   _____

3. He filled the tank with twenty gallons of clat.

   _____

4. The rescue team had to dig its way through waist-high drifts of mish.

   _____

5. The instructor sketched the design on the board with smond.

   _____

6. He hooked the shark using herring for pumb.

   _____

7. The picture was flashed on the prend for all to see.

   _____

8. At night, after pitching tents, they cooked their steaks over a gervr.

   _____

9. The child ran home with the money and put it in his sald.

   _____

10. To win the race the runners had to jump over the dumpers.

    _____

11. As he sat behind the shald of his car, he was hit from behind.

    _____

THE SKILL OF SKIMMING

You may be surprised to hear skimming called a skill. Yet that is exactly what it is.

Flexible Reading

A good reader is flexible. He varies his reading technique to suit the occasion. He knows that there are many kinds of reading and he tries to become skilled in all of them. Some materials demand a slow, analytical approach; insurance policies and contracts are good examples. Light fiction calls for a breezy, casual kind of reading at a fairly rapid rate. Another kind of material permits the reader to run his eyes down the column of print, snatching ideas on the run. This is skimming, and let us examine the kind of material it is appropriate for.

Suitable Material

Often, in the course of a week, we run across articles, accounts, and stories which are of just casual or passing interest to us. These may be unrelated to school or the job; they may contain very little factual content; and they are very simply written. To read these materials analytically like contracts and documents would be a waste of time. To use our study skills and techniques on them would be nonproductive and wasted effort. These materials need only to be skimmed to be comprehended.

Comprehension Level

Comprehension is another aspect of flexible reading. There are degrees or levels of comprehension which are appropriate for certain materials. For example, a very practical and thorough kind is needed to follow directions accurately. Obviously we don't need this for reading the comics. Textbooks require the student to remember concepts and to understand relationships. The student, moreover, is expected to use comprehension as a tool for thinking. But simple articles of passing interest require only a temporary kind of comprehension — the kind that comes from skimming.

COMPREHENSION: For each of the following statements and questions, select the option containing the most complete or most accurate answer.

1. The real work of the conference was done at
(g)
   ☐ a. the forums.
   ☐ b. the workshops.
   ☐ c. the dinner meetings.
   ☐ d. the general sessions.

2. The Berkeley student advocated
(c)
   ☐ a. personal responsibility.
   ☐ b. collective responsibility.
   ☐ c. corporate responsibility.
   ☐ d. executive responsibility.

3. An important group which should have been
(h) represented at the conference was
   ☐ a. corporate management.
   ☐ b. university administrators.
   ☐ c. stockholders.
   ☐ d. government.

4. The University of Houston student made an
(c) appeal for
   ☐ a. organized collective action.
   ☐ b. corporate understanding and response.
   ☐ c. minority rights and revolution.
   ☐ d. radical political action.

5. The words of Henry Ford seem to encourage
(h)
   ☐ a. controlled productivity.
   ☐ b. organized labor.
   ☐ c. enormous profit.
   ☐ d. profit sharing.

6. According to Raymon Mulford, a policy
(f) which fosters social justice favors
   ☐ a. the growth of socialism.
   ☐ b. the financial interests of business.
   ☐ c. the religious climate of the nation.
   ☐ d. the individual at the expense of business.

7. The businessman who spoke on the drawbacks
(c) of affluence felt that young people
   ☐ a. should think of their future and work to secure it.
   ☐ b. should concern themselves with problems they can understand.
   ☐ c. should not be obliged to serve in the armed forces.
   ☐ d. should appreciate the accomplishments of other generations.

8. The remarks leveled at the economic system
(h) were most probably made by
   ☐ a. a student.
   ☐ b. a businessman.
   ☐ c. a politician.
   ☐ d. a stockholder.

9. The comment, "...the first business of Ameri-
(h) can business is to stay in business," suggests that the decisions made by businessmen must be guided by
   ☐ a. hard facts.
   ☐ b. emotion.
   ☐ c. morality.
   ☐ d. social consciousness.

10. The conference succeeded
(c)
   ☐ a. to change the minds of the participants.
   ☐ b. to improve the quality of life in America.
   ☐ c. to generate hope and understanding.
   ☐ d. to improve the image of the corporate business world.

> Comprehension Skills: a—isolating details; b—recalling specific facts; c—retaining concepts; d—organizing facts; e—understanding the main idea; f—drawing a conclusion; g—making a judgment; h—making an inference; i—recognizing tone; j—understanding characters; k—appreciation of literary forms.

The Right To Exist

A Report on Our Endangered Wildlife

A little more than a century ago a man could watch by the hour as millions of passenger pigeons winged overhead, literally shutting out the sun.

A little more than a half a century ago the last passenger pigeon on earth died in a zoo.

A little more than a century ago a man might have watched by the hour as a herd of bison thundered across the land.

A little more than half a century ago the American bison had been reduced to a few hundred stragglers. But a spark of concern caught fire, and the bison was brought back from the edge of oblivion to continue as part of America's wildlife heritage.

Today the future of many kinds of wildlife depends on how brightly burns that spark of concern. We can recall, in shortened form, Aldo Leopold's observation on the extinction of the passenger pigeon: "For one species to mourn the death of another is a new thing under the sun. We, who have lost our pigeons, mourn the loss. Had the funeral been ours, the pigeons would hardly have mourned us. In this fact, rather than in nylons or atomic bombs, lies evidence of our superiority over the beasts." And we can be assured by the bison we see today that imperiled wildlife can be saved when concern is bright enough.

Through the eons of time, who knows how many kinds of animals have lived and died? Why did the huge dinosaurs, the formidable saber-toothed tiger, the diminutive four-toed horse, the gigantic mastodons and mammoths disappear from the earth? They held important places in the wildlife communities of their times, which collectively spanned millions of years. Now they are known only from fossils in the crust of the earth.

These ancient species disappeared along with thousands of others that lived long before man began to dominate the earth. We can only speculate on the cause of their demise on the basis of geologic evidence and our knowledge of species that survived until historic times.

Our wild animals have developed through natural selective processes. Each different form has special characteristics, unique features, that have enabled it to survive. These attributes fit them for specific niches in their environment. If species arise that are better adapted to fill community niches, the original occupants are replaced, and when there is an adverse change in the conditions for which a species is fitted, it faces two alternatives: Adapt or perish.

Before the arrival of man, species disappeared because of gradual climatic changes, glacial advances, or inundation by ancient seas. These changes eliminated or adversely modified their habitats. Some lost out in their fight for life when competition with other species grew too intense.

Changes have been speeded up by civilized man with his technological means of rapidly altering environment, his propensity for introducing competing species, both wild and domestic, and his more direct means of destruction. As a result, species are now disappearing faster than they are evolving.

What Makes a Species Become Extinct?

How can you tell if an animal is in jeopardy? To determine whether a species is in danger, information is needed about the area it originally occupied and its abundance, the changes in its distribution, and the causes of those changes, its present status in numbers and range, and the natural and human factors that may act upon it. We need to know when pollution may be making unlivable the only stream that is the habitat of a race of fish; or when the drying up of the last bit of marsh will wipe out the only source of food or nesting cover for a species of bird; or when expansion by another species will bring about, through interbreeding, the disappearance of the special characteristics that distinguish an interesting subspecies.

Specialists of the Bureau of Sport Fisheries and Wildlife of the U.S. Department of the Interior have suggested the circumstances under which wildlife should be considered in peril and have prepared a list of those considered rare and endangered. The terms used to show the status of wildlife species and subspecies or races are these:

An *endangered* form is one whose prospects of survival and reproduction are in immediate jeopardy. Its peril may result from one or many causes—ravages of disease, predation by other animals, competition from a more aggressive species, or changes in and loss of habitat. Endangered animals must have help, or extinction will probably soon follow. In this classification are about 90 mammals, birds, fish, reptiles, and amphibians.

A *rare* form is one whose numbers are few throughout its range. So long as conditions remain stable and favorable, such species may continue to survive in limited numbers. When such an animal occupies a limited habitat, adverse influences are more critical, and unfavorable changes in its environment may quickly make it endangered. In this classification are nearly 45 mammals, birds, fish, reptiles, and amphibians.

In addition there are *peripheral* forms whose occurrence in the United States is at the edge of their natural range. Such an animal may be found in satisfactory numbers outside our country, but its retention in our Nation's fauna may call for special attention. In this classification the specialists note over 80 mammals, birds, fish, and reptiles.

In *status undetermined* have been placed over 100 mammals, birds, and fish. Biologists have suggested that information be sought on these so that their status can be determined. Some of them may be in danger.

Education

Universal stewardship of wildlife should be a national objective. Responsible citizens must not only obey the laws themselves but must encourage others to obey. Organizations and individuals who have an interest in our native wildlife must take every opportunity to convey the conservation message to everyone. The subject is front page news. Interesting articles and pictures are readily accepted by the press and they form the basis for popular television programs.

Practically untouched are the opportunities for bringing this conservation message to school children. The story of endangered wildlife is the chronicle of much of our wasted natural wealth, though wildlife not yet extinct is a renewable resource.

The Price Is Right

There is even an economic advantage to the perpetuation of endangered animals. Concentrations of wildlife of any kind seem to draw people: Chambers of Commerce often advertise them as local attractions. When people gather, they naturally spend money and prime the local economy. Curiosity draws thousands of visitors to Aransas National Wildlife Refuge in Texas, where the few remaining magnificent whooping cranes gather to spend the winter. Sightseeing boats on the Intracoastal Waterway near the refuge enable people to get a view of these majestic birds. But in our whole national economy this is only a small part.

Many animals whose existence is in jeopardy were once important sources of food or other raw material for human use. The bison and the beaver practically supported the exploration and initial settlement of the West. The passenger pigeon, the sturgeon, and the prairie chicken were staple food items in the markets of yesteryear. Prairie chickens are unlikely to become an important food item again, but the fur seal and the northern sea otter herds have been rescued from the brink of extinction to become important items of commerce.

Americans are notorious for their interest in the underdog. This interest goes out to wildlife struggling for their very existence against obstacles that sometimes are the inevitable results of human progress, but may also be the results of human indifference or greed.

Suppose the last whooping crane quietly gave up the struggle for survival in some lonely marsh. Would it make any difference to you? Chances are you'll never see a live one anyhow—millions of Americans never will. Why worry? The same may be said of many other rare or endangered species. What are the values of these creatures? Why spend time and effort to save them?

Worth the Effort

Coldly appraised, there is little doubt we could get along without most forms of wildlife, be they common, rare, or threatened with extinction. We could get along without baseball or golf or automobiles or many, many other things—if we had to. But each of these helps make life easier or more pleasant or more interesting. It's a question of how many good things we want and can afford.

A businessman, after a period of tense competition, realized he must either slow up or blow up and took off on a fishing trip to the coast. The three game fish he caught were big ones, and figuring what he spent for his trip, they had a value of about $170 apiece. Or was that the value of the fish?

Can we set a value on a whooping crane as the price a zoo might offer on a free and open market?

The American bison or buffalo has been restored to the point that it is necessary to keep some of the herds to manageable size by disposing of a few animals for food. Should we figure the true worth of bison to the American people in food store values?

Can the worth of a city park be calculated in board feet of trees and cubic feet of soil? Or in children's feet at play?

A generation ago there was a vogue for estimating the worth of the chemicals and other elements that make up a human's body. In those days it came to something less than a dollar. Prices are higher now and no doubt a human these days is worth more than a dollar. Isn't he?

Why feel concern for whooping cranes?

History is replete with examples of evolution and change, a matter of considerable import to mankind as an indication or insight into his own future. Threatened forms are visible indicators of some of the changes that are continually occurring but often so subtly as to be otherwise unnoticed and therefore unmeasured.

Man's wisdom and experience have not been extensive enough to grasp the full significance of the loss of a species of wildlife. Each occupies a niche and makes a contribution to the whole of life. The biological impact of forever removing a form from the environment may not always be readily discernible, but something of value has been lost.

Human happiness is the sum total of all the desires and enjoyments and accomplishments of all the individuals who make up the human population. Take one part from the whole and it is no longer complete.

As the numbers of our wildlife grow fewer, their true individual value grows greater, for in the few are concentrated all the worth of one small but valuable part of our whole world.

Starting Time: _____	Finishing Time: _____
Reading Time: _____	Reading Rate: _____
Comprehension: _____	Vocabulary: _____

VOCABULARY: The following words have been taken from the selection you have just read. Put an X in the box before the best meaning or synonym for the word as used in the selection.

1. **formidable**, page 36, column 1, paragraph 6
   "...the formidable saber-toothed tiger, ..."
   □ a. exceptional
   □ b. dreaded
   □ c. pleasant
   □ d. forgotten

2. **habitats**, page 36, column 2, paragraph 2
   "These changes eliminated or adversely modified their habitats."
   □ a. natural environments
   □ b. houses
   □ c. habits
   □ d. wide distribution

3. **propensity**, page 36, column 2, paragraph 3
   "...his propensity for introducing competing species, ..."
   □ a. wish
   □ b. addiction
   □ c. need
   □ d. tendency

4. **inevitable**, page 37, column 2, paragraph 3
   "...obstacles that sometimes are the inevitable results of human progress, ..."
   □ a. required
   □ b. desired
   □ c. unavoidable
   □ d. unfortunate

5. **replete**, page 38, column 1, paragraph 5
   "History is replete with examples of evolution and change, ..."
   □ a. lacking
   □ b. repeat
   □ c. filled
   □ d. finished

PREFIXES

Many English words consist of a base or root word to which prefixes (beginnings) and suffixes (endings) have been added. To the root word **agree** (a verb) we can add both a prefix and a suffix to get **disagreeable** (an adjective) which has an opposite meaning.

A prefix is added to the beginning of a word and causes a change in the meaning of that word. We have just seen how the prefix **dis** reverses the meaning of **agree**.

Two Prefixes

1. **de-** is a Latin prefix which means **down** or **from**. A **deposit** is money the buyer puts down.

2. **inter-** is also Latin and it means **among** or **between**. **International** trade is conducted among nations.

In the following sentences, the words in bold print need prefixes. Add one of these two prefixes to each word and write your word on the line following the sentence.

1. Slow down when driving on ice but **celerate** gradually.

   _____

2. Citing poor health, he **clined** the nomination.

   _____

3. The dictator was **posed** by a band of army officers.

   _____

4. By **fusing** the chemicals, a new compound was developed.

   _____

5. May I **pose** an opinion in this conversation?

   _____

6. Secrets pertaining to space exploration have been **classified**.

   _____

7. The official was found **linquent** in the performance of his duties.

   _____

8. In football hindering the receiving of a pass can be ruled **ference**.

   _____

9. An **mission** was scheduled between Acts II and III, permitting the audience to get up and stretch.

   _____

10. An **-urban** train would reduce commuter traffic between neighboring cities.

   _____

SKIMMING FOR FACTS

Skimming is an art and skill — it is not careless reading.

We mentioned in an earlier lesson that there are certain light and unimportant materials which do not require lasting comprehension. These materials lend themselves well to skimming.

Study-type Material

Another kind of material which permits the reader to skim is study-type matter in which the student wishes to locate certain facts or extract specific data. Actually this is a reference skill—skimming through a chapter or lesson to see if a particular topic is discussed or covered. When the student finds what he is looking for, he then employs his reading and study techniques. Consider this type of skimming a more thorough kind of previewing.

When skimming for facts, here is how to proceed.

1. **Read the Title.** This may tell you if the author's subject is one which might include your information.

2. **Read the Subhead.** Be alert for a word pertaining to your topic. See if the author announces a category or classification which might include it.

3. **Read the Illustration.** Look for graphic information relating to what you are seeking.

4. **Read First Sentences.** Look for paragraphs which contain information and definitions. These are the ones most likely to contain factual data. Skim through these looking for your topic. Paragraphs of introduction may tell you what you are seeking is coming next. Paragraphs of illustration will probably not contain factual data—these may be glossed over or skipped entirely. The closing paragraph is not likely to help, either.

Skimming for facts is a valuable reference skill and one more tool of the flexible reader.

COMPREHENSION: For each of the following statements and questions, select the option containing the most complete or most accurate answer.

1. It was public concern that saved the bison
(b) from extinction. The strength of this concern will
   - ☐ a. encourage the creation of many parks and zoos.
   - ☐ b. determine the future of many kinds of wildlife.
   - ☐ c. limit the great industrial productivity of America.
   - ☐ d. interfere with the survival of small animal species.

2. Aldo Leopold's observation can be inter-
(e) preted to mean which of the following?
   - ☐ a. Man should concentrate solely on his own survival.
   - ☐ b. Man should take pride in his humanity.
   - ☐ c. Technological progress determines man's basic superiority.
   - ☐ d. Pigeons are unworthy of man's concern.

3. The extinction of the dinosaur and the saber-
(h) toothed tiger suggests that
   - ☐ a. they failed to adapt.
   - ☐ b. man destroyed their environment.
   - ☐ c. they became too numerous.
   - ☐ d. pollution was not controlled.

4. Species are presently disappearing faster than
(c) they are evolving because of
   - ☐ a. natural disasters.
   - ☐ b. diminishing funds.
   - ☐ c. population control.
   - ☐ d. human technology.

5. The factors which contribute to the extinction
(c) of a species are
   - ☐ a. stable and unchangeable.
   - ☐ b. easy to control.
   - ☐ c. impossible to determine.
   - ☐ d. involved and complex.

6. Forms of wildlife which require immediate
(f) help are those which are classified as
   - ☐ a. endangered.
   - ☐ b. rare.
   - ☐ c. peripheral.
   - ☐ d. status undetermined.

7. The ultimate responsibility for the preserva-
(g) tion of wildlife lies with
   - ☐ a. the federal government.
   - ☐ b. the public media.
   - ☐ c. the general public.
   - ☐ d. concerned groups.

8. Conservation is
(c)
   - ☐ a. poor economy.
   - ☐ b. good business.
   - ☐ c. a last resort.
   - ☐ d. a necessary evil.

9. Wildlife in its numerous and varied forms
(c)
   - ☐ a. threatens human survival.
   - ☐ b. is too expensive to maintain.
   - ☐ c. enriches human existence.
   - ☐ d. is impossible to control.

10. The selection is written in the form of a
(k)
   - ☐ a. thesis.
   - ☐ b. report.
   - ☐ c. debate.
   - ☐ d. story.

Comprehension Skills: a—isolating details; b—recalling specific facts; c—retaining concepts; d—organizing facts; e—understanding the main idea; f—drawing a conclusion; g—making a judgment; h—making an inference; i—recognizing tone; j—understanding characters; k—appreciation of literary forms.

The New York

Why Are They Saying All Those Horrible Things about It?

Subway System

Nearly two million people ride the New York City subway every day, but very few of them have anything good to say about it. Daily riders make such comments as:

"Personally, I have been on the verge of quitting my job many times due to unfortunate experiences on the subway. Not only are the trains themselves in terrible condition, but lately it seems even the escalators in the stations are out of order."

Another comment concerning how safe people think the subways are came from a secretary: "If you mean 'safe' as it concerns operation, it's a toss-up. If you're referring to the unsavory characters who frequent the subways, you take your life in your own hands when you ride them."

A similar comment was: "I believe every station should bear a sign: 'ENTER AT YOUR OWN RISK.' Sometimes the smoke, from what I assume are electrical fires, is so bad that it's almost impossible to breathe. Do I think the subway is the most efficient way of getting around the city? For Manhattan, yes. If you live in Queens, get a horse."

On the one hand, some of these opinions may be justified. Riding the subway—particularly for out-of-towners—can be a traumatic experience. There is the roar of trains running through sometimes dimly-lit stations, and hordes of jostling people. Taking the subway during rush hour can often seem like an exercise in basic survival. A person may have to fight his way downstairs to a crowded platform, and struggle to find himself a position near the tracks. When a train enters the station and opens its doors, the scene can be somewhat like putting the Oklahoma land rush on the top of a billiard table.

On the other hand, the subway is still the fastest, most efficient and most economical (short of walking or bicycling) way of getting around the city. It is faster than a bus. It is even faster than a taxi in many cases, and certainly is a lot cheaper.

And officials of the Transit Authority go to great lengths to fight the problems that exist—such as crime, overcrowding and litter—with varying degrees of success. To combat crime in the subway, the Transit Authority employs a force of 3,200 transit police who patrol the platforms and ride the passenger cars during the high crime periods from eight in the evening until four in the morning. This is the seventh largest police force in the country.

Contrary to some views, crime in the subways is relatively low compared to that in the city as a whole. In the period from 1965 to 1970, for example, felonies in New York City increased from over 54-thousand to 489-thousand; in the subway, felonies increased from 1.5-thousand to 4.5-thousand. This means that the city felony rate increased over eight times during that period, compared to only three times in the subway.

Police may have an effect on crime, but they can do little about the crowds. It may be pointed out that overcrowding is not a problem peculiar to the subway—overcrowding is peculiar to all of New York.

One prime example of the heavy subway traffic is the Times Square area, the region around the intersection of 42nd Street with Broadway and Sixth, Seventh and Eighth Avenues. A total of 16 different subway lines run through this two-block area, with a total of 4,750 daily trains. During a single day throughout the entire system, some 3,982,200 people pass through the turnstiles.

In an attempt at alleviating this crowding, commerce and industry associations and other civic and employers' groups in New York have experimented with staggered work hours. A third of the people who work in a particular building will work from 8:30 A.M. to 4:30 P.M., another third will come in at 8:45 and leave at 4:45, and the rest from 9 to 5. The Downtown-Lower Manhattan Association and the Port of New York Authority reported recently that this system resulted in a 26 percent reduction in congestion in three major subway stations.

Many subway riders complain about litter. Often cars and stations are strewn with newspapers and the walls are covered with graffiti. This situation exists in spite of the fact that each of the Transit Authority's 7,000 cars are swept clean each morning before it leaves the yard. According to the Transit Authority, the cleanup of the subway has increased considerably. In 1969, as an example, the exteriors of 6,856 cars were scrubbed each month. Last year, the cleanups were stepped up to 14,401.

In addition, heavy scrubbing went up from 2,100 to 4,000 a month—four out of every seven cars were given an additional interior cleaning.

A staggering 32 tons of trash are removed from the subway every day by a force of 2,000 men who work from 10 P.M. to 6 A.M. when the platforms are relatively free of passengers and the trains run at longer intervals. And the Transit Authority spent over $500,000 last year alone to remove spray-painted graffiti from the walls of the stations.

While crime, overcrowding and litter are among the concerns of subway riders, perhaps a major source of irritation has been recent fare increases, following what the TA terms "years of politically dictated, unrealistically low fares." In 1966, the price of a subway ride was 20 cents. In 1970, this was increased to 30 cents. And in 1972, the fare was upped again to 35 cents—an increase over a 6-year period of 15 cents. Some New Yorkers felt that an increase in fare should have been accompanied by an upgrading of service, but the Transit Authority countered by saying that the fares still lagged far behind what it costs to provide the subway service.

A spokesman for the Metropolitan Transportation Authority said recently that while the subways have made great progress in the past few years in overcoming long-existing problems, the key to further improvements is the money to pay for them.

The crux of the problem with the subway is that it simply is not capable of paying its own way. The Transit Authority faces a financial crisis. This crisis grew out of years of decisions by the City of New York—which owns the subway—to hold the fare at an artificially low level, and at the same time refusing to subsidize subway operations. There are two alternatives: you either allow the fare to rise, or you subsidize. If you don't take one of those two alternatives, your subway service will deteriorate.

When you have a combination of an artificially low fare and a lack of other sources of operating funds, you simply cannot maintain the system at the levels you'd like. This accounted for the steady deterioration of the system during the 50s and 60s when the fare was arbitrarily held at 15 or 20 cents.

The State took over in 1968, added a lot of money, and effected a turn-around. But the problem was so enormous and the deterioration had been so great during those long decades of lack of maintenance and financial starvation that to fully correct the situation requires enormous leverage. The state is now in a financial crisis of its own, and asking the federal government for the first time to come in and subsidize to help hold the fare down.

Most subway costs are labor costs. Seven dollars out of every eight of the subway's expense budget is a direct labor cost. To pay that seven dollars out of every eight absorbs more money than the subway takes in the fare box. It's as simple—and as complicated—as that.

Dr. William J. Ronan, Chairman of the Metropolitan Transportation Authority and president of the Institute for Rapid Transit, testified before the Subcommittee on Housing of the Committee on Banking and Currency of the U.S. House of Representatives in a bid to receive a federal subsidy.

Dr. Ronan said that a transit emergency exists, "not just in the New York Metropolitan Region, but in all of urban America . . . . The problem to which I address myself today, gentlemen, is the product of economic inflation, rising operating costs, changing patterns of travel and other factors that have arisen in the past decade . . . .

"The transit system losses experienced throughout this country—amounting to some $400-million last year—are not exclusively big city losses. We are witnessing an epidemic situation throughout our cities, large and small, across the nation. Bus and rapid transit facilities can no longer carry out the function of moving people to their jobs, to their schools, to recreation, and to shopping districts, without material assistance outside the fare box."

Starting Time: _____		Finishing Time: _____	
Reading Time: _____		Reading Rate: _____	
Comprehension: _____		Vocabulary: _____	

VOCABULARY: The following words have been taken from the selection you have just read. Put an X in the box before the best meaning or synonym for the word as used in the selection.

1. **unsavory**, page 41, column 1, paragraph 3
" 'If you're referring to the unsavory characters who frequent...' "
☐ a. unfortunate
☐ b. sickly
☐ c. tasteless
☐ d. objectionable

2. **frequent**, page 41, column 1, paragraph 3
" '...characters who frequent the subways, ...' "
☐ a. resort to
☐ b. seldom appear in
☐ c. are often in
☐ d. visit occasionally

3. **alleviating**, page 41, column 2, paragraph 5
"In an attempt at alleviating this crowding, ..."
☐ a. satisfying
☐ b. increasing
☐ c. relieving
☐ d. controlling

4. **countered**, page 42, column 1, paragraph 3
"...but the Transit Authority countered by saying that the fares..."
☐ a. answered
☐ b. encountered
☐ c. objected
☐ d. agreed

5. **subsidize**, page 42, column 2, paragraph 1
"...either allow the fare to rise, or you subsidize."
☐ a. charge
☐ b. finance
☐ c. substitute
☐ d. increase

SYLLABICATION

Syllabication (frequently written syllabification) refers to the process of dividing a word into its parts or syllables.

Knowing how to reduce words to their syllables aids both reading and spelling. Frequently a long word can be recognized and understood if pronounced by syllables. And in spelling, of course, knowledge of syllables contributes to accuracy.

There are rules or generalizations which we can follow when dividing words. One rule tells us that when one consonant comes between two vowels in a word, the word is divided before the consonant. In the word **climate**, the consonant **m** comes between the vowels **i** and **a**; therefore, we divide the word into **cli** and **mate**, before the **m**.

In the following sentences, divide the words in bold print according to this rule. Write the word on the line to the right, inserting hyphens (-) between the syllables.

1. Give no **credence** to rumors. _____

2. School closes on **Friday**. _____

3. The **debate** ran on. _____

4. **Details** are essential. _____

5. **Dilute** the solution. _____

6. The chimney **ejects** smoke. _____

7. The **female** is prettier. _____

8. A **glacial** appearance resulted. _____

9. The **grotesque** repels. _____

10. **Human** rights must prevail. _____

11. His friends are **legion**. _____

12. A **lesion** caused blindness. _____

13. Seek **recourse** for injustice. _____

14. **Savor** victory. _____

15. **Unite** for strength. _____

16. Don't **desert** us. _____

17. File tax **returns** early. _____

18. Read the **label** first. _____

DYNAMIC SKIMMING

We can label another type of high speed skimming dynamic skimming. We call it dynamic because of the impressive results it yields at such high speeds. You may have seen demonstrations of this type of reading on television or have read about it somewhere. The fact that some reading courses charge fees close to two hundred dollars testifies to the value of this kind of reading as a tool in the repertory of the flexible reader. The steps to dynamic skimming are these.

1. **Preview.** As you no doubt have begun to realize, previewing is a prerequisite to reading of any kind. In dynamic skimming, previewing is more essential than ever. Before skimming, the reader must perform a thorough and comprehensive preview of the entire article. The steps to previewing do not change. Just more time is spent learning as much as possible to use as a mental outline for skimming.

2. **Skim.** This time let your eyes flow down the column of print, snatching ideas on the run. Do not stop to read—do not pause to reflect. Strive to let the words trigger your mind as you skim by.

This kind of skimming is difficult at first because we've been in the habit of reading line by line. To overcome this natural tendency, use your finger as a pacer, to force your eyes down the page. You may wish to move your finger in a zigzag fashion, letting the eyes fixate (stop and read) twice on each line. Gradually speed up until you are able to cover the page in ten or twelve seconds.

3. **Reread.** This is the third step to dynamic skimming. Rereading is done like previewing, attempting to fill any gaps in your understanding of the article.

To be successful, you must have easy material and perform each of the three steps: preview, skim, and reread.

COMPREHENSION: For each of the following statements and questions, select the option containing the most complete or most accurate answer.

1. The critics of the New York subway system
(h) seem to think that it

☐ a. costs too much to operate.
☐ b. cannot be salvaged.
☐ c. does not serve enough people.
☐ d. costs too much to use.

2. The officials of the Transit Authority are
(g) strong in their determination

☐ a. to keep fare prices down.
☐ b. to rebuild the entire system.
☐ c. to reduce operating expenses.
☐ d. to make the subways safe.

3. The crowded condition on New York subways
(c) is directly related to

☐ a. overpopulation.
☐ b. crime.
☐ c. poor service.
☐ d. faulty equipment.

4. The staggered work hour experiment is an
(g) example of

☐ a. creative thinking.
☐ b. oppressive regimentation.
☐ c. futile effort.
☐ d. financial independence.

5. Many problems experienced by the New York
(f) transit system are related to

☐ a. official indifference.
☐ b. juvenile delinquency.
☐ c. public abuse.
☐ d. insufficient patronage.

6. It seems that the best interests of the transit
(h) system and the people who use it can be
served if

☐ a. the police put an end to crime.
☐ b. the Transit Authority is replaced.
☐ c. the fare is increased realistically.
☐ d. the city assumes control.

7. The financial crisis faced by the Transit
(b) Authority is directly related to

☐ a. state subsidy.
☐ b. labor costs.
☐ c. federal neglect.
☐ d. public demands.

8. The present state of the New York transit
(e) system is the result of

☐ a. poor service and unwise management.
☐ b. population growth and public apathy.
☐ c. inflation and political expediency.
☐ d. long neglect and increased profits.

9. New York's transportation problem is
(c) ☐ a. common across the country.
☐ b. peculiar to New York City.
☐ c. common to large cities.
☐ d. related to high unemployment.

10. Transit systems across the United States
(c) ☐ a. operate with a low margin of profit.
☐ b. require time to recuperate.
☐ c. should be nationalized.
☐ d. must be subsidized.

Comprehension Skills: a—isolating details; b—recalling specific facts; c—retaining concepts; d—organizing facts; e—understanding the main idea; f—drawing a conclusion; g—making a judgment; h—making an inference; i—recognizing tone; j—understanding characters; k—appreciation of literary forms.

The Duck Man of Venice

A Roly-poly Tuba Player Has Become a Waterfowl Benefactor and Doctor

Skip Ferderber

To several hundred ducks and geese living in the stagnant salty waters which fill the once elegant canals of Venice, California, a roly-poly tuba player has become their benefactor, their doctor—and literally their connection to life itself.

To a visitor to Southern California, the colorful Venice Canals—a sleepy decaying neighborhood located a half-mile from the Pacific Ocean with graffiti-scrawled walls, ill-kempt buildings, long-haired hippies and an abundance of dirty children who play loudly beside the crumbling seawalls—somehow become more quaint with the constant honking of the water fowl that have made the old and rundown area their home.

Their charm, however, masks their desperate state. With salt water from the ocean filling the canals being anathema to the fresh water birds; with little or no vegetation to sustain them; and with too many birds and too many hazards such as dogs and cruel human beings, the quackers and honkers are faced with a desperate situation.

It would be far worse without the Duck Man of Venice.

His name is Buddy Hayes, or, more formally, Theodore Hayes. He has taken on the enormously complex job of providing food, water and medical attention for Venice's troubled waterfowl community.

Twice a day, at 11 A.M. and 5 P.M., the usually quiet neighborhood reverberates with the rasping sound of hundreds of quacking birds who throng and gawk outside the white picket fence surrounding Hayes' two-story house, situated on the corner of a canal intersection.

The ducks, acting like quibbling ladies at a clothing sale, vie for space near where Hayes or his wife, Jean, will offer a smorgasbord of duck pellets, hard corn kernels, lettuce leaves and other greens.

The door opens and out marches Hayes, a chubby, smiling elf of a man dressed in a gray jumpsuit and poncho, bright red boots and a wreath of graying hair topped with a pony tail tied with a rubber band.

He approaches the fence, waits for the appropriate moment, and flings the food in a grainy

shower. The birds heave to their meal with a vengeance.

And while they eat, Hayes changes their water, providing fresh water for the birds to drink and to bathe in—the only way they have to wash the deathly salt off their feathers, salt which tends to make it increasingly hard for them to fly or to live.

It's been this way seven days a week for seven years for the 54-year-old musician, a former regular with the Lawrence Welk ensemble, who views the survival of the ducks as a labor of love—even though the cost of purchasing food, water and veterinarian services runs over $600 a year, money he can ill afford.

"It's an unnatural place for the ducks to live," said Hayes one day recently, slouched in a chair, his hands on his pot belly, watching with fondness as his charges loudly gobbled their midday meal. "They're fresh water creatures, not salt water, and yet people insist on dumping their ducks here in the canals."

"Every year, around Easter especially, we get a lot of ducks, kids having let them go in the canals after getting them for gifts and getting tired of them real fast.

"And they start multiplying and, well, you know, here they are." He looked thoughtful for a moment. "I sure wish these pet shop owners would stop selling them. Maybe some of them don't know that the animals they sell are going to wind up down here. I don't know. . . ."

When he came to the canals following a long career as a tuba player, a bass player and a comedian, he bought a house and began the process of transforming it into a delightful two-story local landmark with a gray-painted roof, white stucco and red trimming.

After years of traveling with bands—including Welk's and at one time, his own—it was time to settle down and enjoy life.

He reckoned, however, without the ducks.

"It was about the time I moved here that I noticed the ducks starting to come," he reminisced. "I began feeding them along with some others in the neighborhood. I'm about the only one left, I guess."

He also converted an empty lot adjacent to his house into a duck shelter and hospital for birds injured by overexposure to salt water or that have been injured by neighborhood dogs and cats.

Over the years, Hayes has pulled through dozens of the waterfowl by providing a recuperation area and by footing veterinarian bills which average as high as $20 a month. He is not sure exactly how high: "I don't dare look at them," he winces.

Aside from the natural dangers, which have included a severe botulism attack, he faces the duck's own reproductive cycle, a problem which continues to create an overpopulation problem in the canals.

On occasion, he has enlisted the help of sympathetic young people who have combed the canal banks for birds' nests, breaking any eggs they found. But he is not always too successful, and the results are tragic when he is not.

"Not too long ago," he said, "I picked up ten baby geese and raised them in my backyard. I released them and it was only a couple of days later that I looked out into the canal near my backyard and I found five of them dead, floating in the water. So I got the other five and I've got them here in my backyard. I don't know what I'm going to do with them."

One solution he tried was to give them away to Hollywood Park, one of Southern California's largest racetracks which features an infield area with an extensive waterfowl collection. The park shied away from any outside donations, other than those arranged by the waterfowl manager. Hayes is still looking for some people who would like to become foster parents to the geese.

The ducks and geese are also easy prey to neighborhood pets. To prevent this, Hayes has planted heavy shrubbery around his property in an effort to ward off any marauding dogs and cats. His three dogs, in addition, have voluntarily taken over the job of "watchdog" for the ducks. "Whenever the ducks quack a sort of a warning signal, a sound that the dogs recognize, they'll go over and help to chase intruders off the property."

One danger that he has little control over is the most dangerous animal of all: man. "The street people eat them once in a while," he said, shaking his head sadly. "I've never seen anyone actually picking up any of the ducks, but every so often I'll see something in a trash can that looks suspiciously like duck feathers."

He added that he didn't think they would be good eating: "With all the salt water they've drunk, the meat is probably too salty."

Another problem facing the Duck Man of Venice is a massive reconstruction of the canals, financed by property owners by assessments to the tune of $24.5 million, and which will include draining of the canals. Although the starting date may be as much as four years away, owing to a series of recently filed lawsuits, Hayes still feels obligated to try to make some sort of arrangements for the birds.

"If the draining of the canals doesn't get them," he said, "the dogs will. I'm just going to try to keep them alive until the project starts and take them somewhere else so they'll have some sort of protection.

"They can't go and join their fellow birds because most of them are domesticated and they don't know how to fly."

Over the years, he has received complaints from some neighbors who become incensed by the rat-tat-tat sound of a gaggle of geese and ducks calling for their food. Hayes threw up his hands. "You know, they were really the ones who helped encourage the ducks. They started putting out food and water and the ducks multiplied and then the people stopped and the ducks were still here."

He has asked for cooperation from the city of Los Angeles—Venice being a suburb of the megalopolis—but he has received little help. According to his wife, Jean, the city was asked to transport some of the ducks elsewhere to avoid overcrowding and to lessen the chance of a botulism epidemic—an ever-current possibility with the presence of even one duck infected with the killer disease.

But waterfowl, she explained, are under the control of the state fish and game commission and the city apparently has been unable to make arrangements to transport the ducks. "They can't place them locally because every place around here is loaded with ducks," she said.

While the Hayes have been the ducks' chief supporters, they hasten to add that some of the long-haired young people in the neighborhood have eagerly responded to help care for the ducks when help has been requested, especially during a botulism attack.

But by and large, the main responsibility still falls on Buddy Hayes. And he does not shirk that task. Even though his current job—playing in a downtown Los Angeles dance ballroom four nights a week—pays him a somewhat limited wage, and even though he faces paying a hefty assessment on his property as a result of the canals reconstruction project, he is determined to do what he can for as long as he can.

"As long as I have a dime in my pocket," said Hayes with a gleam in his eye, "I'll feed the ducks. I might lose my house"—and he laughed—"but I'll feed the ducks."

Starting Time: _____	Finishing Time: _____
Reading Time: _____	Reading Rate: _____
Comprehension: _____	Vocabulary: _____

VOCABULARY: The following words have been taken from the selection you have just read. Put an *X* in the box before the best meaning or synonym for the word as used in the selection.

1. **ill-kempt,** page 46, column 1, paragraph 2
"...graffiti-scrawled walls, ill-kempt buildings, ..."
☐ a. unsanitary
☐ b. unruly
☐ c. rough
☐ d. neglected

2. **anathema,** page 46, column 1, paragraph 3
"With salt water from the ocean filling the canals being an anathema to the fresh water birds;..."
☐ a. curse
☐ b. ban
☐ c. anesthesia
☐ d. blessing

3. **sustain,** page 46, column 1, paragraph 3
"...with little or no vegetation to sustain them;..."
☐ a. encourage
☐ b. support
☐ c. bother
☐ d. retain

4. **reverberates,** page 46, column 1, paragraph 6
"...the usually quiet neighborhood reverberates with the rasping sound, ..."
☐ a. argues
☐ b. recoils
☐ c. returns
☐ d. echoes

5. **marauding,** page 47, column 1, last paragraph
"...an effort to ward off any marauding dogs and cats."
☐ a. invading
☐ b. hungry
☐ c. malicious
☐ d. meandering

TOPICS FOR THE RESTLESS

PREFIXES

Many English words consist of a base or root word to which prefixes (beginnings) and suffixes (endings) have been added. To the root word **agree** (a verb) we can add both a prefix and a suffix to get **disagreeable** (an adjective) which has an opposite meaning.

A prefix is added to the beginning of a word and causes a change in the meaning of that word. We have just seen how the prefix **dis** reverses the meaning of **agree**.

Two Prefixes

1. sub- is a Latin prefix which means **under** or **below**. A **submarine** is an underwater craft.

2. super- is also Latin and it means **over, above,** or **extra.** **Superior** grades are above average.

In the following sentences the words in bold print need prefixes. Add one of these two prefixes to each word and write your word on the line following the sentence.

1. **Soil** is the layer of soil beneath that which is on the surface.

   _____

2. A second image was **imposed** on the first to create the illusion of motion.

   _____

3. Construction companies often **contract** the installation of certain items.

   _____

4. The land was **divided** into parcels suitable for development.

   _____

5. High speed automobile travel is now possible on **highways.**

   _____

6. Lake **ior** is the largest of the Great Lakes.

   _____

7. Read the **heads** at the beginning of each chapter, too.

   _____

8. **Chargers** improve automotive power by increasing the supply of air to the engine.

   _____

9. Our **sidiary** company manufactures the component parts.

   _____

10. The bullet caused a **ficial** wound; fortunately it did not enter the body.

    _____

PATTERNS OF THOUGHT

Authors use different patterns of thought in developing their paragraphs. The reader who understands these patterns has the key to selective reading—the art of extracting the topic sentence or key statement from each paragraph.

You recall from your English classes that a paragraph is defined as a group of sentences developing one idea. Authors use certain methods of developing this idea, and these methods can be classified into identifiable patterns. Recognizing the pattern permits the reader to find the main idea quickly and see how it has been developed. Students who have difficulty distinguishing between main ideas and subordinate details will find the use of paragraph patterns of immense value.

Selective Reading

We have been told of the late President Kennedy's ability to read at speeds of 1200 words-a-minute, picking out the key ideas. This kind of reading is called selective reading.

Selective reading techniques are additional skills needed by the flexible reader. Good reading is really many different kinds of reading, each suitable for a particular reading occasion. Many of the techniques we have been discussing in this text encourage flexible reading, and many of the skills taught contribute to flexibility in reading.

The skills of using patterns of paragraph development are part of the selective reading techniques needed to become a flexible reader. We will discuss the eleven popular patterns employed by authors to present and develop their main ideas. The student who can master the techniques of recognizing and using patterns of thought will have at his disposal the ability to pick out the key ideas in any material he is reading.

Plan now to study and learn the paragraph patterns which will be discussed in this text.

COMPREHENSION: For each of the following statements and questions, select the option containing the most complete or most accurate answer.

1. It can be inferred from the selection that
(h)
- ☐ a. Californians are cruel to wildlife.
- ☐ b. the ducks cannot adapt to conditions in the canal.
- ☐ c. long-haired hippies spoiled the once elegant canals.
- ☐ d. the canals cannot be improved.

2. The duck problem in the Venice Canals could
(g) be reduced and possibly solved by
- ☐ a. an organized effort to educate people.
- ☐ b. a ban on the sale of ducks in pet shops.
- ☐ c. pumping fresh water into the canals.
- ☐ d. following the example of Buddy Hayes.

3. The ducks in the Venice Canals are mostly
(f)
- ☐ a. the multi-colored wild species.
- ☐ b. the sea-going variety.
- ☐ c. prized for their tasty meat.
- ☐ d. the common white variety.

4. Buddy Hayes seems to have become involved in
(g)
- ☐ a. a strange sort of hobby.
- ☐ b. a publicity stunt.
- ☐ c. a useless undertaking.
- ☐ d. a one-man crusade.

5. The future of Buddy Hayes' ducks is
(c)
- ☐ a. uncertain.
- ☐ b. encouraging.
- ☐ c. bright.
- ☐ d. destruction.

6. Which of the following expresses the attitude
(e) behind Buddy Hayes' efforts?
- ☐ a. All life is precious.
- ☐ b. Recognition takes time.
- ☐ c. Children are cruel.
- ☐ d. Government is uncaring.

7. The ducks which populate the Venice Canal are
(a)
- ☐ a. dangerous.
- ☐ b. wild.
- ☐ c. domesticated.
- ☐ d. protected.

8. Buddy Hayes and his wife Jean are
(j)
- ☐ a. inconsistent.
- ☐ b. compassionate.
- ☐ c. bothersome.
- ☐ d. headstrong.

9. A solution must be found before
(f)
- ☐ a. the Hayes lose interest.
- ☐ b. the canals are drained.
- ☐ c. the Fish and Game Commission takes over.
- ☐ d. the public loses patience.

10. The selection is written in the form of
(k)
- ☐ a. a report.
- ☐ b. an interview.
- ☐ c. an open letter.
- ☐ d. an editorial.

Comprehension Skills: a—isolating details; b—recalling specific facts; c—retaining concepts; d—organizing facts; e—understanding the main idea; f—drawing a conclusion; g—making a judgment; h—making an inference; i—recognizing tone; j—understanding characters; k—appreciation of literary forms.

The Selling of the Flesh, I

Prostitution Is Growing. Its Sadness Fills the Land.

Rog Halegood

It is impossible to say how many individuals in the United States are selling their bodies in full or part-time employment for the purposes of sex. One estimate is that there are a minimum of 75,000 professional prostitutes at work during any given evening in the land of free enterprise. But it is the amateurs in the trade that are swelling the figure to perhaps ten times that estimate. These are the female and male hustlers who are turning "tricks" on street corners all across the nation with a rising frequency that has outstripped the capabilities of the law enforcement agencies to control the traffic. It is these "amateurs" that are posing the most serious threat of disease and crime ever known in the annals of American prostitution.

Whores and Americana

For all the stringencies exercised by the "Puritan ethic," America has always had a soft spot in its history and art for the ladies of horizontal pleasure.

From Dreiser through Capote, our literature is dotted with more-or-less unabashed paeans to the services and personalities of glamorous whores. As often as not, the girls and madams are portrayed as rough-and-tumble creatures of easy virtues but solid hearts. And, outside of fiction, real life accounts of ex-prostitutes and madams have held a solid sway over the interests of the reading public. Polly Adler, the fun-and-games proprietress of New York's best known bordello during the '20s and '30s, scored a success with her best seller, *A House Is Not a Home.* And speaking of Miss Adler, her establishment was a favorite haunt of George S. Kaufman, the hypochondriacal playwright who was able to overcome his fastidiousness to the point where he enjoyed a monthly charge account at Adler's. Those were the golden days of whoredom.

Our national myth, too, has been heavily influenced by the accounts of great prostitutes and greater houses. Surely the queen of all brothels was the 50-room mansion maintained in Chicago at the turn of the century by the winsome Everleigh

sisters, Ada and Minna. So lavish was their establishment that guests could enjoy the amenities of champagne suppers and music recitals played on a gold-leafed piano.

And, of course, what self-respecting frontier town would allow itself to be caught with its pants down by not offering an accommodating bordello? Whores and gun-slingers are as much a part of the lore of the West as the Forty-Niners and the sourdoughs.

Hollywood has oiled the dream-machine with whoring epics such as *The Revolt of Mamie Stover, Sadie Thompson, A Walk on the Wild Side, The Owl and the Pussycat* (wherein Barbra Streisand played a working girl without so much as having to sing a note), and *Klute* with Jane Fonda in a fully-exposed role.

It is easy to see why whores exert such a stronghold on literature and art (Rimbaud was their greatest poet; Lautrec and Hogarth their best artists). For one thing, it is such a basic, albeit base profession. It is the one calling open to all women. It is also, in a sense, the epitome of self-made professions. A girl, dealing solely on her wits (some famous prostitutes have been appallingly ugly) can work her way up from a two-buck hooker to a woman splendidly kept in a fashionable penthouse. At least, that's the theory. Today, however, the realities of prostitution—and the chances for advancement—are of a far grimmer nature than those of our past fantasies.

Exploding the Myth

In real life, there is nothing glamorous about prostitution. It is a terrifying existence of pimps and cops, of scared young girls and callous "johns," the trade sobriquet for the patrons of prostitutes.

Lorrie X. is a 17-year-old prostitute in Washington, D.C. Even at this age, she is a street "pro" with three years' experience. That means she turned her first "trick" when she was fourteen. She is black and services customers in the Southwest ghetto where she was raised. Her first sexual experience was at age 12 when she was raped by an uncle.

It would be comforting to think that 17-year-old Lorrie was an exception. She is not. She is but one of hundreds—perhaps, thousands—of young girls who exist today in what is a true white-slavery trade. The problem is so vast that vice-squads are at a loss as to how to stem the traffic.

Runaways are frequent targets for the pimps and assorted panders. Scared, broke, a long way from home, the girls are literally trapped into prostitution by the inducement of drugs, money and roofs over their heads. In New York City, there have been cases of runaway girls being kidnapped as they stepped off the buses at the sprawling Port Authority bus terminal!

Since accurate records cannot be kept on such a subrosa activity as white-slavery, it is impossible to estimate how many runaway girls listed on missing person dossiers across the country are engaged in prostitution. Certainly, from arrest reports alone, the figures are staggeringly high—perhaps more than 200 in New York City. Percentages are equally grim in Washington, Chicago, Los Angeles and San Francisco.

Not only are the girls becoming prostitutes, but they're becoming desperately vicious as well. In New York, they have taken to cruising in cars and mugging unsuspecting "johns" as they walk the streets. Last year, two hookers accosted a foreign diplomat in front of the New York Hilton and fatally stabbed him.

New York's East Village, the quiet haven of the Flower Children of the early '60s, has turned into a sinkhole of depravity and crime surpassing any of the legendary flesh-pits of the Middle East. The girls come from Dubuque and Kansas City, Terre Haute and Denver. They have no place to go, no money, no friends. They're afraid to call home for fear of parental reprisals, so they drift to the East Village. There the promise of easy drugs and quick money lure them into dead end streets of prostitution, disease, muggings, and all too frequently, death.

For years, prostitution in the United States was in the hands of hard-bitten professionals: women who had made the conscious decision to sell their bodies for one reason or another. Now, the part-time hookers, spurred on by drug habits in 80 percent of the cases, walk the streets in desperate search for a "john." When the "john" trade is slow, they frequently resort to robberies and muggings performed, usually, with two or more comrades.

The incidence of venereal disease among "free-lancing" street walkers—girls who do not use the services of a pimp or syndicate—is appallingly high. According to a New York doctor who has treated many East Village hookers, "The chance of a girl who works the street by herself having gonorrhea or syphilis is almost 100 percent. There's simply no way they can avoid it. They're usually too 'strung-out' to seek medical aid from one of the free clinics and, most of the time, they just don't give a damn. I've had 15-year-old girls tell me that they enjoyed the thought of passing 'clap' on to their tricks. It's a sort of a way of getting even for all the wrongs which they feel have been done to them."

The vagrant girls who come under the "protection" of a pimp fare slightly better in some areas, but their lives remain an unremitting hell. Since most pimps like to build a trade, they are usually somewhat concerned about VD and take precautions to keep their girls "clean." Usually they do not allow the girls to roll the clients. Of course, some pimps are interested in one-time setups only wherein the client is physically coerced, robbed or blackmailed. There is no way to determine in advance whether or not a pimp is "honest."

Pimps keep their girls in line by three methods: physical threats, drugs, and money. All earnings go to the pimp with the pimp picking up living expenses, furnishing an apartment, and giving the girls limited amounts of pocket money. Woe to the girl who attempts to hold out on her pimp: She is burned with heated coat hangers, her drug supply is terminated, and she may even face death.

The traffic in these young people is one of the saddest chapters in contemporary American history. A massive program of social action on all fronts is needed immediately to eliminate this horror. Few problems cry out for solution with the urgency of this one. No country can live with itself that allows slavery. And no slavery is more heinous than that which is being practiced in the dark recesses of the metropolitan alleys of our nation. It must end.

Starting Time: _____	Finishing Time: _____
Reading Time: _____	Reading Rate: _____
Comprehension: _____	Vocabulary: _____

VOCABULARY: The following words have been taken from the selection you have just read. Put an X in the box before the best meaning or synonym for the word as used in the selection.

1. **annals**, page 51, column 1, paragraph 1
"...most serious threat of disease and crime ever known in the annals of American prostitution."
☐ a. publications
☐ b. history
☐ c. stories
☐ d. years

2. **haunt**, page 51, column 1, paragraph 3
"...her establishment was a favorite haunt of George S. Kaufman, ..."
☐ a. resort
☐ b. spirit
☐ c. place
☐ d. hunch

3. **winsome**, page 51, column 1, bottom line
"...maintained in Chicago at the turn of the century by the winsome Everleigh sisters,..."
☐ a. charming
☐ b. wistful
☐ c. wholesome
☐ d. beautiful

4. **callous**, page 51, column 2, paragraph 5
"...of scared young girls and callous 'johns,' ..."
☐ a. dull
☐ b. soft
☐ c. sophisticated
☐ d. insensitive

5. **heinous**, page 52, column 2, last paragraph
"And no slavery is more heinous than that which is being practiced..."
☐ a. admirable
☐ b. excessive
☐ c. illegal
☐ d. wicked

CONTEXTUAL AIDS: ADJECTIVE CLAUSES

Studies of good readers show that they are aware of the context of what they are reading. This means that they are anticipating what is coming next by what has gone before.

The many ways in which context functions to help the reader recognize words are called contextual aids.

Contextual Aid. Words can be understood when used with adjective clauses. Frequently an unknown word modified by an adjective clause can be understood through the relationship of the clause to the rest of the sentence. In the sentence, **She went to a _____, which was located in a shopping center**, the reader can correctly guess that the missing word is **store**. The adjective clause following the blank is the clue.

In the following sentences, similar contextual aids have been used to modify nonsense words. Underline the nonsense word and write the correct word on the line following each sentence.

1. He opened the penk which had been presented to him on his birthday.

   _____

2. The child scribbled all over the trelp which had just been withdrawn from the library.

   _____

3. The Malsentrep, who is also the commander-in-chief, spoke to the soldiers.

   _____

4. The blurps which shine in the sky at night have always fascinated man.

   _____

5. The child climbed the pullen which had been left leaning against the house.

   _____

6. The frantz which had just been floated as a new issue sold right away.

   _____

7. The tob, whose tires had all gone flat, was stripped.

   _____

8. The hankprat, who was supposed to frighten away the birds, was stolen.

   _____

9. The pasend, which alerted the police, was not heard by the burglars.

   _____

THE FABLE PARAGRAPH

The first pattern of paragraph development that we are going to examine is called the Fable. This pattern begins with a story or illustration and then presents the conclusion, moral, or generalization drawn from that illustration. In this sense it is like a fable: a story comes first to illustrate the moral presented at the end.

Graphically the Fable paragraph looks like this:

Here is an example of the Fable:

In my student days, I once knew a professor, an eminent psychologist, who was a little daft on the subject of the Roosevelt administration. Every act of the president, every program proposed, every law enacted was interpreted by him as a bid for more power, an example of creeping socialism, a collaboration with communists. You need not be sympathetic to New Deal policies or practices to understand why I sat rapt when he spoke on psychology and only psychology.

Once the reader recognizes a Fable paragraph, he knows where to find the main idea. This is the author's point — this is what he wants the reader to understand and learn. The story illustrating his point may be interesting but it is not important in itself. It is not to be memorized or remembered.

COMPREHENSION: For each of the following statements and questions, select the option containing the most complete or most accurate answer.

1. Judging by the number of people engaged in
(h) prostitution, it can be inferred that it is
   - ☐ a. controllable.
   - ☐ b. lucrative.
   - ☐ c. legal.
   - ☐ d. ethical.

2. Traditionally, America's attitude toward pros-
(c) titution has been
   - ☐ a. restrained.
   - ☐ b. critical.
   - ☐ c. enthusiastic.
   - ☐ d. tolerant.

3. The realities of prostitution
(c)
   - ☐ a. contradict the fantasies of the profession.
   - ☐ b. make it a popular profession.
   - ☐ c. frighten young people.
   - ☐ d. discourage public officials.

4. Which of the following are easy victims
(b) of white-slavery?
   - ☐ a. Runaway girls
   - ☐ b. East Village hookers
   - ☐ c. Glamorous girls
   - ☐ d. Young amateur prostitutes

5. The selection is written in the form of
(k)
   - ☐ a. an exposition.
   - ☐ b. a review.
   - ☐ c. an interview.
   - ☐ d. a documentary.

6. Prostitution seems to be
(h)
   - ☐ a. accepted as a fact of life.
   - ☐ b. tolerated by the public.
   - ☐ c. connected with organized crime.
   - ☐ d. exploited by poor people.

7. A relationship seems to exist between prosti-
(e) tution and
   - ☐ a. glamor.
   - ☐ b. social background.
   - ☐ c. poverty.
   - ☐ d. native intelligence.

8. Part-time prostitutes engage in prostitution
(a)
   - ☐ a. to support a drug habit.
   - ☐ b. to steal from unsuspecting victims.
   - ☐ c. to live in comfortable luxury.
   - ☐ d. to provide for the necessities of life.

9. Girls who work the streets by themselves are
(c) extremely
   - ☐ a. hard-bitten professionals.
   - ☐ b. vulnerable to disease.
   - ☐ c. abused and robbed.
   - ☐ d. protected and "clean."

10. The selection ends with an appeal for
(f)
   - ☐ a. higher morals.
   - ☐ b. legalizing prostitution.
   - ☐ c. police protection.
   - ☐ d. positive action.

> Comprehension Skills: a—isolating details; b—recalling specific facts; c—retaining concepts; d—organizing facts; e—understanding the main idea; f—drawing a conclusion; g—making a judgment; h—making an inference; i—recognizing tone; j—understanding characters; k—appreciation of literary forms.

The Selling of the Flesh, II

Officialdom Has Knitted Its Brows over Prostitution—All to Fruitless Ends

Rog Halegood

The Professionals

When we move out of the white-slavery arena (and the term should include black) into "normal" prostitution, i.e. women who choose to prostitute of their own free will, we are dealing with more subtle questions. Should a woman have the right to ask for payment for sexual services rendered? Is prostitution rightfully anyone's business besides the prostitute and the patronizer? Is arrest for prostitution an example of a "victimless crime?" Should clients of prostitutes be as subject to arrest as the prostitutes themselves? Should adult prostitution be legalized?

These are old questions regarding prostitution and the arguments pro and con have been hotly debated. Some facts are highly interesting.

Storey County, Nevada, legalized prostitution in 1971. It is too early for statistics to be available, but indications point up that crimes related to prostitution have declined drastically. Also, because of mandatory health checkups, the VD rate is dropping.

Prostitution was legal in New York City until 1870. In effect, prostitution is once again "legal" in New York as witnessed by the open advertising of numerous "massage parlors." These are an old play on the "quickie" brothel. For a usual charge of $30.00, and under the guise of a "massage," a patron is masturbated by a scantily-clad "masseuse." At last count, there were 18 such "parlors" operating openly in midtown Manhattan alone. One "manager-madam" stated that her business consisted mainly of out-of-town businessmen and Manhattan businessmen on their lunch hours.

The FBI Uniform Crime Reports released on August 31, 1971 stated total arrests for prostitution for 1970 of 40,323. This broke down to 13,387 white arrests (33.2 percent) and 26,498 black arrests (65.7 percent).

The 1969 Marchio bill made prostitution a Class B misdemeanor in New York City with a maximum sentence of 91 days per conviction.

In one year San Francisco, according to a crime commission estimate, spent $375,000 in arresting, processing and jailing 2,116 prostitutes.

Twenty-two percent of the prostitutes arrested in New York City in 1971 had prior records of arrests for violent crimes.

Sacramento Assemblyman Leroy Greene polled 15,000 California constituents in 1971 regarding their opinion on legalizing prostitution. Sixty-nine percent were in favor of legalization.

What do the above facts tell us? Only that prostitution is a large-scale operation, and that we are floundering in an attempt to piece together the total picture.

Prostitution is a difficult subject to grasp because it is compounded of three very different types of operation:

1. The syndicate or mob-controlled forms of prostitution;

2. The independent madam and/or pimp operation employing two or more girls;

3. The prostitutes operating their own businesses.

Syndicate-controlled prostitution is impossible to break until the mobs themselves are destroyed. Prostitution is but one of the four major revenue sources of the mobs, the other three being drugs, numbers, and "protection." Arrests of prostitutes working for a syndicate (many times they don't know that they are) are sporadic owing to the influence of the syndicates in many areas of law enforcement. Syndicates, by and large, limit their prostitution efforts to the teeming ghettoes, preying on the low-income male who can muster the price of a cheap, assembly-line brothel or the one-to-one meetings arranged by pimps working for the syndicates. Hence, gang-controlled prostitution flourishes with blacks preying on blacks in black ghettoes. It is a self-renewing cycle of greed and viciousness.

In the second category are the prostitutes who align themselves with a well-known madam in a modern day bordello, or who work as call girls using an appointment and referral system administered by pimps.

The "fashionable" red-light district of New York City today is York Avenue in the middle and upper Sixties. Here, madams operate out of highrise apartments with a "stable" of four or more resident prostitutes with additional girls

"on call." The madams maintain the all-important "john book" listing regular, trustworthy clients. The girls are never shown this book for it might prove the passkey in allowing a girl to open her own business. Occasionally, a girl will save enough out of her own earnings to buy a copy of the book from the madam. Such copies have been known to sell for as high as $20,000!

In "reputable" New York houses, live-in girls receive 25 percent of their earnings, while girls "on call" from a madam receive about 60 percent. Some suburban housewives have been known to take up residence in a brothel for two or three months at a time, thereby earning enough extra cash to finance the family's second car or even to send the husband through school.

The average price for one-time service in a "good" house ranges between $30.00 and $50.00. The days of champagne suppers have long since passed. There is little real "class" left in today's whoring establishments. Arrests are infrequent in well-organized houses, and "johns" are almost never arrested. In New York, arrests for "patronizing a prostitute" were less than six percent of all morals arrests in 1971; the conviction rate was less than one percent.

The highest calling for most prostitutes is the upwardly mobile, upwardly middle-class All-American dream of hitting the big time. Of climbing to the top of the heap. Of silk sheets and overhead mirrors. Of negliges from Saks, and perfume from Paris. Of a penthouse and a sugar daddy who is the chairman of the board of Wiedt International. Every self-respecting whore with brains and drive hopes for the day when she can make it on her own. No madams. No pimps. Just one fat "john book" with a list of men who are not afraid to pay $300 a night for a little feminine solace. A Valhalla of Fallen Virtue.

Some girls make it. There is a well known, elegant restaurant in Atlanta where the hatcheck girl, provided a client's credentials are in order, will be happy to arrange an escort for the evening in the three-figure category. Similarly, certain members of the night staff of some of New York's most prestigious hotels are more than happy to provide a telephone number where a guest might reach some engaging company. None of this sleazy bellhop-slipping-a-hooker-into-the-room jazz. Strictly appointment only arrangements for the well-heeled.

The earnings of a top call girl are open to debate. Dr. David Reuben, the self-appointed Whiz Kid of sex, estimates that the best prostitutes in New York earn $20,000 after all expenses and taxes. This may be true if one considers that such a girl is almost certain to spend an equal amount a year on clothing, frills and baubles necessary to maintain her standing within the trade. Again, arrests of this type of prostitute are marginal owing to the great care exercised by the girl in selecting her clientele. And while it's a dirty thought to law enforcement establishments, payoffs are not unknown in the profession.

So, when all is said and done, prostitution remains. Investigating-bodies, such as the Knapp Commission, come and go, spewing thousands of pages of testimony in their wake. Legislators harangue for hours on the "evil vice" then go off to conventions "looking for the girls." Since the days of Hammurabi, officialdom has knitted its brows over prostitution—all to fruitless ends.

Like death and taxes, the whores are with us forever. When they ply their trade alone, and of their own *free* volition—in short, when other avenues to gainful employment are open to them—then their work is probably not of too much concern to society. But when mobs and pimps control their lives, when young girls are *forced* into service, then society is very much involved. It is this traffic which must be stopped.

Prostitution will only diminish when two things happen: 1. When organized crime is driven from this country; 2. When law enforcement agencies are supplied with sufficient funds, and public guidance, to effectively wipe out on-street pimps.

First of all, the public must demand an end to prostitution. Historically, this has never been a popular battle cry. Whores are so "nasty." It is much easier to "save" the well-behaved poor. No one wants to take a whore to lunch.

Starting Time: _____	Finishing Time: _____
Reading Time: _____	Reading Rate: _____
Comprehension: _____	Vocabulary: _____

VOCABULARY: The following words have been taken from the selection you have just read. Put an *X* in the box before the best meaning or synonym for the word as used in the selection.

1. **mandatory**, page 56, column 1, paragraph 3
"...because of mandatory health checkups, ..."
☐ a. obligatory
☐ b. frequent
☐ c. unnecessary
☐ d. rigorous

2. **guise**, page 56, column 1, paragraph 4
"...under the guise of a 'massage,'..."
☐ a. guidance
☐ b. attire
☐ c. pretense
☐ d. expense

3. **sporadic**, page 56, column 2, paragraph 8
"Arrests of prostitutes working for a syndicate are sporadic owing to the..."
☐ a. unusual
☐ b. continuous
☐ c. infrequent
☐ d. unnecessary

4. **solace**, page 57, column 2, paragraph 1
"...to pay $300 a night for a little feminine solace."
☐ a. comfort
☐ b. solidity
☐ c. company
☐ d. assistance

5. **harangue**, page 57, column 2, paragraph 4
"Legislators harangue for hours on the 'evil vice' then go off..."
☐ a. agree
☐ b. spout
☐ c. research
☐ d. instruct

SUFFIXES

Many English words consist of a base or root word to which prefixes (beginnings) and suffixes (endings) have been added. To the root word **agree** (a verb) we can add both a prefix and a suffix to get **disagreeable** (an adjective) which has an opposite meaning.

A suffix is added to the end of a word and changes the part of speech of that word. We have just seen how the suffix **able** changes **agree** from a verb to an adjective.

Two Suffixes

1. -ess is a Greek noun suffix. It can be added to words which are already nouns, like **prince**, to give a feminine character to the word, as in **princess**, still a noun.

2. -ism is also a Greek noun suffix and it also can be added to nouns, like **vandal**, to make **vandalism**, still a noun.

In the following sentences, root words have been set in bold print. Add one of these suffixes to each root and write the new word in the space following the sentence. As you add suffixes to words, you may have to drop or change letters.

1. Her ambition was to be known as a **patron** of the Arts.

   _____

2. He spent more time with his **govern** than with his parents.

   _____

3. The other panel members were not amused at his **witty**.

   _____

4. The **actor** has appeared in three recent movies.

   _____

5. Movies strive for the quality of **real**.

   _____

6. The effects of **alcohol** are severe and debilitating.

   _____

7. The most famous **poet** of our time read her works.

   _____

8. **Social** is widely endorsed by emerging nations.

   _____

9. In the pride the **lion** hunts and provides food.

   _____

10. The gang's practices were clearly acts of **terror**.

    _____

THE SALESTALK PARAGRAPH

The next pattern of paragraph development we wish to consider is called the Salestalk. This pattern presents facts and details and closes with a generalization. Like a good salesman, this pattern gives the arguments first and then makes the pitch.

Graphically the Salestalk looks like this:

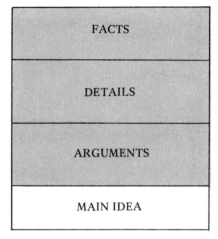

Here is an example of the Salestalk:

Finally, strive constantly to judge the truth and value of the ideas you encounter in your reading. Do not act like a blotter, passively sopping up whatever the author has to offer. Maintain at all times a critical attitude. Criticism, after all, is only "the act or art of judging by some standard." When you weigh, you judge the pro and con evidence of an issue. In other words, you think—and that is why you come to college: to learn how to think effectively.

This pattern is used a great deal in textbook paragraphs of information. The author will give details and facts and then present to the reader the main idea based on those facts.

Your job as reader is to recognize the pattern and locate the main idea. With this in mind, you can read the facts and details critically, understanding how they relate to the whole and to each other.

COMPREHENSION: For each of the following statements and questions, select the option containing the most complete or most accurate answer.

1. The difference between white-slavery and
(c) "normal" prostitution is
☐ a. higher fees.
☐ b. free will.
☐ c. insignificant.
☐ d. academic.

2. The questions arising from prostitution
(g) ☐ a. have serious social implications.
☐ b. should not be discussed in public.
☐ c. should be decided by prostitutes.
☐ d. have simple and obvious answers.

3. If prostitution were legalized
(h) ☐ a. syndicate crime would disappear.
☐ b. society would be destroyed.
☐ c. it would quickly disappear.
☐ d. health standards could be enforced.

4. History shows that prostitution
(h) ☐ a. cannot be legalized.
☐ b. is here to stay.
☐ c. is a seasonal menace.
☐ d. contributes to the economy.

5. Prostitution and crime
(f) ☐ a. are mutually exclusive.
☐ b. protect each other.
☐ c. are socially acceptable.
☐ d. go hand-in-hand.

6. The overall tone of the selection is
(i) ☐ a. critical.
☐ b. light and amusing.
☐ c. factual and direct.
☐ d. offensive.

7. Gang controlled prostitution flourishes in
(d) ☐ a. high-rise apartments.
☐ b. poor neighborhoods.
☐ c. massage parlors.
☐ d. prestige hotels.

8. An important point is made concerning
(e) ☐ a. the need to regulate prostitution.
☐ b. the importance of arrests and convictions.
☐ c. the legal rights of professional prostitutes.
☐ d. the moral climate of the nation.

9. The arrest and conviction rate of all moral
(h) arrests in New York in 1971 suggests
☐ a. a decreasing crime rate in New York.
☐ b. a reaction to public indignation.
☐ c. a tolerant attitude toward prostitution.
☐ d. a tough police reaction to prostitution.

10. Whether prostitution diminishes or is allowed
(c) to remain really depends on
☐ a. the public.
☐ b. the courts.
☐ c. the police.
☐ d. the prostitutes.

Comprehension Skills: a—isolating details; b—recalling specific facts; c—retaining concepts; d—organizing facts; e—understanding the main idea; f—drawing a conclusion; g—making a judgment; h—making an inference; i—recognizing tone; j—understanding characters; k—appreciation of literary forms.

Topics for the Restless

Dr. Batman

A Colorado Microbiologist Studies the Stratified Evidence of Environmental Misuse

Anthony Wolff

In most folk, a fascination with bats might be thought morbid. Bats, after all, are bizarre creatures: dog-faced, bird-winged mammals that frequent the night. Count Dracula's mythic consorts, they still inspire nightmare sleep and waking fear in normal folk. But for Dr. Michael Petit, a sane, sociable microbiologist at Colorado State University in Fort Collins, bats are a professional obsession. With modest support from the Rockefeller Foundation, he pursues them throughout the Southwest, from Colorado to Mexico.

In fact, it is not the bats themselves that fascinate Dr. Petit, though he likes them well enough. His special interest is reserved for what the bats leave behind in their dark, isolated caves. Each year—generation after generation, sometimes for centuries—the migratory bat colonies carpet the floors of their summer homes with droppings (known politely as "guano," from the Spanish), as well as with corpses and other souvenirs. In that accumulated debris, Dr. Petit is seeking an index to the past. The bats' leavings contain traces of various environmental poisons—mercury, lead, etc.—that the mammals have ingested along with their food and excreted in the guano. Left undisturbed, the guano accumulates on the floors of the caves, forming discrete annual strata. Dr. Petit's theory is that the quantities of environmental poisons in a layer of guano are accurate measures of their concentrations in the area surrounding the cave when the guano was deposited.

Some of the bat colonies, especially the Mexican free tails, have returned yearly to the same cave for three centuries and more. A precise record of pollutants in this relatively near past—too recent for most other techniques to date with sufficient accuracy—would reveal the year-by-year impact of industrialized man on the environment. By the same token, Dr. Petit's research may establish a sensitive technique for establishing realistic standards of pollution control in the future. Dr. Petit explains:

For example, suppose we find that over the next ten years pollution-control techniques can reduce the level of mercury at Carlsbad Caverns by a factor of ten. This may be meaningless if we learn from analysis of guano in the caverns that the level existing there 300 years ago was down by a factor of 10,000. If, on the other hand, we find that ambient levels in the area today are no greater than they were 300 years ago, the unreasonableness of initiating costly pollution-control measures and setting unrealistic standards for that area will be apparent.

Pursuing the bats to their inner sanctums demands both ingenuity and stamina. To locate likely caves, Petit collects lore from local old-timers, hunters, and gas-station attendants, as well as from fellow scientists. He also has been able to enlist the bats themselves in revealing their hideaways. During all-night vigils he snares thirsty bats in a gossamer "mist net," stretched like a tennis net over likely watering places. To his tiny captives he attaches even tinier radio transmitters of his own devising, powered by hearing-aid batteries. Just before dawn on successive nights, he releases the "bugged" bats from two different locations. If he has netted members of the same colony, Petit can track their signals as they wing homeward and thereby triangulate the approximate spot where they disappear into their cave.

But tracking bats is easier on maps than over the rugged relief of the southwestern mountains. One early morning last May, under an Iberian sky of bottomless blue, Petit forsook a comfortable Tucson motel to search for a cave hidden somewhere along a remote, rocky ridge in the Patagonia range. During two days of painstaking mountaineering around the highest rock outcroppings the previous fall, Petit had failed to find it.

This time, the search covered the slightly lower altitudes, just below the three peaks that punctuated the ridgeline. The two-rut road ended far below; Petit had to make the climb on foot. Near the top of a meadow so steep that the ascent required a series of traverses, his tiring pace quickened, refreshed by a breeze perfumed with guano coming from a fissure no more than six inches high at the back of a shallow rock overhang. After

a short scramble uphill around the base of the peak, Petit found the cave's front door, a man-high portal invisible from above and below.

Petit also found disheartening evidence that he was not the first visitor to the cave: The floor was littered with the debris of modern trespassers—tin cans and odds and ends of plastic. Clearly the disturbed guano on the floor would be useless for dating, which depends on strict stratification of annual deposits. Searching the dark recesses of the main chamber, however, Petit discovered a narrow chimney leading to a second story. Exploring cautiously, careful not to disturb the deep carpet of guano, he made his way into the upper room. The narrow beam from his headlamp divided the utter darkness. As Petit's gaze swept the room, the light revealed, stroke by stroke, a world apart—a bat's sanctuary locked in the fastness of the rock. This upper chamber showed no sign of previous human intruders.

The same expedition included a return visit to a cave in Eagle Creek Canyon, in the Gila mountain range. The cave was especially valuable for validating Petit's techniques, because it had been literally vacuum-cleaned of its guano deposits for commercial fertilizer in 1954. Thus, its present layers of guano could be dated with certainty from that year. Moreover, the operation of a massive copper mine and smelter nearby provided a clear test of Petit's hypothesis that the guano would reveal changes through time in the concentrations of industrial effluents in the environment.

Inside the cave the sibilant voice of Eagle Creek gave way to the caterwauling of Mexican free-tailed bats, the vanguard of the summer population. They huddled head down, shoulder-to-shoulder on the ceiling, dropping off in squadrons to fly swift, tight formations in the gloom. Petit estimated three hundred thousand of them, darting through the upturned beam of his light like warplanes on a night raid, miraculously avoiding certain suicide against the cave walls. Later in the season, he knew, the population might explode to several million, feeding on local insects by night, breeding, dying. On the wing inside the huge cavern, they would crowd the air, colliding with intruders and each other despite their sensitive sonar. Their droppings would saturate the top layer of guano on the floor, and the smell of concentrated ammonia would make the cave inhospitable to visiting scientists. Now, however, early in the season, they had plenty of airspace for their maneuvers, and their droppings floated down like the gentlest rain. Petit's baseball cap was protection enough from above, and the smell from underfoot was no worse than the bouquet of common garden fertilizer.

Dr. Petit's scientific guano-sampling kit consists of nothing more than a length of common stovepipe, which he drives down into the deposit with any handy rock. He then shovels the surrounding

TOPICS FOR THE RESTLESS

guano away so that the stovepipe can be sealed with wax, top and bottom, for the journey back to the Fort Collins laboratory. There the sample is impregnated with paraffin to prevent crumbling before the stovepipe is slit open lengthwise, laying bare the strata for consecutive dating. A sample of the guano from each layer is subjected to sophisticated testing procedures for measuring its burden of environmental poisons.

His test results so far lend support to Dr. Petit's hypothesis. Analysis of the guano samples from Eagle Creek Canyon shows evidence of the mercury wastes associated with the nearby copper industry, correlating closely with fluctuations in the smelter's activity. The correlation is so sensitive that Dr. Petit's graph of the mercury content in his guano samples dips sharply to correspond to the two years when strikes crippled the smelter.

If Dr. Petit can carry his measurements far enough into the past—into guano deposited before man's industrial by-products were added to the environment—his technique will offer a standard for measuring the impact of industry on the environment and on ourselves.

Starting Time: _____	Finishing Time: _____
Reading Time: _____	Reading Rate: _____
Comprehension: _____	Vocabulary: _____

VOCABULARY: The following words have been taken from the selection you have just read. Put an X in the box before the best meaning or synonym for the word as used in the selection.

1. **frequent**, page 63, column 1, paragraph 1
"...dog-faced, bird-winged mammals that frequent the night."
☐ a. visit
☐ b. inhabit
☐ c. avoid
☐ d. fly

2. **ingenuity**, page 63, column 2, paragraph 2
"Pursuing bats to their inner sanctums demands both ingenuity and stamina."
☐ a. strength
☐ b. skill
☐ c. genius
☐ d. persistence

3. **validating**, page 64, column 2, paragraph 2
"The cave was especially valuable for validating Petit's techniques, ..."
☐ a. disproving
☐ b. legalizing
☐ c. practicing
☐ d. confirming

4. **hypothesis**, page 64, column 2, paragraph 2
"...provided a clear test of Petit's hypothesis that the guano would reveal changes..."
☐ a. hope
☐ b. guess
☐ c. belief
☐ d. theory

5. **impregnated**, page 65, column 1, paragraph 1
"There the sample is impregnated with paraffin..."
☐ a. saturated
☐ b. infected
☐ c. fertilized
☐ d. imprecated

EXPECTANCY CLUES

The most important aids to word recognition and, therefore, fluency in reading are meaning clues. Good readers use these clues effectively and automatically. Meaning clues permit the reader to anticipate words before actually reading them.

Expectancy clues are one type of meaning clue. These clues refer to the sorts of words and concepts one might expect to encounter in a given subject. For example, in a story about big city life, the reader should expect to meet words like *subway, traffic congestion, urban renewal, ghetto, high-rise apartments,* and so on. Anticipating these words enables the reader to move along the printed lines rapidly, with understanding.

The following words except two all appeared in a story about housing. Think first about the kinds of words you would find in such a story and then examine the words below. Underline the two words you would *not* expect to find in this story.

1. contractor	5. plat	9. foundation
2. zoning	6. carburetor	10. property
3. dressmaking	7. tenant	11. occupy
4. upkeep	8. apartment	12. siding

Which of the following phrases would you expect to read in a newspaper account of a safe driving campaign? Put an *X* in the box before them.

☐ 1. safety belts and harnesses

☐ 2. highway fatigue

☐ 3. season's tickets

☐ 4. safety inspection

☐ 5. rubbing blemishes off

☐ 6. drunk behind the wheel

☐ 7. right of way

☐ 8. exceeding recommended speeds

☐ 9. horse with one lame foot

☐ 10. stop and rest

☐ 11. framework of beams

☐ 12. courtesy of the road

☐ 13. road and traffic conditions

☐ 14. consideration of the other driver

☐ 15. major cause of deaths

☐ 16. renewal of licenses

☐ 17. driver qualifications

☐ 18. sudden, unexpected stops

☐ 19. turning the pages slowly

☐ 20. driving defensively

THE THEREFORE PARAGRAPH

The next pattern of paragraph development we want to examine is called the Therefore. It is used anytime the author wishes to present successive steps to an argument or a conclusion. The author's purpose is persuasion—his pattern is to lead you logically to his conclusion by presenting the sucessive premises on which it is based.

Graphically the Therefore looks like this:

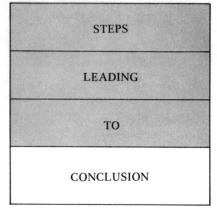

| STEPS |
| LEADING |
| TO |
| CONCLUSION |

Here is an example of the Therefore:

In any event many skills and habits cannot be gained without practice. But practice itself may be blundering, incidental, and accidental: or it may be intelligent, formal, and planned. Life is too short, and time too limited to be spent in wasteful trial and error practice.

(therefore)

This is why we have schools, for it is under directed, regular and supervised drill that students most rapidly acquire proper mental habits.

In the Therefore pattern, the reader is led logically to the author's conclusion. The evidence is there; you have no alternative but to accept the logical statement that follows.

In textbooks, this pattern is used to demonstrate the validity of certain principles of the subject.

COMPREHENSION: For each of the following statements and questions, select the option containing the most complete or most accurate answer.

1. Dr. Petit can draw significant conclusions from his research by using which of the following techniques?
(e)
   ☐ a. Carbon dating
   ☐ b. Photosynthesis
   ☐ c. Comparative analysis
   ☐ d. Radio biology

2. Dr. Petit's cave explorations suggest that bats are
(h)
   ☐ a. dangerous.
   ☐ b. supernatural.
   ☐ c. harmless.
   ☐ d. destructive.

3. The droppings of bats
(c)
   ☐ a. reflect man's effect on the environment.
   ☐ b. pollute natural scenic wonders.
   ☐ c. interfere with nature's delicate balance.
   ☐ d. interfere with scientific investigation.

4. Bats are
(a)
   ☐ a. birds.
   ☐ b. mammals.
   ☐ c. reptiles.
   ☐ d. canine.

5. Dr. Petit's theory seems to be
(g)
   ☐ a. confusing to the untrained person.
   ☐ b. unlikely, considering the habits of bats.
   ☐ c. resented by business and industry.
   ☐ d. based on reasonable assumptions.

6. The technique used by Dr. Petit is useful in dealing with the
(f)
   ☐ a. recent past.
   ☐ b. bat population.
   ☐ c. prehistoric past.
   ☐ d. daily guano accumulation.

7. The reduction of pollution in an area is meaningless unless
(c)
   ☐ a. present levels are compared to past levels.
   ☐ b. people cooperate with local conservation groups.
   ☐ c. legal measures are taken to protect the environment.
   ☐ d. funds are provided to support scientific research.

8. Dr. Petit seems to be
(j)
   ☐ a. a resented meddler.
   ☐ b. a popular teacher.
   ☐ c. a thorough investigator.
   ☐ d. a misunderstood scientist.

9. Dr. Petit's field work requires
(h)
   ☐ a. sophisticated equipment.
   ☐ b. unusual courage.
   ☐ c. unlimited funds.
   ☐ d. physical stamina.

10. Test results indicate that Dr. Petit's technique is
(c)
   ☐ a. potentially unsafe.
   ☐ b. economically wasteful.
   ☐ c. probably questionable.
   ☐ d. scientifically sound.

Comprehension Skills: a—isolating details; b—recalling specific facts; c—retaining concepts; d—organizing facts; e—understanding the main idea; f—drawing a conclusion; g—making a judgment; h—making an inference; i—recognizing tone; j—understanding characters; k—appreciation of literary forms.

Sickle Cell Anemia

The Problem Is Finding Out Who Has It

Bern Gentry

In 1970 four United States black soldiers died while on maneuvers. Surprising? No, not really, except the soldiers were not in Vietnam, Laos, or Cambodia. They were at Fort Bliss, Texas. Their deaths resulted from ignorance and neglect not from an over-zealous drill instructor but from the failure of the general public and the medical community to recognize a major health problem—sickle cell disease. With knowledge of the disease, of its effects and with proper counseling, the deaths of those four young men could have been lastingly prevented.

Sickle cell disease is a disease of the blood that can cause grave injury and death. Hemoglobin, the fluid in our blood cells that makes them red, is the substance that takes oxygen from our lungs to the rest of our bodies. With exertion and muscle usage, hemoglobin uses oxygen and in most of us remains a fluid while returning to the lungs for more oxygen. Sickle cell hemoglobin is fluid when carrying oxygen, but when oxygen is absent the hemoglobin becomes solid changing the normally doughnut-shaped red blood cells into a sickle, or new-moon, shape. The result is painful, damaging, and sometimes fatal. When the cells sickle they no longer pass freely through smaller blood vessels; thus, a "log jam" occurs within the vessels. This causes pain and destruction of the cells resulting in anemia. In more severe instances it causes tissue loss or even "necrosis"—the loss of an entire organ. Should this "jamming" occur extensively throughout the body, death will result.

Understanding the Disease

Sickle cell disease is not contagious; it is inherited through the parents. While sickle cell disease can cause the damage mentioned above, it does not happen to every sufferer of "sickling." The majority of "sicklers" have two sorts of hemoglobin: sickle cell and normal, with the type depending on the genes inherited from the parents. Half of one's hemoglobin is received from the mother and half from the father. Assuming both parents have normal hemoglobin then their offspring will have hemoglobin type AA. If one parent has "sickling" hemoglobin and the other has normal hemoglobin the child will be a "sickler" typed as AS. This

child then has "sickle cell trait" and is almost always healthy. Sickle cell trait is *usually* harmless. But not always. It can be harmful, even fatal, if there is a severe reduction of oxygen like that occurring at high altitudes, from a complicating anaesthetic, from severe lung disease, from lengthy obstructed blood flow after unusually strenuous exercise, from the result of extreme exposure to cold, or complications from other serious diseases. The four soldiers at Fort Bliss had sickle cell trait, not sickle cell disease. An individual with sickle cell disease, typed SS, had parents who both had sickle cell traits: AS + AS = SS. Such an individual will have anemia and attacks of pain and fever. He may be underdeveloped. He may die at a young age. The disease first causes illness between six months and five years of age. Sickle cell disease is inherited predominately by Blacks. It is believed to have come from Africa where people with sickle cell hemoglobin had a natural immunity to malaria. Mediterranean anemia which affects Greeks and Italians is similar to sickle cell, and is likewise a preventive against malaria. Sickle cell anemia is a genetic problem among Blacks just as cystic fibrosis, hemophilia and leukemia are genetic problems predominant in Whites.

While sickle cell disease is not contagious, it also is not readily preventable or curable, although it is treatable. Only the *symptoms* of sickle cell disease, or sickle cell anemia, can be treated. When the cells sickle and blood flow ceases, drugs are used to ease pain and to alleviate dehydration and constriction of the blood vessels. New, more immediate forms of treatment are being researched. At present, the only form of prevention is testing for sickle cell trait in individuals. It is estimated that there are two million people in the United States with sickle cell trait. If two people with sickle cell trait marry, one-fourth will be normal and one-half will have sickle cell trait. Each individual should know if they have inherited the sickle type of hemoglobin not only to make reasoned decisions in family planning but, also, to avoid conditions that might bring on a crisis precipitated by high altitudes and over-exertion.

What Should Be Done

At present, the most effective means of controlling sickle cell disease are improved communication and education, plus large-scale testing programs. The average person has limited knowledge about sickle cell disease, its cause, its symptoms, its dangers and its treatment. Black communities need more in-depth information and counseling as does the general public. Less than half of the black population has ever heard of this disease. The economic, educational, social and psychological effects of sickle cell disease affect all of us. Mass education along with massive testing programs can alleviate much of sickle cell's dangers. As mentioned earlier, awareness that one has the disease prevents problems. Unfortunately, one can live an entire lifetime and be unaware that he has sickle cell trait. For instance, Indiana University tested 275 persons in a six-month span and found that 112 of them needed to return to the University for genetic counseling. A similar test conducted by the same institution at a foundry in Indianapolis revealed 10 out of 113 employees with sickle cell trait—all were totally unaware of it. The point? Now these people can avoid situations which might bring on a crisis and have other family members tested and counseled.

At present there are special blood tests used to detect sickle cell disease but only one that is truly thorough. In recent years, a test has been devised and improved upon by Dr. Robert M. Nalbandian, M.D., that requires only a small drop of blood from a finger. Called the Sickledex, it shows sickling if it is present; yet, to establish the specific type of sickle cell condition, whether full-disease or a trait, a test using blood drawn from the arm, electrophoresis, is a must. Besides being more thorough, electrophoresis has the added advantage of being cheaper than Sickledex and equally efficient for primary screening. The extensive equipment used by Indiana University cost approximately $1,000. To equip a smaller community, clinic or mobile lab would cost a fraction of the above. Cost can no longer be cited as too prohibitive to mount an attack on sickle cell anemia.

The goals of such organizations as the Foundation for Research and Education in Sickle Cell Disease and the Southeastern Wisconsin Sickle Cell Center should and can be the viable goals of any community's clubs and concerned organizations. They can conduct community information programs for patients and the public. They can encourage health officials and legislators to provide increased funds for research and health services. They can initiate and develop facilities for testing and counseling.

Tragedies like the one that occurred at Fort Bliss are preventable. Alleviating the problem of sickle cell disease does not necessarily require money; however, it does require effort, information, time and genuine concern. And work should begin now.

The Blacks in the United States have enough problems; infirmity and death from sickle cell conditions should not be one of them.

Starting Time: _____	Finishing Time: _____
Reading Time: _____	Reading Rate: _____
Comprehension: _____	Vocabulary: _____

VOCABULARY: The following words have been taken from the selection you have just read. Put an *X* in the box before the best meaning or synonym for the word as used in the selection.

1. **zealous**, page 68, column 1, paragraph 1
"...an over-zealous drill instructor..."
☐ a. friendly
☐ b. anxious
☐ c. eager
☐ d. qualified

2. **immunity**, page 68, column 2, paragraph 1
"...had a natural immunity to malaria."
☐ a. protection
☐ b. proneness
☐ c. hatred
☐ d. fear

3. **alleviate**, page 68, column 2, paragraph 2
"...to ease pain and to alleviate dehydration..."
☐ a. encourage
☐ b. permit
☐ c. aggravate
☐ d. relieve

4. **precipitated**, page 68, column 2, paragraph 2
"...a crisis precipitated by high altitudes..."
☐ a. slowed down
☐ b. brought about
☐ c. condensed
☐ d. preceded

5. **viable**, page 69, column 2, paragraph 1
"...can be the viable goals of any community's clubs..."
☐ a. visible
☐ b. vivid
☐ c. practicable
☐ d. unusual

SUFFIXES

Many English words consist of a base or root word to which prefixes (beginnings) and suffixes (endings) have been added. To the root word **agree** (a verb) we can add both a prefix and a suffix to get **disagreeable** (an adjective) which has an opposite meaning.

A suffix is added to the end of a word and affects the part of speech of that word. We have just seen how the suffix **able** changes **agree** from a verb to an adjective.

Two Suffixes

1. **-ment** is a Latin noun suffix. It changes a verb like **establish** to a noun, **establishment**.

2. **-ry** is also a Latin noun suffix. It can be added to words which are already nouns, like **forest**, to make **forestry**, still a noun.

In the following sentences, root words have been set in bold print. Add one of these suffixes to each root and write the new word in the space following the sentence. As you add suffixes to words, you may have to drop or change letters.

1. The sounds of **merry** carried throughout the building.

   _____

2. In tribal cultures, animal skins are worn as **adorn**.

   _____

3. **Dentist** as a profession is gaining in stature.

   _____

4. She paraded as though dressed in elegant **fine**.

   _____

5. The neighborhood mothers marched, demanding **improve** of the playground facilities.

   _____

6. The new **move** enlisted many supporters on the campus.

   _____

7. We were called to testify as witnesses to the **robber**.

   _____

8. We could scarcely conceal our **disappoint** over the Supreme Court decision.

   _____

9. In some places more money is spent on **jewel** than on food.

   _____

10. Work in the prison kitchen can only be described as **drudge**.

    _____

THE PROCEEDER PARAGRAPH

The next pattern of paragraph development we wish to examine is the Proceeder. This paragraph builds on successive facts, proceeding from the lesser to the greater point until the main idea is developed. It proceeds from the specific to the general.

Graphically the Proceeder looks like this:

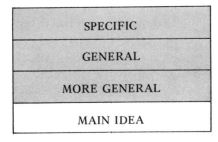

SPECIFIC
GENERAL
MORE GENERAL
MAIN IDEA

Here is an example of the Proceeder:

The Freshman is fairly sure that he knows many things quite well. The Sophomore is absolutely certain that he knows most things very well. The Junior has begun to have serious doubts about the quantity and quality of what he knows. The Senior is quite convinced that he knows almost nothing about anything. Then he graduates and tries to get an employer to pay him for what he knows.

This pattern is different from the others we have been examining in that the main idea statement is not the inclusive generalization that it is in the others. The statement here is simply a broader or more general concept which the preceding ones have been expanded into.

It's value to the reader is that it encourages him to accept the general statement because he has been able to see it progress and build from its humble beginnings.

In textbooks this pattern will be employed when the author has to present broad concepts to the student and he wishes to lead the student progressively to them.

COMPREHENSION: For each of the following statements and questions, select the option containing the most complete or most accurate answer.

1. The Fort Bliss tragedy could have been
(c) avoided if

☐ a. the soldiers had been in Vietnam.
☐ b. the area doctors had been alert.
☐ c. the military had been less demanding.
☐ d. the soldiers had received proper food.

2. Sickle cell anemia is
(c)
☐ a. a fatal condition.
☐ b. a disease of the blood.
☐ c. a tropical disease.
☐ d. a common sickness.

3. Hemoglobin
(c)
☐ a. conducts oxygen.
☐ b. destroys white blood cells.
☐ c. solidifies when exposed to air.
☐ d. prevents anemia.

4. Which of the following causes sickle cell hemo-
(c) globin to solidify?

☐ a. Loss of body temperature
☐ b. Absence of red blood cells
☐ c. Improper sanitation
☐ d. Lack of oxygen

5. The passage, "...thus, a 'log jam' occurs within
(k) the vessel,' is an example of

☐ a. a metaphor.
☐ b. a simile.
☐ c. an alliteration.
☐ d. a hyperbole.

6. Sickle cell anemia is
(a)
☐ a. contracted especially by adults.
☐ b. transmitted by parents.
☐ c. highly contagious.
☐ d. rarely fatal.

7. Which of the following represents the most
(c) damaging form of the sickle cell disease?

☐ a. AA
☐ b. AS
☐ c. SA
☐ d. SS

8. It can be concluded that
(f)
☐ a. certain races are predisposed to certain diseases.
☐ b. persons of African descent are immune
to malaria.
☐ c. the Mediterranean part of the world
is unhealthy.
☐ d. military doctors lack professional ethics.

9. Sickle cell anemia
(c)
☐ a. resists all known treatment.
☐ b. affects one-half of the Black population.
☐ c. is difficult to detect.
☐ d. cannot be cured.

10. The main thrust of the selection is di-
(e) rected at

☐ a. alarming the Black population.
☐ b. criticizing the medical profession.
☐ c. disseminating information.
☐ d. resisting change.

Comprehension Skills: a—isolating details; b—recalling specific facts; c—retaining concepts; d—organizing facts; e—understanding the main idea; f—drawing a conclusion; g—making a judgment; h—making an inference; i—recognizing tone; j—understanding characters; k—appreciation of literary forms.

Police Brutality:
Answers to Key Questions

How Much Force Is Necessary or Proper?

Albert J. Reiss, Jr.

"For three years, there has been through the courts and the streets a dreary procession of citizens with broken heads and bruised bodies against few of whom was violence needed to effect an arrest. Many of them had done nothing to deserve an arrest. In a majority of such cases, no complaint was made. If the victim complains, his charge is generally dismissed. The police are practically above the law."

The statement was published in 1903, and its author was the Hon. Frank Moss, a former police commissioner of New York City. Clearly, today's charges of police brutality and mistreatment of citizens have a precedent in American history—but never before has the issue of police brutality assumed the public urgency it has today. In Newark, in Detroit, in Watts, in Harlem, and, in fact, in practically every city that has had a civil disturbance, "deep hostility between police and ghetto" was, reports the Kerner Commission, "a primary cause of the riots."

Whether or not the police accept the words "police brutality," the public now wants some plain answers to some plain questions. How widespread is police mistreatment of citizens? Is it on the increase? Why do policemen mistreat citizens? Do the police mistreat Negroes more than whites?

To find some answers, 36 people working for the Center of Research on Social Organization observed police-citizen encounters in the cities of Boston, Chicago, and Washington, D.C. For seven days a week, for seven weeks, these observers, with police permission, sat in patrol cars and monitored booking and lockup procedures in high-crime precincts.

Obtaining information about police mistreatment of citizens is no simple matter. National and state civil-rights commissions receive hundreds of complaints charging mistreatment—but proving these allegations is difficult. The few local civilian-review boards, such as the one in Philadelphia, have not produced any significant volume of complaints leading to the dismissal or disciplining of policemen for alleged brutality. Generally, police chiefs are silent on the matter, or answer charges of brutality with vague statements that they will investigate any complaints brought to their attention. Rank-and-

file policemen are usually more outspoken: They often insinuate that charges of brutality are part of a conspiracy against them, and against law and order.

The Meaning of Brutality

What citizens mean by police brutality covers the full range of police practices. These practices, contrary to the impression of many civil-rights activists, are not newly devised to deal with Negroes in our urban ghettos. They are ways in which the police have traditionally behaved in dealing with certain citizens, particularly those in the lower classes. The most common of these practices are:

☐—the use of profane and abusive language,
☐—commands to move on or get home,
☐—stopping and questioning people on the street or searching them and their cars,
☐—threats to use force of not obeyed,
☐—prodding with a nightstick or approaching with a pistol, and
☐—the actual use of physical force or violence itself.

Citizens and the police do not always agree on what constitutes proper police practice. What is "proper," or what is "brutal," it need hardly be pointed out, is more a matter of judgment about what someone did than a description of what police do. What is important is not the practice itself but what it means to the citizen. What citizens object to and call "police brutality" is really the judgment that they have not been treated with the full rights and dignity owing citizens in a democratic society. Any practice that degrades their status, that restricts their freedom, that annoys or harasses them, or that uses physical force is frequently seen as unnecessary and unwarranted. More often than not, they are probably right.

Many police practices serve only to degrade the citizen's sense of himself and his status. This is particularly true with regard to the way the police use language. Most citizens who have contact with the police object less to their use of four-letter words than to *how* the policeman talks to them. Particularly objectionable is the habit policemen have of "talking down" to citizens, of calling them names that deprecate them in their own eyes and those of others. More than one Negro citizen has complained: "They talk down to me as if I had no name—like 'boy' or 'Man' or whatever, or they call me 'Jack' or by my first name. They don't show me no respect."

To be treated as "suspicious" is not only degrading, but is also a form of harassment and a restriction on the right to move freely. The harassing tactics of many policemen—dispersing social street-gatherings, the indiscriminate stopping of Negroes on foot or in cars, and commands to move on or go home—are particularly common in ghetto areas.

Young people are the most likely targets of harassing orders to disperse or move on. Particularly in summer, ghetto youths are likely to spend lots of time in public places. Given the inadequacy of their housing and the absence of community facilities, the street corner is often their social center. As the police cruise the busy streets of the ghetto, they frequently shout at groups of teenagers to "get going" or "get home." Our observations of police practices show that *white as well as Negro youths* are often harassed in this way.

Frequently the policeman may leave the car and threaten or force youths to move on. For example, one summer evening as the scout car cruised a busy street of a white slum, the patrolman observed three white boys and a girl on a corner. When told to move on, they mumbled and grumbled in undertones, angering the police by their failure to comply. As they slowly moved off, the officers pushed them along the street. Suddenly one of the white patrolmen took a lighted cigarette from a 15-year-old boy and stuck it in his face, pushing him forward as he did so. When the youngsters did move on, one policeman remarked to the observer that the girl was "nothing but a whore." Such tactics can only intensify resentment toward the police.

Police harassment is not confined to youth. One in every four adult Negroes in Detroit claims he has been stopped and questioned by the police without good reason. The same proportion claim they have been stopped in their cars. One in five says he has been searched unnecessarily; and one in six says that his car was searched for no good reason. The members of an interracial couple, particularly a Negro man accompanying a white woman, are perhaps the most vulnerable to harassment.

What citizens regard as police brutality many policemen consider necessary for law enforcement. While degrading epithets and abusive language may no longer be considered proper by either police commanders or citizens, they often disagree about other practices related to law enforcement. For example, although many citizens see "stop and question" or "stop and frisk" procedures as harassment, police commanders usually regard them merely as "aggressive prevention" to curb crime.

Physical Force—or Self-Defense?

The nub of the police-brutality issue seems to lie in police use of physical force. By law, the police have the right to use such force if necessary to make an arrest, to keep the peace, or to maintain public order. But just how much force is necessary or proper?

This was the crucial problem we attempted to answer by placing observers in the patrol cars and in the precincts. Our 36 observers, divided equally between Chicago, Boston, and Washington, were responsible for reporting the details of all situations where police used physical force against a citizen. To ensure the observation of a large number of encounters, two high-crime police precincts were monitored in Boston and Chicago; four in Washington. At least one precinct was composed of primarily Negro residents, another primarily whites. Where possible, we also tried to select precincts with considerable variation in social-class composition. Given the criterion of a high-crime rate, however, people of low socio-economic status predominated in most of the areas surveyed.

The law fails to provide simple rules about what—and how much—force that policemen can properly use. The American Bar Foundation's study *Arrest,* by Wayne La Fave, put the matter rather well, stating that the courts of all states would undoubtedly agree that in making an arrest a policeman should use only that amount of force he reasonably believes necessary. But LaFave also pointed out that there is no agreement on the question of when it is better to let the suspect escape than to employ "deadly" force.

Even in those states where the use of deadly force is limited by law, the kinds of physical force a policeman may use are not clearly defined. No kind of force is categorically denied a policeman, since he is always permitted to use deadly force in self-defense.

This right to protect himself often leads the policeman to argue self-defense whenever he uses force. We found that many policemen, whether or not the facts justify it, regularly follow their use of force with the charge that the citizen was assaulting a policeman or resisting arrest. Our observers also found that some policemen even carry pistols and knives that they have confiscated while searching citizens; they carry them so they may be placed at a scene should it be necessary to establish a case of self-defense.

Of course, not all cases of force involve the use of *unnecessary* force. Each instance of force reported by our observers was examined and judged to be either necessary or unnecessary. Cases involving simple restraint—holding a man by the arm—were deliberately excluded from consideration, even though a policeman's right to do so can, in many instances, be challenged. In judging when police force is "unwarranted," "unreasonable," or "undue," we rather deliberately selected only those cases in which a policeman struck the citizen with his hands, fist, feet, or body, or where he used a weapon of some kind—such as a nightstick or a pistol. In these cases, had the policeman been found to have used physical force improperly, he could have been arrested on complaint and, like any other citizen, charged with a simple or aggravated assault. A physical assault on a citizen was judged to be "improper" or "unnecessary" only if force was used in one or more of the following ways:

☐ If a policeman physically assaulted a citizen and then failed to make an arrest; proper use involves an arrest.
☐ If the citizen being arrested did not, by word or deed, resist the policeman; force should be used only if it is necessary to make the arrest.
☐ If the policeman, even though there was resistance to the arrest, could easily have restrained the citizen in other ways.

☐ If a large number of policemen were present and could have assisted in subduing the citizen in the station, in lockup, and in the interrogation rooms.
☐ If an offender was handcuffed and made no attempt to flee or offer violent resistance.
☐ If the citizen resisted arrest, but the use of force continued even after the citizen was subdued.

In the seven-week period, we found 37 cases in which force was used improperly. In all, 44 citizens had been assaulted. In 15 of these cases, no one was arrested. Of these, 8 had offered no verbal or physical resistance whatsoever, while 7 had.

An arrest was made in 22 of the cases. In 13, force was exercised in the station house when at least four other policemen were present. In two cases, there was no verbal or physical resistance to the arrest but force was still applied. In two other cases, the police applied force to a handcuffed offender in a field setting. And in five situations, the offender did resist arrest, but the policemen continued to use force even after he had been subdued.

Starting Time: _____	Finishing Time: _____
Reading Time: _____	Reading Rate: _____
Comprehension: _____	Vocabulary: _____

VOCABULARY: The following words have been taken from the selection you have just read. Put an X in the box before the best meaning or synonym for the word as used in the selection.

1. **precedent**, page 73, column 1, paragraph 2
"...police brutality and mistreatment of citizens have a precedent in American history—"
☐ a. priority
☐ b. precept
☐ c. basis
☐ d. right

2. **monitored**, page 73, column 1, paragraph 4
"...sat in patrol cars and monitored booking and lockup procedures..."
☐ a. observed
☐ b. supervised
☐ c. criticized
☐ d. allowed

3. **insinuate**, page 73, column 2, paragraph 1
"They often insinuate that charges of brutality are part of a conspiracy..."
☐ a. insist
☐ b. instigate
☐ c. imply
☐ d. deny

4. **deprecate**, page 74, column 1, paragraph 1
"...calling them names that deprecate them in their own eyes..."
☐ a. appreciate
☐ b. confuse
☐ c. satisfy
☐ d. belittle

5. **predominated**, page 74, column 2, paragraph 3
"...people of low socio-economic status predominated in most of the areas surveyed."
☐ a. prevailed
☐ b. filled
☐ c. disturbed
☐ d. worked

CONTEXTUAL AIDS: ADJECTIVE CLAUSES

Studies of good readers show that they are aware of the context of what they are reading. This means that they are anticipating what is coming next by what has gone before.

The many ways in which context functions to help the reader recognize words are called contextual aids.

Contextual Aid. Words can be understood when used with adjective clauses. Frequently an unknown word modified by an adjective clause can be understood through the relationship of the clause to the rest of the sentence. In the sentence, **She went to a _____, which was located in a shopping center**, the reader can correctly guess that the missing word is **store**. The adjective clause following the blank is the clue.

In the following sentence similar contextual aids have been used to modify nonsense words. Underline the nonsense word and write the correct word on the line following each sentence.

1. We said goodbye to our pellidants who had lived next door for ten years.

   _____

2. He drove the dramp which was used to make deliveries all over the city.

   _____

3. The lapton which connects the two cities has just been resurfaced.

   _____

4. The dentelpot who directs both the junior high and the high school is new this year.

   _____

5. He picked up the maft who had been barking noisily.

   _____

6. The fastelmod, who could type and take dictation, was hired last year.

   _____

7. Krampers, whose job it is to cut hair, talk knowledgeably on everything.

   _____

8. The pasterband, whose daily circulation is tremendous, influences public thinking.

   _____

9. The buntelpot who is campaigning for the office of mayor addressed the crowd.

   _____

THE FOR EXAMPLE PARAGRAPH

The fifth pattern of paragraph development is called the For Example. It is an inversion of the Fable paragraph—the main idea or generalization comes first, followed by the illustration or story.

Graphically the For Example looks like this:

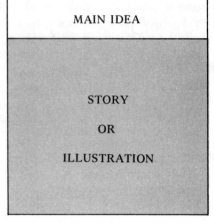

Here is an example of the For Example:

Conversationalists of the low-level or high-level variety are uniformly dull. As Wendell Johnson observes: "The low-level speaker frustrates you because he leaves you with no directions as to what to do with the basketful of information he has given you. The high-level speaker frustrates you because he simply doesn't tell you what he is talking about—being thus frustrated, and being further blocked because the rules of courtesy (or of attendance at class lectures) require that one remain quietly seated until the speaker has finished, there is little for one to do but daydream, doodle, or simply fall asleep."

Like the Fable this pattern presents a story or anecdote to illustrate the main point. Observe too that there are no facts or data presented in the illustration for the student to digest and retain. The story is there simply to help the reader get the point.

COMPREHENSION: For each of the following statements and questions, select the option containing the most complete or most accurate answer.

1. The first paragraph
(i)
  □ a. is an irresponsible statement.
  □ b. defends the actions of the police.
  □ c. accuses the public of indifference.
  □ d. sets the tone of the selection.

2. The relationship between police brutality
(f) and civil disobedience is
  □ a. uncertain.
  □ b. unknown.
  □ c. absent.
  □ d. direct.

3. Police attitude to the public's demand for
(h) plain answers has been generally
  □ a. suspicious.
  □ b. cooperative.
  □ c. negative.
  □ d. hostile.

4. Police practices which many civil rights ac-
(a) tivists label as police brutality have
  □ a. been developed to deal with Blacks.
  □ b. been accepted by most citizens.
  □ c. always been standard procedures.
  □ d. been defended by citizen groups.

5. The author points out that the definition of
(h) what constitutes police brutality often depends on
  □ a. subjective interpretation.
  □ b. police reports.
  □ c. eye witnesses.
  □ d. medical testimony.

6. All police enforcement agencies would do well
(e)
  □ a. to treat suspects politely and patiently.
  □ b. to hesitate before making an arrest.
  □ c. to respect a suspect's self-image.
  □ d. to avoid the use of undercover procedures.

7. Police harassment is generally looked upon by
(f) ghetto youths as
  □ a. an invasion of privacy.
  □ b. unfortunate but necessary.
  □ c. a proper police technique.
  □ d. helpful and reasonable.

8. The relationship between crime and poor liv-
(b) ing conditions is
  □ a. not convincing.
  □ b. totally absent.
  □ c. low.
  □ d. high.

9. The answer to the question, "How much
(g) physical force should be used by the police?"
is often
  □ a. a matter of careful thought.
  □ b. a question of conscience.
  □ c. a decision reached by all policemen.
  □ d. an interpretation of a legal definition.

10. It seems reasonable to conclude that
(f)
  □ a. the question of police brutality will always be with us.
  □ b. policemen guilty of brutality will never be punished.
  □ c. the citizen's charge of police brutality is usually exaggerated.
  □ d. the courts can do nothing to help the average citizen.

> Comprehension Skills: a—isolating details; b—recalling specific facts; c—retaining concepts; d—organizing facts; e—understanding the main idea; f—drawing a conclusion; g—making a judgment; h—making an inference; i—recognizing tone; j—understanding characters; k—appreciation of literary forms.

Women of Lesbos

Shelley Discusses the Male Hatred and Social Abhorrence of Lesbianism

Martha Shelley

Lesbianism is one road to freedom—freedom from oppression by men.

To see lesbianism in this context—as a mode of living neither better nor worse than others, as one which offers its own opportunities—one must abandon the notion that deviance from the norm arises from personal illness.

It is generally accepted that America is a "sick society." There is an inevitable corollary to this statement, which has not been generally accepted: that people within our society are all crippled by virtue of being forced to conform to certain norms. (Those who conform most easily can be seen as either the most healthy, because adaptable, or most sick because least spirited.) Blacks are struggling to free themselves not only from white oppression, but from the sickness of self-contempt and the sick sexual roles. It is clear that the self-abasing, suffering, shuffling black is not someone with a personal neurosis, but society's victim—and someone who has been forced to learn certain techniques for survival. Few people understand that the same is true of the self-abnegating passive housewife. Fewer understand this truth about the homosexual.

For women, as for other groups, there are several American norms. All of them have their rewards—and their penalties. The nice girl next door, virginal until her marriage—the Miss America type—is rewarded with community respect and respectability. She loses her individuality and her freedom to become a toothpaste smile and a chastity belt. The career woman gains independence and a larger margin of freedom—IF she is willing to work twice as hard as a man for less pay, and IF she can cope with emotional strains similar to those that beset the black intellectual surrounded by white colleagues. The starlet, call-girl, or bunny whose source of income is directly related to her image as a sex object, gains some financial independence and freedom from housework. She doesn't have to work as hard as the career women, but she pays through psychological degradation as a sex object, and through the insecurity of knowing that her career—based on youthful good looks—is short-lived.

The lesbian, through her ability to obtain love and sexual satisfaction from other women, is freed of dependence on men for love, sex and money. She does not have to do menial chores for them (at least at home) nor cater to their egos, nor submit to hasty and inept sexual encounters. She is freed from fear of unwanted pregnancy and the pains of childbirth, and from the drudgery of child raising.

On the other hand, she pays three penalties. The rewards of child raising are denied her. This is a great loss for some women, but not for others. Few women abandon their children, as compared with the multitudes of men who abandon both wives and children. Few men take much interest in the process of child raising. One suspects that it might not be much fun for the average person, and so the men leave it to the women.

The lesbian must compete with men in the job market, facing the same job and salary discrimination as her straight sister. On the other hand, she has more of a chance of success since her career is not interrupted by childbirth.

Finally, she faces the most severe contempt and ridicule that society can heap on a woman.

A year ago, when Women's Liberation picketed the 1968 Miss America pageant, the most terrible epithet heaped on our straight sisters was "lesbian." The sisters faced hostile audiences who called them "commies," "tramps," etc., and they faced these labels with equanimity; but they broke into tears when they were called lesbians. When a woman showed up at a feminist meeting and announced that she was a lesbian, many women avoided her. Others told her to keep her mouth shut, for fear that she would endanger the cause. They felt that men could be persuaded to accept some measure of equality for women—as long as these women would parade their devotion to heterosexuality and motherhood.

A woman who is totally independent of men—who obtains love, sex and self-esteem from other women—is a terrible threat to male supremacy. She doesn't need them, and therefore they have very little power over her.

I have met many, many feminists who were not lesbians—but I have never met a lesbian who was not a feminist. Straight women by the millions have been sold the belief that they must subordinate themselves to men, accept less pay for equal work, and do all the shit work around the house. I have met straight women who would die to preserve their chains. I have never met a lesbian who believed that she was innately less rational or capable than a man.

Lesbians, because they are not afraid of being abandoned by men, are less reluctant to express hostility towards the male class who are oppressors of women. Hostility towards your oppressor is healthy—but the guardians of modern morality, the psychiatrists, have interpreted this hostility as an illness, and they say this illness causes and is lesbianism.

If hostility to men causes lesbianism, then it seems to me that in a male-dominated society, lesbianism is a sign of mental health.

The psychiatrists have also forgotten that lesbianism involves love between women. Isn't love between equals healthier than sucking up to an oppressor? And when they claim we aren't capable of loving men, even if we want to—I ask you, straight man, are you capable of loving another man so deeply that you aren't afraid of his body or afraid to put your body in his hands? Are you really capable of loving women, or is your sexuality just another expression of your hostility? Is it an act of love or sexual conquest? An act of sexual imperialism?

I do not mean to condemn all males. I have found some beautiful, loving men among the revolutionaries, among the hippies, and the male homosexuals. But the average man—including the average student male radical—wants a passive sex-object cum domestic cum baby nurse to clean up after him while he does all the fun things and bosses her around—while he plays either bigshot executive or Che Guevara—and he is my oppressor and my enemy.

Society has taught most lesbians to believe that they are sick and has taught most straight women to despise and fear the lesbian as a perverted, diseased creature. It has fostered the myth that lesbians are ugly and turn to each other because they can't get that prize, that prince, a male! In this age of the new "sexual revolution," another myth has been fostered—the beautiful lesbians who play games with each other on the screen for the titillation of heterosexual males. They are not seen as serious people in love—but as performers in the "let's try a new perversion" game.

Freud founded the myth of penis envy, and men have asked me, "But what can two women do together?" As though a penis were the sine qua non of sexual pleasure! Man, we can do without it, and keep it going longer, too!

Women are afraid to be without a man's protection—because other men will assault them on the streets. And this is no accident, not an aberration performed by a few lunatics. Assaults on women are no more an accident than are lynchings of blacks in Mississippi. Men have oppressed us, and like most oppressors, they hate the oppressed and fear their wrath. Watch a white man walking in Harlem and you will see what I mean. Look at the face of a man who has accidentally wandered into a lesbian bar.

Men fear lesbians because they are less dependent, and because their hostility is less controlled.

Straight women fear lesbians because of the lesbian inside them, because we represent an alternative. They fear us for the same reason that uptight middle class people fear hip people. They are angry at us because we have a way out that they are afraid to take.

And what happens to the lesbians under all this pressure? Many of my sisters, confused by the barrage of anti-gay propaganda, have spent years begging to be allowed to live. They have come begging because they believed they were psychic cripples, and that other people were healthy and had the moral right to judge them. Many have lived in silence, burying themselves in their careers, like name-changing Jews and blacks who passed for white. Many have retreated into an apolitical domesticity, concerning themselves only with the attempt to maintain a love relationship in a society which attempts to destroy love and replace it with consumer goods—flowers, mouthwashes, diamond rings, automobiles—and which attempts to completely destroy any form of love outside the monogamous marriage.

This, by the way, is an important point for all kinds of revolutionaries. If you love your brothers and sisters you are less willing to stand by and watch them get crushed under the relentless pressures of the rat race, of the doctor bills and the furniture bills. If you love your brothers and sisters you won't try to swindle them. Restricting love to the immediate family group isolates each family from the community—each ethnic group from the others—and makes all these isolated frightened people more willing to settle for fancy furniture on the installment plan, for grudgingly bestowed respectability, because they can't get the real thing, real love.

To return to the lesbian—because LESBIAN has become such a vile epithet, we have been afraid to fight openly. We can lose our jobs—we have fewer civil rights than any other minority group. Because we have few family ties and no children, for the most part, we have been active in many causes—but always in secret, because our name contaminates any cause that we work for.

To the radical lesbian, I say that we can no longer afford to fight for everyone else's cause while ignoring our own. Ours is a life style born out of a sick society—so is everyone else's. The revolution must be fought for us, too, as well as Blacks, Indians, welfare mothers, grape pickers, SDS people, Puerto Ricans, or mine workers. We must have a revolution for human rights.

Maybe after the revolution, people will be able to love each other regardless of skin color, ethnic origin, occupation, or type of genitals. But if that's going to happen, it will only happen because we make it—starting right now.

Starting Time: _____	Finishing Time: _____
Reading Time: _____	Reading Rate: _____
Comprehension: _____	Vocabulary: _____

VOCABULARY: The following words have been taken from the selection you have just read. Put an X in the box before the best meaning or synonym for the word as used in the selection.

1. **mode**, page 78, column 1, paragraph 2
"...as a mode of living neither better nor worse than others, ..."
☐ a. appearance
☐ b. manner
☐ c. model
☐ d. rule

2. **deviance**, page 78, column 1, paragraph 2
"...one must abandon the notion that deviance from the norm arises from personal illness."
☐ a. departure
☐ b. adherence
☐ c. devious
☐ d. criticism

3. **inevitable**, page 78, column 1, paragraph 3
"There is an inevitable corollary to this..."
☐ a. undesirable
☐ b. unimportant
☐ c. enviable
☐ d. necessary

4. **equanimity**, page 78, column 2, paragraph 5
"...they faced these labels with equanimity; ..."
☐ a. force
☐ b. anger
☐ c. calmness
☐ d. equality

5. **innately**, page 79, column 1, paragraph 1
"...believed that she was innately less rational or capable than a man."
☐ a. intimately
☐ b. naturally
☐ c. generally
☐ d. unconsciously

SUFFIXES

Many English words consist of a base or root word to which prefixes (beginnings) and suffixes (endings) have been added. To the root word **agree** (a verb) we can add both a prefix and a suffix to get **disagreeable** (an adjective) which has an opposite meaning.

A suffix is added to the end of a word and affects the part of speech of that word. We have just seen how the suffix **able** changes **agree** from a verb to an adjective.

Two Suffixes

1. **-en** is an Old English verb suffix. It changes nouns and adjectives to verbs, like **dark** and **darken**.

2. **-ize** is a Greek verb suffix. It also changes nouns and adjectives to verbs, like **sterile** and **sterilize**.

In the following sentences, root words have been set in bold print. Add one of these suffixes to each root and write the new word in the space following the sentence. As you add suffixes to words, you may have to drop, change or add letters.

1. Are you certain it's time? The sun hasn't even **rise**.

   _____

2. His voice **soft** when the little girl burst into tears.

   _____

3. **Fast** this bracket to the other side of the door.

   _____

4. It seemed to **material** before our very eyes.

   _____

5. Ice cream **crystal** in root beer.

   _____

6. The suspense was **height** by his earlier remarks.

   _____

7. Exposure to cold weather **weak** his resistance to disease.

   _____

8. We **theory** that he must have come and gone before we arrived.

   _____

9. Many immigrant children become **American** in just a short time.

   _____

10. Let me **emphasis** this point.

   _____

THE COUNT-THEM PARAGRAPH

Number six in our discussion of patterns of paragraph development is the Count-Them. This pattern is an inverted Salestalk—the "pitch" comes first, followed by the facts supporting it.

Graphically the Count-Them looks like this:

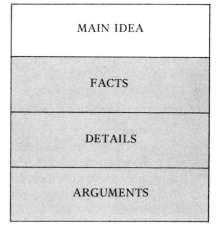

Here is an example of the Count-Them:

College learning deals in abstractions, ideas, principles, laws, theorems, whole movements in history, and so on. This kind of intellectual work requires understanding, the perception of relationships, judgment and reasoning. None of these processes is possible without sustained attention or concentration. Where the mind cannot be held riveted to an idea or principle, understanding falters or fails completely. Then the necessary connections that must be apprehended are not perceived and the educative process quickly degenerates into rote learning or verbalizing.

In this pattern a formal approach is used. The generalization or main idea is presented first for the reader to see and read. Then the facts and details supporting it are given. This is a pattern used most often in textbooks. The author wants the student to see his main point first and then examine the evidence supporting it.

COMPREHENSION: For each of the following statements and questions, select the option containing the most complete or most accurate answer.

1. The author looks upon lesbianism as
(c)
   - ☐ a. a type of degradation.
   - ☐ b. a personal illness.
   - ☐ c. a social disease.
   - ☐ d. a form of liberation.

2. Americans would enjoy better mental and emotional health if
(f)
   - ☐ a. they were given a better standard of living.
   - ☐ b. doctors were more easily available.
   - ☐ c. hospital rates were reasonable.
   - ☐ d. they were not made to conform.

3. The author concludes that whatever life styles a woman chooses
(f)
   - ☐ a. she is bound to succeed.
   - ☐ b. society exacts its toll.
   - ☐ c. she tends to dominate.
   - ☐ d. society supports her efforts.

4. From the point of view of professional success
(h)
   - ☐ a. a lesbian has a distinct advantage over a non-lesbian.
   - ☐ b. a woman has more drive and ambition than a man.
   - ☐ c. society makes allowances for a woman's family responsibilities.
   - ☐ d. a lesbian cannot be expected to compete satisfactorily.

5. The woman's liberation movement refuses to become identified with
(c)
   - ☐ a. professed lesbians.
   - ☐ b. traditional motherhood.
   - ☐ c. career women.
   - ☐ d. minority groups.

6. The author states that lesbianism is
(b)
   - ☐ a. a form of female chauvinism.
   - ☐ b. an abnormal manifestation.
   - ☐ c. a threat to male supremacy.
   - ☐ d. a threat to the human race.

7. Lesbians would agree to which of the following ideas?
(a)
   - ☐ a. All homosexuals are accepted.
   - ☐ b. All men are heterosexuals.
   - ☐ c. All feminists are lesbians.
   - ☐ d. All lesbians are feminists.

8. The article suggests that lesbians are
(j)
   - ☐ a. constantly terrified.
   - ☐ b. fiercely independent.
   - ☐ c. completely unreasonable.
   - ☐ d. overly emotional.

9. The author expresses her views with
(i)
   - ☐ a. haughty arrogance.
   - ☐ b. frank conviction.
   - ☐ c. careful reserve.
   - ☐ d. veiled resentment.

10. An important point made in the selection is that
(e)
   - ☐ a. women liberationists lack conviction.
   - ☐ b. the best men are homosexuals.
   - ☐ c. all women are frustrated lesbians.
   - ☐ d. society should accept and respect alternate life styles.

> Comprehension Skills: a—isolating details; b—recalling specific facts; c—retaining concepts; d—organizing facts; e—understanding the main idea; f—drawing a conclusion; g—making a judgment; h—making an inference; i—recognizing tone; j—understanding characters; k—appreciation of literary forms.

TOPICS FOR THE RESTLESS

The Plight of the Porpoise

If Porpoises Are Intelligent, They Will Soon Discover Who Their Real Enemies Are

Robert Benkovitch

Drifting in the warm shark-infested waters of the Indian Ocean on a Sunday in 1971, a cabin cruiser with a stalled engine was suddenly struck by a huge wave, overturned, and immediately sank. Three persons drowned as a result, but a determined 23-year-old Yvonne Vladislavich, with an open cut on her foot, began to swim toward the coast. A half dozen marauding sharks picked up the scent of blood and were soon trailing her. As the sharks began circling toward their prey, two porpoises suddenly appeared at her side. The sharks, knowing the speed and agility of their natural enemy, withdrew.

Miss Vladislavich, a strong swimmer, had a 25-mile distance ahead of her before reaching safety. Her strength began failing, but the porpoises helped her stay afloat. Eventually she reached a buoy, climbed on, and waited to be rescued.

Miss Vladislavich insists that she owes her life to the two porpoises—but their lives, unfortunately, may now be in the hands of man and his modern technology.

For centuries, porpoises have been recognized as man's closest aquatic friend. Briny tales have passed from sailor to sailor, telling how they guided lost boats through dense fog, or of rescuing drowning swimmers from dangerous waters. Even early Greek pottery often depicted a human riding on the back of a smiling porpoise.

One Greek myth suggests that some porpoises were once men. The story claims that Dionysus, the God of wine, was kidnapped and taken out to sea. When he realized his fate, the god made the boat's mast sprout grape vines. As the fearful and panicstricken crew jumped overboard, Dionysus changed them into porpoises and forced the evil sailors to remain in the sea forever.

Evolutionary theory, based on studies done with fossil skeletons, slightly support the ancient Greek tale—but only to the point that porpoises were once land-dwelling animals. Fifty million years ago, after adapting to life on land, the early ancestors of porpoises gave today's scientists a genuine mystery by returning to the sea. Although the real reason remains unknown, practicality appears to be the only explanation because, at that time, a greater portion of the earth's surface was covered with water.

During the long process of readapting to sea life, porpoises exchanged legs for flippers and grew streamlined, averaging in length between five to 12 feet. However, finger bones can still be found in their flippers and they must breathe air through lungs while surfacing. Unlike man, porpoises breathe consciously every six minutes by inhaling two gallons of air within a half-second.

A porpoise's brain is 20 to 40 percent larger than that of man. With that in mind, some scientists believe that in addition to performing desultory tricks, porpoises probably have the basic capabilities of learning language.

In water, a porpoise communicates by producing sounds originating from air passages in its head. The waterborne sounds move at a speed four times faster than the airborne sounds man is accustomed to. When two porpoises are together, they will exchange long series of sounds that vary in frequency and length. One remains courteously silent while the other is "talking."

When in the presence of human beings, porpoises politely revert to using mostly airborne sounds that resemble clicks and whistles containing elements of human speech. In fact, porpoises produce humanoid sounds when they hear human speech and come in close contact with people. Aristotle, in 300 B.C., insisted that "the voice of the porpoise in air is like that of a human; that he pronounces vowels and combinations of vowels." A porpoise's initiative deserves priase, considering that few, if any, humans have ever attempted to place their heads in water and attempt water-borne communication.

Some scientists have experimented with creating an interspecies language. Vocal sounds in consecutive chains ranging from one to ten were given to several porpoises. Each was rewarded if it correctly repeated the exact series. Out of an average of 1000 of the syllables, one porpoise mimicked the vocalizations with few mistakes in both resembling pronunciation and timing between each sound. A human being's memory span limits most to remembering and repeating chains containing only seven consecutive sounds.

Although concerned scientists seriously study porpoises, other people seriously study profit and have exploited the porpoise's intelligence for both commercial and military use.

The United States Navy, for example, has been attempting to train porpoises to locate underwater objects, such as sunken ships, submarines, or torpedoes by following acoustic signals reflected by the objects. The Navy also trains porpoises to attack sharks that threaten personnel engaged in underwater salvage or rescue work. A porpoise's hard boney snout and high speed acts as an effective battering-ram that has earned the respect of sharks.

Commercial enterprises have also exploited the talents of the porpoise. There are more than a dozen aquariums, marinelands or oceanariums from Florida to California that buy porpoises, then make them earn their keep by jumping through fiery hoops, dancing, raising flags, and playing basketball. In Hawaii, a pair of trainers, who noted that Christmas was only a few weeks away, wanted a porpoise to pull a brightly colored sled mounted on styrofoam runners. Whatever the gimmick, porpoises are successfully used to entice curious tourists to part with millions of dollars each year.

Hollywood and television have also made their bid for a piece of the action. One bottlenose porpoise was trained to play a leading role in a movie entitled "Flipper." The film was later stretched out into a weekly TV series with the same name, using several porpoises for the starring role.

Porpoises have become box office, and Florida supplies the demand. About 190 are captured each year from Florida waters and used to supply 80 percent of the American oceanariums and all of Europe's. A freshly captured porpoise brings between $400 to $800. A 12-foot adult weighing over 700 pounds might add shipping and handling charges of about $1700. Regulations make it illegal to capture any porpoise less than six feet.

Fortunately, concerned conservationists recently aimed their attention on limiting the number of captures. Last year, one marine organization netted ten porpoises off the coasts of Naples and Marco Islands in Florida to be sold to exhibits. Though a permit had been issued by the Florida Department of Natural Resources allowing the organization to capture 22, several protests were made by local residents.

The group insisted that 22 porpoises was a significant number when caught in a limited area. The protests were brought to the attention of the county commissioner who called the captures "crass commercialism." He has been attempting to set a trend in the right direction by asking for an ordinance forbidding the transporting of porpoises "in any manner" from his county.

The Japanese have usually been portrayed as the major killers of porpoises because they use them for food. Between 11,000 to 16,000 are caught for this purpose each year, according to the Japanese government fishing agency. A porpoise is individually valued at about $20 in Japan with variations in price depending upon the annual catch.

Despite international complaints about using porpoises as a food source, the Japanese continue their fishing and defend themselves by pointing an accusing finger at the American tuna industry.

United States tuna fishermen operating out of the West Coast catch up to 45,000 tons of tuna each year. However, because tuna are often inseparable traveling companions with porpoises in Pacific waters, and both feed on similar small fish, porpoises are inadvertently netted, too. In the process, as many as 250,000 porpoises are consciously killed in a year, in addition to those killed by the French, Spanish and Scandinavian fishing industries.

In 1971 a Congressional subcommittee conducted hearings on proposed legislation designed to stop the useless slaughter of aquatic mammals. Environmentalists insisted that one porpoise death might be too many because so little is known about the size and composition of the porpoise population, or whether those accidental deaths threaten the existence of the species.

As a compromise between environmentalists and commercial fishermen, California representatives introduced a bill that would allow the killing of ocean mammals "if the harrassment, hunting, capturing or killing is incidental to commercial fishing operations."

On October 21, 1972, the President signed the Federal Marine Mammal Protection Act. In addition to forbidding United States fishermen from deliberately killing porpoises, it also demands that no marine mammal may be taken or imported by any United States citizen or organization; or by any person in United States waters.

The law is of little comfort to the porpoise because it provides the United States tuna industry with a loophole that still allows them to kill porpoises "accidentally" or "incidentally," and, in addition, keeps fishermen from reverting back to their older method of pole and line fishing that was effectively used in the early 60s.

The plight of porpoises proves once again that technology in the hands of man becomes a tool used for conquering nature, instead of helping man live with it. As a result, another species becomes threatened with needless extinction because of man's bottomless greed and perverted sense of entertainment. If a porpoise's intelligence is what it is reputed to be, then they will soon discover who their real enemies are. And what will happen then?

Starting Time:	_____	Finishing Time:	_____
Reading Time:	_____	Reading Rate:	_____
Comprehension:	_____	Vocabulary:	_____

VOCABULARY: The following words have been taken from the selection you have just read. Put an X in the box before the best meaning or synonym for the word as used in the selection.

1. **marauding**, page 83, column 1, paragraph 1
"A half dozen marauding sharks picked up the scent of blood..."
☐ a. vicious
☐ b. desperate
☐ c. roving
☐ d. lost

2. **agility**, page 83, column 1, paragraph 1
"The sharks, knowing the speed and agility of their natural enemy, withdrew."
☐ a. talent
☐ b. liveliness
☐ c. agitation
☐ d. aggressiveness

3. **aquatic**, page 83, column 1, paragraph 4
"...porpoises have been recognized as man's closest aquatic friend."
☐ a. faithful
☐ b. water-dwelling
☐ c. known
☐ d. animal

4. **depicted**, page 83, column 1, paragraph 4
"Even early Greek pottery often depicted a human riding on the back of a smiling porpoise."
☐ a. portrayed
☐ b. required
☐ c. depleted
☐ d. imitated

5. **desultory**, page 83, column 2, paragraph 3
"...some scientists believe that in addition to performing desultory tricks, ..."
☐ a. methodical
☐ b. debilitating
☐ c. disconnected
☐ d. spectacular

SYLLABICATION

Knowing how to reduce words to their syllables aids both reading and spelling. Frequently a long word can be recognized and understood if pronounced by syllables. And in spelling, of course, knowledge of syllables contributes to accuracy.

There are rules or generalizations which we can follow when dividing words. One such rule tells us that when two consonants come between two vowels the word is divided between the consonants. For example, the word **window** is divided into **win** and **dow** because the two consonants, **n** and **d**, come between the two vowels, **i** and **o**.

In the following sentences divide the words in bold print according to this rule. Write the word on the blank line following each sentence, inserting hyphens (-) between the syllables.

1. Improve your **diction**. _____

2. Be **earnest** in your dealings. _____

3. Crops need **fertile** soil. _____

4. Not everything **glitters**. _____

5. **Hermits** live alone. _____

6. The **impact** took lives. _____

7. Germs **infect** everyone. _____

8. **London** swings. _____

9. **Martial** law was imposed. _____

10. The **monsoons** come in April. _____

11. No **offense** was meant. _____

12. Tell **only** me. _____

13. **Passions** overcome reason. _____

14. The **robber** was caught. _____

15. Wear the **scarlet** hat. _____

16. **German** autos wear well. _____

17. Watch your **language**. _____

18. The **puppy** whined all night. _____

19. **Maintain** a calm appearance. _____

20. **Connect** the two parts. _____

THE BECAUSE PARAGRAPH

The Because pattern of paragraph development is the same as the Therefore, turned upside down. The conclusion or generalization is presented first, followed by the sequential arguments leading to it.

Graphically the Because looks like this:

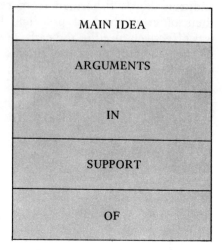

| MAIN IDEA |
| ARGUMENTS |
| IN |
| SUPPORT |
| OF |

Here is an example of the Because:

Concentration, then, narrows your consciousness to some object and heightens your awareness of that object. There are a thousand things that might enter consciousness if you let them. The fact is you allow only a few things into your consciousness at any one time. Those things, moreover, are in some way bound up with your wants, needs, hopes, interests and purposes. Thus concentration functions something like a spotlight. It highlights things that are of significance to you so that they stand out in sharp relief. At the same time, it throws into shadow (i.e., to the background of consciousness) items of experience that are not of particular interest or importance at the moment.

The Because paragraph and its opposite, the Therefore, are used in the same way by the student: find and read the conclusion first; then read and evaluate the steps leading to it.

COMPREHENSION: For each of the following statements and questions, select the option containing the most complete or most accurate answer.

1. Sharks have a highly developed sense of
(h)
   - □ a. sight.
   - □ b. hearing.
   - □ c. taste.
   - □ d. smell.

2. A porpoise has
(f)
   - □ a. a fearful reputation.
   - □ b. a voracious appetite.
   - □ c. a superior intellect.
   - □ d. a highly developed brain.

3. The origin of the porpoise is
(c)
   - □ a. explained by the theory of evolution.
   - □ b. lost in a cloak of mystery.
   - □ c. explained by Greek mythology.
   - □ d. strange beyond belief.

4. A porpoise's manner of breathing is to man's
(g) manner of breathing as
   - □ a. natural is to unnatural.
   - □ b. quality is to quantity.
   - □ c. land is to sea.
   - □ d. deliberate is to automatic.

5. Compared to the human brain, the porpoise's
(b) brain is
   - □ a. larger.
   - □ b. smaller.
   - □ c. superior.
   - □ d. equal.

6. A porpoise has
(c)
   - □ a. a need to communicate with man.
   - □ b. a natural fear of man.
   - □ c. an uncanny sensitivity to sound.
   - □ d. a preference for land over sea.

7. Compared to some other people, the attitude
(h) of scientists toward porpoises is
   - □ a. commercial.
   - □ b. enlightened and humane.
   - □ c. selfish.
   - □ d. scientific and militaristic.

8. The attitude of the author toward the com-
(i) mercial exploitation of porpoises is
   - □ a. understanding.
   - □ b. critical.
   - □ c. shocked.
   - □ d. financial.

9. Based on the information supplied in the
(f) selection, the greatest threat to the porpoise comes from
   - □ a. the fishing industry.
   - □ b. the entertainment world.
   - □ c. the military establishment.
   - □ d. the scientific community.

10. The present plight of the world's porpoise
(e) population results from
   - □ a. Japanese fishing techniques.
   - □ b. public indifference.
   - □ c. Hollywood's film industry.
   - □ d. human greed.

Comprehension Skills: a—isolating details; b—recalling specific facts; c—retaining concepts; d—organizing facts; e—understanding the main idea; f—drawing a conclusion; g—making a judgment; h—making an inference; i—recognizing tone; j—understanding characters; k—appreciation of literary forms.

Mononucleosis: The Overtreated Disease

Infectious Mono Is a Common Disease and Only Rarely a Serious One

William A. Nolen, M.D.

At a party I attended recently I overheard a woman telling a group of people about her daughter. "Kathy has mononucleosis," the woman said. "She's going to have to drop out of college for the rest of this semester. Doctor Jones says she'll have to stay home and take it easy until her blood tests are normal, and that may take a couple of months. Meantime, I'm going to have to wash her dishes and silverware separately from the rest of the family's; 'mono' is very contagious."

Her listeners nodded in agreement. Then another woman chipped in with a horror story about how her son, when he came down with mono, had to drop out of college not just for a semester but for an entire year. When a third woman started on *her* mono story, I moved out of hearing range. Who wants to watch a grown man cry?

There is more erroneous information floating around about infectious mononucleosis (or "mono," for short) than about any other disease I know. These misconceptions are the property not only of the lay public but even of some doctors—like Kathy's Dr. Jones—who haven't read an article or listened to a lecture on the disease in 20 years. As a result, hundreds of patients with infectious mononucleosis are being *mis*treated, rather than treated, every year.

Consider Kathy's case. First, she dropped out of school, something that should very seldom be necessary. Second, her doctor ordered her to stay at home and rest till her blood tests were normal— when, in fact, it is the symptoms and not the blood tests that should determine the extent of a patient's activity. Third, Kathy's mother is doing a lot of unnecessary work attempting to protect the rest of the family; in actuality, infectious mononucleosis is not a very contagious disease, and only rarely does more than one case occur in a family at any one time. Kathy is being overtreated for her illness: another victim of "infectious-mono overkill."

Rather than cite a lot of other cases of infectious mononucleosis that have been mistreated, I think it might be best to present the facts, as we know them, about the disease. You can then apply these facts to any cases with which you may be acquainted (and it's a rare person who doesn't know, or hasn't known, a patient with mono) and decide for yourself whether the treatment has been proper.

1. Infectious mononucleosis is almost certainly caused by a virus (the Epstein-Barr virus, if you're interested). I have to say "almost" because the evidence incriminating this virus, although very strong, is circumstantial. However, from the patient's point of view, the only important point to be made here is this: Until we have isolated this virus and proved that it causes infectious mono and *only* infectious mono, it will be impossible to prepare a vaccine to immunize patients against the disease.

2. Ninety-seven percent of infectious-mononucleosis cases occur in patients under 35. Most cases (77 percent) seem to occur between the ages of 12 and 22, and most of these occur in college students. I say "seem to occur" because it's highly likely that infectious mononucleosis occurs frequently in young children in a mild form that goes unrecognized. The apparent peak in the college years may be partly due to the close medical supervision college students usually receive.

3. Infectious mononucleosis is not very contagious. It is popularly known as the "kissing disease," and it's true that you can acquire it by kissing, but not from a brotherly or sisterly peck. There has to be transmission of saliva.

If you're a college student, you might also acquire mono by using your roommate's toothbrush, but you won't catch it simply from breathing the same air. Stories of an entire dormitory's coming down simultaneously with mono are invariably based on unfounded rumors.

4. The usual signs and symptoms of infectious mono are sore throat, fever, swollen glands at the back of the neck and a general feeling of tiredness. Since these signs and symptoms occur in many other ailments, blood tests must be done to establish that the patient does indeed have mono. One test is a blood smear, which will show—if the patient has mono—that the percentage of lymphocytes in the blood (usually around 20 percent of the total white-blood-cell count) has risen to about

70 percent, and some of the lymphocytes will be abnormal in appearance. Another test, which takes about two minutes, is done by mixing a drop of the patient's blood with a special solution: Clumps will form if the patient has mono. A third test measures the level of the patient's blood's reaction to the mono virus and may serve as a guide to the severity of the infection. This procedure takes about three hours.

5. The treatment of the ordinary case of infectious mononucleosis consists of rest, a wholesome diet and aspirin for the fever. As a rule, doctors recommend that the patient stay in bed as long as the fever lasts—usually from one to two weeks. After that, the patient can resume routine activities, avoiding overtiredness. Patients who return to their activities early generally get over their weak, tired feeling faster than those who are very cautious about activity. Only rarely should the weakness of infectious mono persist for more than six weeks.

6. Complications can and do occur in some cases. Most of these complications are mild—slight enlargements of the spleen and liver, for example—and require no special treatment.

When the complications are serious (for example, massive enlargement of the spleen and/or severe involvement of the liver), longer periods of rest may be required. With marked enlargement of the spleen, the patient must be kept quiet and out of active contact sports, which could possibly result in rupture of the spleen. A doctor can determine, usually by a physical examination, whether or not the spleen is enlarged.

Sometimes a streptococcus infection of the throat will become superimposed on the infectious-mono inflammation; a doctor can find out whether this has happened by taking a throat culture. If there *is* such a complication, antibiotics should be used to cure the strep infection. But antibiotics have no effect on infectious mononucleosis itself and they should not be used—as some doctors occasionally use them—"prophylactically"; that is, to ward off infections that do not even exist.

For the patient whose throat becomes so sore and swollen that eating and even breathing are difficult, a short course of cortisone therapy may be useful, but only very seldom does this become necessary.

7. Once you have had infectious mono, you become immune to it.

8. If the patient's symptoms—tiredness, depression, general weakness—persist longer than six weeks, it's wise to look for some cause other than infectious mono.

For example, college students who are bored with studying, afraid of examinations, fed up with the whole college scene, will sometimes use a case of mono as an excuse to drop out of the rat race. Whether consciously or unconsciously, they refuse to part with their symptoms until they are able to get out of the taxing situation they are in. Studies have shown that athletes, anxious to get back to their teams, recover from mono much more quickly on the average than do students who have no comparable ambitions. It's a shame—and it happens frequently—to continue to treat a boy or girl for infectious mononucleosis if what is *really* needed is intelligent counseling and advice on how to cope with the stresses of life.

Infectious mono is a common disease and only rarely a serious one. Overtreatment of patients is a far more common cause of disability than is undertreatment. Rest, a balanced diet, aspirin to relieve discomfort and liberal applications of common sense—this is all the treatment most mononucleosis patients need.

Starting Time: _____   Finishing Time: _____

Reading Time: _____   Reading Rate: _____

Comprehension: _____   Vocabulary: _____

VOCABULARY: The following words have been taken from the selection you have just read. Put an *X* in the box before the best meaning or synonym for the word as used in the selection.

1. **contagious**, page 88, column 1, paragraph 1
   "...'mono' is very contagious."
   □ a. contiguous
   □ b. serious
   □ c. catching
   □ d. rare

2. **erroneous**, page 88, column 1, paragraph 3
   "There is more erroneous information floating around about infectious mononucleosis..."
   □ a. incorrect
   □ b. accurate
   □ c. erratic
   □ d. scientific

3. **incriminating**, page 88, column 2, paragraph 2
   "...the evidence incriminating this virus, although very strong, is circumstantial."
   □ a. encouraging
   □ b. arresting
   □ c. dismissing
   □ d. implicating

4. **invariably**, page 88, column 2, paragraph 5
   "Stories of entire dormitory's coming down simultaneously with mono are invariably based on unfounded rumors."
   □ a. usually
   □ b. consistently
   □ c. often
   □ d. rarely

5. **taxing**, page 89, column 2, paragraph 4
   "...until they are able to get out of the taxing situation they are in."
   □ a. costly
   □ b. relaxing
   □ c. burdensome
   □ d. embarrassing

ROOTS

Many English words consist of a base word or root word to which prefixes (beginnings) and suffixes (endings) have been added. To the root word **agree** (a verb) we can add both a prefix and a suffix to get **disagreeable** (an adjective) which has an opposite meaning.

Roots are Latin and Greek stems on which our English words are based. For example, **bio** (life) is a Greek root on which the word **biology** (the study of plant and animal life) is built.

Two Roots

1. **capt**, **cept** are variants of the Latin root for **take** or **seize**. A **captive** has been taken.

2. **pend**, **pens** are variants of the Latin root for **hang** or **weigh**. A **suspension** bridge hangs over the water.

In the following sentences, these two roots have been left out. Space has been left indicating where the root belongs. Add one of these two roots and write your word on the line following the sentence.

1. Since its **in—ion**, the new elective program has been popular.

    _____

2. The college notified the students of their **ac—ance**.

    _____

3. **—ant** type earrings are the latest fashion.

    _____

4. The customary restrictions will be **sus—ed** in this one case.

    _____

5. The closed mind is not **re—ive** to new ideas.

    _____

6. The expulsion of the overdue members is **—ing** before this committee.

    _____

7. Her excellent performance **—ivated** the young audience.

    _____

8. Don't keep us hanging in **sus—e**; tell us the outcome.

    _____

9. The **—ive** look on his face indicated the thought he was giving the matter.

    _____

10. The **pre—** was issued to direct the conduct of the students.

    _____

THE COME-ON PARAGRAPH

This pattern of paragraph development is different from those we have already seen in that the main idea comes at neither the beginning nor the end; it comes in the middle.

This pattern leads the reader into the paragraph first and then presents the main idea. This is usually followed by additional thoughts pertaining to the generalization.

Graphically, the Come-On looks like this:

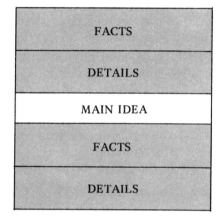

Here is an example of the Come-On:

Every scholar is plagued with the problem of distraction (it is really counter-attraction) during study. What should be done about it? Well, one good practical rule is to be on the alert for the first wavering of your concentration. You can then nip wool-gathering in the bud. If you try to understand each thought as the author presents it, there is little danger that your mind will wander. Reading an abstruse passage without understanding it, breaks the continuity of your thought. There is then a tendency to substitute your own fancies for the author's ideas.

This pattern makes for interesting reading. The introductory ideas entice the reader and lead him into the paragraph. Then the author lets his reader see the main idea and some additional facts relating to it.

COMPREHENSION: For each of the following statements and questions, select the option containing the most complete or most accurate answer.

1. Mononucleosis affects a person's
(c)
   □ a. nerves.
   □ b. blood.
   □ c. skin.
   □ d. liver.

2. The selection supports which of the follow-
(f) ing conclusions?
   □ a. Doctors should update their knowledge of mononucleosis.
   □ b. Hospitalization is recommended for persons with mononucleosis.
   □ c. Persons with mononucleosis should not frequent public places.
   □ d. Mononucleosis is a rare disease about which little is known.

3. The purpose of the selection is
(e)
   □ a. to criticize the medical profession.
   □ b. to encourage further research.
   □ c. to reassure the victims of mononucleosis.
   □ d. to educate the public-at-large.

4. The author develops his point of view by
(k) means of
   □ a. philosophical discussions.
   □ b. factual information.
   □ c. scientific theories.
   □ d. alarming examples.

5. Before a vaccine against mononucleosis can
(c) be developed
   □ a. circumstantial evidence is needed.
   □ b. more study and research are necessary.
   □ c. doctors must read about the disease.
   □ d. victims must report early symptoms.

6. Mononucleosis occurs especially among which
(h) of the following age groups?
   □ a. The very young
   □ b. The early teens
   □ c. The late teens
   □ d. The middle-aged

7. Mononucleosis is usually transmitted by
(b)
   □ a. physical contact.
   □ b. breathing.
   □ c. saliva.
   □ d. contaminated water.

8. The presence of mononucleosis can be posi-
(h) tively identified as a result of
   □ a. a short stay in the hospital.
   □ b. consulting the family doctor.
   □ c. observing obvious symptoms.
   □ d. a series of tests.

9. The length of time a person suffers from
(c) mononucleosis may depend upon the severity of the infection as well as his
   □ a. state of mind.
   □ b. geographic location.
   □ c. sex and age group.
   □ d. personal physician.

10. Most mononucleosis patients require
(f)
   □ a. complete isolation.
   □ b. intelligent counseling.
   □ c. relatively simple treatment.
   □ d. strong doses of antibiotics.

Comprehension Skills: a—isolating details; b—recalling specific facts; c—retaining concepts; d—organizing facts; e—understanding the main idea; f—drawing a conclusion; g—making a judgment; h—making an inference; i—recognizing tone; j—understanding characters; k—appreciation of literary forms.

The Anatomy of Drink, I

Everything You Should Know about Alcohol, but Didn't Want To Ask

Rog Halegood

Alcoholism appears to be as old as the history of alcoholic beverages—a history which is ancient indeed. In the *Wisdom of Ani,* an ancient Egyptian book of proverbs and moral codes, warnings are given against the unwise imbibing of too much drink. The Bible, too, is dotted with references to the misuse of alcohol; the "drunkenness of Noah" is a story known to every school child. The Moslems forbid alcohol all together, and in some countries of that faith the mere possession of it is a capital offense. Yet, stern legislation against alcohol seems never to have deterred the general populace from having its full share. The English were at a loss to stem the phenomenal addiction to gin that ravaged British society during the 18th century; the Volstead Act in the United States was a total fiasco and introduced an element of organized crime which still plagues us. In fact, history has proven that the more a society tries to repress alcohol consumption, the more that consumption is desired and sought after. Plainly, the safe use of alcohol lies in the successful implementation of sensible drinking programs, not wholesale policies of repression and enforced abstinence.

Man likes to drink. The fact is made evident when one considers the incredible list of ingredients that man has fermented and cheerfully ingested: bananas, grapefruit, persimmons, mare's milk, honey, animal blood, rice, all grains, dandelions—the list is endless and limited only by imagination. Thousands of organic substances are capable of fermentation, and man appears to have fermented just about everything, at one time or another, in the search for a "better" potable. Few areas of human endeavor seem to have brought as much ingenuity to bear as some of the ways by which man has arrived at something new to drink; indeed, many men have devoted their entire lives to the pursuit of one new and glorious distillation. Some, like the Catholic abbot Dom Perignon, succeeded brilliantly. (Perignon is credited with the invention of champagne.)

The reason man has devoted such an exorbitant amount of time to such a non-essential pursuit is quite obvious; alcoholic beverages are a pleasure to drink. Alcohol is nature's own tranquilizer—

Everyman's Librium. Taken in small quantities, it eases life's many pains and troubles. It provides relaxation and good cheer; a sense of well-being and comradeship. These beneficial properties of alcohol have been realized by man since recorded history, and probably long before that. At the same time, man has realized also that alcohol is a terrifying double-edged sword. Used unwisely, it is capable of destroying everything it enhances: sociability, marriage, livlihood, productivity. It can reduce a man to a state lower than an animal, and it can kill him ultimately through a hundred deaths. Alcohol *is* a great destroyer, but it need not be such. The fault is not that of alcohol itself, but in the way it is used. All programs of sensible drinking must start with that ultimate fact.

What happens when I drink?

Alcohol is a drug. It acts on the central nervous system as a depressant (*not as a stimulant*). Normally, it first produces euphoria or a feeling of well-being, then a certain amount of sedation interpreted as relaxation, then intoxication and, finally, death. Each of these stages is governed by the amount and rate of alcohol entering the bloodstream of the drinker. There is no hocus-pocus involved here. The amount of alcohol in the system can be precisely determined at any time by means of a common blood test. However, the degree of effect of alcohol upon any given person is determined by many factors: weight, amount of food in the stomach at the time alcohol is ingested, the emotional outlook of the person at the time he is drinking, previous drinking history, and overall tolerance to the drug. These factors, and others, can alter the absorption rate of alcohol into the system. Still, the level of alcohol in the blood is the final determinant for assaying states through sobriety into full-fledged drunkenness. As the alcohol level rises, specific physiological and psychological changes can be safely predicted.

The formula works this way: one shot of liquor (one and one-half ounces) will place the alcohol concentration in the blood at approximately 0.03 percent, or 0.03 grams of alcohol for every 100 c.c. of blood. These figures are based on an average adult male of about 150 pounds; the concentration would be higher for most women and children, of course. Now, at this level, it is virtually impossible to label anyone as intoxicated. However, the second drink, if taken within an hour of the first, will raise the alcohol in the blood to a little more than 0.05 percent, and we begin to experience alcohol's first plateau: we feel relaxed, more talkative. Our problems don't seem quite as pressing, and the company around us suddenly seems more pleasant, more "fun to be with." We are still not drunk in any legal sense, and our judgment and physical coordination is virtually unimpaired. So far, so good.

Somewhere between the third and fourth drink, things begin to happen rapidly. With the fourth drink, our alcohol concentration has reached 0.10 percent, or more, and we can at last be classified as legally drunk. The people we are with may still be "fun," but we're not noticing them as much as we did earlier. We are really becoming more introspective, although we may be the "life of the party" since our normal inhibitions against outrageous or scatological conduct have been repressed. It is at this point that we make the pass at the cocktail waitress, or guffaw too loudly at a dirty joke. Our brain is reacting to the soporific effects of alcohol, and our motor functions are becoming "loose" and uncoordinated. It is at this level that we are a definite hazard on the highway, and most states now consider a blood-alcohol analysis of 0.10 percent as legal evidence for drunkenness.

But it's New Year's, or Armistice Day, or the boss-just-fired-me day, or the mother-in-law-is-here-to-stay day, so we have a few more. The sixth drink, or the seventh beer (we'll see in a moment why they are about the same), jumps our alcohol level to between 0.15 and 0.20 percent. At this level, we are almost unrecognizable, both to ourselves and others. If sleep doesn't overtake us, we are likely to undergo violent changes in our mood and behavior. We may laugh one minute, cry the next. We may pick a fight, or take our clothes off on Main Street. We are no longer in control of our actions, and our behaviour is completely unpredictable. If we drive in this state, we stand a high chance of killing ourselves and others.

But let's really tie one on, okay? It's very easy to do. The only requirement is that we stay awake long enough to keep pouring back the hootch. At about the eighth continuous drink, the alcohol level in our blood will rise to somewhere around 0.35 percent. Most of us can't walk at this level, so we had better just stay at the bar provided we can still get service. Better still, we can check into a hotel with a bottle and there'll be no one to bother us. The company we were with lost their

charm a long time ago, and it's better to be by ourselves.

Somewhere between the eleventh and thirteenth drink, our alcohol level jumps to 0.50 percent and we suddenly can't drink another drop. Reason: We have passed out. However, if we drink very quickly, we might be able to down two or three more before the curtain descends. By doing this, we can pretty well assure ourselves that we may hit the alcohol bull's eye with a blood concentration of 0.55 to 0.60 percent. At this point, we will die in an acute alcoholic coma and our little drinking bout comes to a sudden close.

We are talking here of facts, not fiction. While tolerance to alcohol, and other factors, may allow one person to drink more than another, the alcohol concentrations mentioned above will produce the effects exactly as described, plus hundreds of others not mentioned. Alcohol is a drug. It cannot be played with without endangering life itself. It can be consumed *safely*, and that is the whole purpose of sane drinking practices.

I'm drunk. What do I do now?

When you become drunk, the only cure is to stop drinking. Coffee will not sober you up. Steam baths will do nothing. Exercise is of no avail. Only time can bring you back to a sober state.

The body's system must oxidize all the alcohol which is ingested. It does this at a rate of approximately .015 percent an hour. The rule of thumb is to allow about one hour of sobering up time for each drink, or beer, consumed. It takes this long for alcohol to be eliminated within the system. Beyond the one drink an hour limit, alcohol accumulates in the bloodstream and only time (and the liver) can remove it. There are no short cuts.

There are, however, ways in which the absorption rate can be slowed. The principal method is by food. It is always better to drink with food in the stomach than to drink on an empty stomach. While this will not save you from over-indulgence, it will provide some moderate protection against the first couple of drinks. Similarly, sipping a drink over a long period of time will reduce its net effect.

And that's about it. Anything else you may have heard is probably an old wive's tale. If you drink, alcohol will enter your bloodstream. If you continue to drink, it will accumulate in your bloodstream. That's the pure fact, and anything else is myth.

Starting Time: _____	Finishing Time: _____
Reading Time: _____	Reading Rate: _____
Comprehension: _____	Vocabulary: _____

VOCABULARY: The following words have been taken from the selection you have just read. Put an *X* in the box before the best meaning or synonym for the word as used in the selection.

1. **deterred**, page 93, column 1, paragraph 1
   "Yet, stern legislation against alcohol seems never to have deterred the general populace..."
   □ a. deterioriated
   □ b. discouraged
   □ c. encouraged
   □ d. allowed

2. **fiasco**, page 93, column 1, paragraph 1
   "...the Volstead Act in the United States was a total fiasco..."
   □ a. success
   □ b. fiesta
   □ c. disgrace
   □ d. failure

3. **assaying**, page 93, column 2, paragraph 2
   "...is the final determinant for assaying states through sobriety into..."
   □ a. trying
   □ b. analyzing
   □ c. attacking
   □ d. assigning

4. **scatological**, page 94, column 1, paragraph 2
   "...our normal inhibitions against outrageous or scatological conduct..."
   □ a. obscene
   □ b. unusual
   □ c. scattered
   □ d. logical

5. **soporific**, page 94, column 1, paragraph 2
   "Our brain is reacting to the soporific effects of alcohol, ..."
   □ a. sophisticated
   □ b. sordid
   □ c. sleep-inducing
   □ d. enchanting

CONTEXTUAL AIDS: APPOSITIVES

Studies of good readers show that they are aware of the context of what they are reading. This means that they are anticipating what is coming next by what has gone before.

The many ways in which context functions to help the reader recognize words are called contextual aids.

Contextual Aid. A word can be understood through another word or phrase used in apposition to it. An appositive is a word or phrase which explains the word it is placed next to. Appositives give the reader a clue to the meaning of the unknown word. In the sentence, **He wanted to be _____, the elected head of the state,** the appositive phrase clues the reader that the missing word is **governor.**

In the following sentences, similar contextual aids have been used in apposition to nonsense words. Underline the nonsense word and write the correct word on the line following each sentence.

1. Faldrons, armed fighting men, protect the security of our nation.

    _____

2. The warden called out the clodphers, special tracking dogs.

    _____

3. The bald podget, symbol of our nation, is almost extinct.

    _____

4. Brunkelsnaps, courageous space pilots, have landed on the surface of the moon.

    _____

5. The glasentran, also called the mouth organ, is more a toy than an instrument.

    _____

6. Contors, or steel pots, protect the soldiers' heads.

    _____

7. The plint, symbol of Christianity, is displayed in many homes.

    _____

8. Fongebs, wasps with very painful stings, built a nest in our garage.

    _____

9. Fralls, religious songs, were sung by the marchers.

    _____

10. Patners, horses of the desert, go for long periods without water.

    _____

THE SWITCH PARAGRAPH

This pattern of paragraph development is also different from the others in that its main idea, too, comes at neither end but in the middle.

Graphically, the Switch looks like this:

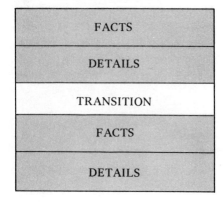

Here is an example of the Switch:

In other instances, the automobile at college is a pure luxury. Under this heading would fall: short hops to beaneries, taverns, and other nearby resorts; long jaunts to root the team on; travel for the sheer joy of keeping on the move, and driving for the sake of dating. All these pleasures help to make college life worth living, but they do eat into a student's time; and they also eat into his pocketbook. Of course, Dad is sometimes persuaded that a car is one of those uncatalogued but necessary expenses of higher education; and so he unwittingly contributes to his son's academic delinquency. At other times it is not unheard of for a student to be so smitten with a desire for the social prestige conferred by the possession of a car that he will take a part time job in order to pay for its upkeep.

Notice how this example of the Switch is effectively used to discuss the pros and cons of having an automobile on campus. The writer's main idea statement is used to make the transition from one side to the other.

TOPICS FOR THE RESTLESS

COMPREHENSION: For each of the following statements and questions, select the option containing the most complete or most accurate answer.

1. Which of the following attitudes should society adopt toward alcohol?
(c)
   - ☐ a. Abstinence
   - ☐ b. Repression
   - ☐ c. Moderation
   - ☐ d. Submission

2. The search for the ultimate drink has produced
(g)
   - ☐ a. trash as well as excellence.
   - ☐ b. temperance along with enjoyment.
   - ☐ c. quality and high prices.
   - ☐ d. confusion and rivalry.

3. The motivation behind man's production of alcoholic beverages is
(b)
   - ☐ a. evil.
   - ☐ b. humanitarian.
   - ☐ c. financial.
   - ☐ d. pleasure.

4. The proper use of alcohol requires
(f)
   - ☐ a. social acceptance.
   - ☐ b. self-restraint.
   - ☐ c. financial independence.
   - ☐ d. congenial company.

5. The logical progression of uncontrolled alcoholic intake
(c)
   - ☐ a. will produce a feeling of well-being.
   - ☐ b. can result in death.
   - ☐ c. can encourage complete relaxation.
   - ☐ d. will result in drunkenness.

6. The degree to which alcohol affects people
(c)
   - ☐ a. is entirely predictable.
   - ☐ b. cannot be determined.
   - ☐ c. depends on many variables.
   - ☐ d. depends on social status.

7. As the alcohol level rises in the bloodstream, its effects
(h)
   - ☐ a. level off gradually.
   - ☐ b. baffle medical science.
   - ☐ c. heighten mental awareness.
   - ☐ d. can be predicted mathematically.

8. A person is legally drunk when the alcohol content of his blood measures
(a)
   - ☐ a. 0.03 percent.
   - ☐ b. 0.05 percent.
   - ☐ c. 0.10 percent.
   - ☐ d. 0.15 percent.

9. The more a person drinks the more he
(b)
   - ☐ a. becomes introspective.
   - ☐ b. is fun to be with.
   - ☐ c. enjoys his friends.
   - ☐ d. wants to walk.

10. Which of the following best expresses the main idea of the selection?
(e)
   - ☐ a. Never drink on an empty stomach.
   - ☐ b. If you drink, don't drive.
   - ☐ c. Social drinking leads to alcoholism.
   - ☐ d. Alcohol should be used, not abused.

Comprehension Skills: a—isolating details; b—recalling specific facts; c—retaining concepts; d—organizing facts; e—understanding the main idea; f—drawing a conclusion; g—making a judgment; h—making an inference; i—recognizing tone; j—understanding characters; k—appreciation of literary forms.

The Anatomy of Drink, II

Alcoholism Is a Disease That Cannot Be Cured, Only Arrested

Rog Halegood

Every year, doctors treat patients for alcoholism who swear that they can't be alcoholics. They base this belief on the premise that all they've ever drunk in their lives is beer. So they have one or two six-packs a day, so what? Beer, after all, has almost "no alcohol." On first glance, it seems a pretty logical argument. Beer does contain only four percent alcohol. But the alcohol is by volume, and therein lies the rub. An ounce of beer contains four percent alcohol. An ounce of 86 proof whiskey contains 43 percent alcohol. While many people stop drinking after one ounce of whiskey, who has ever drunk just one ounce of beer? You drink 10 ounces, or 20 ounces, and you have increased your alcohol ingestion in direct proportion to the alcohol content by *volume.* Therefore, one average mug-and-a-half of beer equals, in alcohol content, about that of one drink. Likewise, a normal sized glass of wine equals one beer, or approximately one drink.

The effects of wine and beer are slightly less noticeable because the alcohol is more diluted by volume than in straight spirits. Similarly, one can retard the effects of hard liquor by mixing it with water or a commercial mixer. On the other hand, about the fastest acting popular cocktail is the straight-up martini, either of the gin or vodka variety. The proof is high, and the drink unadulterated; consequently, robbed of any "buffering" agent such as water, the alcohol from such a drink enters the bloodstream very quickly. Few are the men, boasts to the contrary, who can imbibe two martinis at lunch and have their work for the rest of the day unimpaired. It would be impossible to calculate the number of man hours lost every week in the United States as a direct result of the martini luncheon.

Who drinks, and why?

Ninety-five million Americans drink something alcoholic at least once a year; that leaves about 32 percent of the adult United States populace as absolute teetotalers. Of the ninety-five million drinkers, at least nine million develop serious alcohol-related problems. But, most startling fact of all, the nine million problem drinkers affect the lives of more than 36 million people! This is the awful legacy of the problem drinker. If his drinking harmed only himself, his problem would not fall too heavily upon the shoulders of society. But when 36 million people are involved as a result of his problem, the situation becomes an urgent one.

The fact is that heavy drinking kills—and not just the drinker. Fully half of all highway fatalities are alcohol-related. This means that on the average more than 28,000 people lose their lives on the United States highway system a year as a partial contribution to alcohol misuse. This fact alone is enough to rivet us all into a position of taking a serious look at alcohol in the daily pattern of our social fabric.

But the statistics don't end on the highway. Fully one-third of all homicides in our country are also alcohol-related. And arrests where alcohol is a factor average close to two million a year.

In dollars, something we are fond of considering, alcohol costs industry, and the American worker and taxpayer, more than $15 billion annually in medical expenses, lost time, accidents, and impaired job efficiency.

On the other side of the coin, Americans spend more than $20 billion each year on alcoholic beverages. In the years between 1934 and 1967, taxes collected on alcoholic beverages by various federal, state, and local governments totaled in excess of *$100 billion!* During the same period, the federal government spent less than $4 million a year on alcohol research and alcohol facilities.

Grim as these statistics are, they do not mean that alcohol should once again be prohibited. Clearly, the majority of United States drinkers drink in a sane and safe way. What the figures do prove is that urgent work is needed on the gigantic problem of alcoholism. Nine million lives are directly at stake, plus millions of others who suffer, in one form or another, from the consequences of the alcoholic's problem.

Virtually all medical groups, including the AMA, now recognize alcoholism as an illness. So do many insurance companies and health groups.

We must first instruct the general public in ways of safe drinking, then we must reach the alcoholic himself. Prevention of alcoholism is the first and most important step. This prevention can come about only when all are made aware of the problem. After this, treatment of the alcoholic becomes a much simpler process.

I drink. Am I an alcoholic?

One of the most insidious aspects of the disease of alcoholism is its ability to completely mask itself. Few alcoholics, while in the grips of alcoholism, can admit to themselves that they are diseased. Since no one opens their mouths and physically pours drinks down them, they can always delude themselves that they are in control; i.e. to drink they must make the conscious decision to put glass or bottle in hand, and then to raise that hand to their lips. Since this action is seemingly a voluntary one, alcoholics are provided with the comforting notion that they are operating under their own steam. They can stop drinking any time by closing their fists and their mouths. Nothing could be further from the truth. Alcoholism, regardless of what form it may take, is a physical and/or psychological addiction, and the alcoholic is no more capable of altering his disease than a heroin addict is capable of taking one fix for the day. The disease itself demands alcohol, and an alcoholic cannot be written off as a person with poor will power. Will power has nothing to do with the disease itself, although will power has a lot to do with treatment. There is a very subtle, but very vital difference contained in the last statement. We do not tell cancer patients to cure their disease through will power, and alcoholism cannot be cured by that approach. Cancer and alcoholism are diseases. Both are treatable, although alcoholism cannot be cured, only arrested.

So, who is the safe drinker? And the question can be a difficult one to answer. Simplistically speaking, the safe drinker is one within whom no rationalization, regardless of how subtle, is necessary for the taking of a drink. Whenever rationalization for drinking comes into play, the danger signal should go up.

If you have a drink because you are offered a drink, and think nothing more beyond that, it's probably quite all right for you to have that drink. If you attend a cocktail party and have one or two drinks, that's probably all right too. *But* if you habitually desire a drink before one is offered, or if you attend that cocktail party solely because you want to drink, then these are potential danger signals. Preoccupation with alcohol—planning when you will drink, what you will drink—are sure signs that alcohol may be playing too large a part in your life. Here again is where the rationalizations become so simple. It is so easy to say, "I'll just have these drinks to be sociable," or, "Of course I want a drink. I've had such a lousy day." The safe drinker is one who does not drink because an excuse is handy. He drinks. Or he doesn't drink. And he doesn't think of the why and wherefores. He takes it, or he leaves it—and one situation is as easy for him to do as the other. Alcohol makes absolutely no difference in his life.

Alcoholism is difficult to define because there are so many types of the disease. It is impossible to give hard-and-fast rules that say this is alcoholism, and this is not. Even the person who drinks daily will not necessarily become an alcoholic, although such a pattern would certainly predispose one to the disease.

Most medical authorities now agree that it is not necessarily how much one drinks that may lead to alcoholism, but *why* one drinks. And this goes right back to the fact of rationalizing drinking behavior. If you must think about booze, then you should probably give it up. If you crave a drink, you should give it up. If drink is more important than food, stop now and seek help. If alcohol in any way alters your life or work, you're facing trouble. If a lunch without a drink sounds dull, booze has become too much a part of your life. All these things, and many more, are urgent red flags on the road to alcoholism; only the foolhardy—or the alcoholic—will fail to notice them.

If you drink frequently to relieve problems, soothe tensions, forget cares, get happy, have a fight, go to bed, calm your stomach, increase your sex life, take a trip, meet people—you are drinking for wrong reasons. Drink for the wrong reasons long enough, and you will have a real reason to drink—alcoholism. Nine million Americans are all drinking for the wrong reasons.

Think all alcoholics are skid row bums? Not so. Less than three percent of all United States derelicts have drinking problems. Today's alcoholic individual is likely to be bright, well educated, middle or top management, 35 to 50 years of age, a family man, and well respected in his community and profession. He simply drinks too much, for all

the wrong reasons, and his drinking has led to alcoholism.

Starting Time: _____	Finishing Time: _____
Reading Time: _____	Reading Rate: _____
Comprehension: _____	Vocabulary: _____

VOCABULARY: The following words have been taken from the selection you have just read. Put an *X* in the box before the best meaning or synonym for the word as used in the selection.

1. **premise,** page 98, column 1, paragraph 1
"They base this belief on the premise that all they've ever drunk..."
☐ a. promise
☐ b. testimony
☐ c. grounds
☐ d. condition

2. **ingestion,** page 98, column 1, paragraph 1
"...you have increased your alcohol ingestion in direct proportion..."
☐ a. intake
☐ b. indigestion
☐ c. stupor
☐ d. capacity

3. **insidious,** page 99, column 1, paragraph 2
"One of the most insidious aspects of the disease of alcoholism..."
☐ a. diplomatic
☐ b. obvious
☐ c. intriguing
☐ d. treacherous

4. **delude,** page 99, column 1, paragraph 2
"...they can always delude themselves that they are in control;..."
☐ a. delete
☐ b. deceive
☐ c. trust
☐ d. doubt

5. **predispose,** page 99, column 2, paragraph 2
"...such a pattern could certainly predispose one to the disease."
☐ a. commit
☐ b. predict
☐ c. immunize
☐ d. incline

TOPICS FOR THE RESTLESS

ROOTS

Many English words consist of a base or root word to which prefixes (beginnings) and suffixes (endings) have been added. To the root word **agree** (a verb) we can add both a prefix and a suffix to get **disagreeable** (an adjective) which has an opposite meaning.

Roots are Latin and Greek stems on which our English words are based. For example, **bio** (life) is a Greek root on which the word **biology** (the study of plant and animal life) is built.

Two Roots

1. man, manu is a Latin root which means **hand**. A handbook is called a **manual**.

2. rupt is also Latin and it means **break**. A **ruptured** blood vessel has broken.

In the following sentences these two roots have been left out. Space has been left indicating where the roots belong. Add one of these two roots and write your word on the line following the sentence.

1. An **inter—ion** of electrical power resulted from the storm.

   _____

2. The author eagerly submitted his **—script** to the publishers.

   _____

3. Relations between the two nations have **—ured**.

   _____

4. The natives themselves **—facture** these handbags using simple materials.

   _____

5. Don't **inter—** when someone's talking.

   _____

6. The violent prisoner was **—acled** to the cell door.

   _____

7. The proceedings were **dis—ed** by shouts from the gallery.

   _____

8. The console operator must **—ipulate** several controls to raise and lower the bridge.

   _____

9. The mechanism is broken; change records **—ally**.

   _____

10. **Cor—** practices are forbidden by law.

    _____

THE CLASSIC PARAGRAPH

This next pattern of paragraph development differs also from those we have been discussing but in a different way. The Classic paragraph presents the generalization on both ends.

In the Classic paragraph, the main idea statement appears first, followed by the facts, details, etc. Then at the end, the main idea is repeated or restated.

Graphically the Classic looks like this:

MAIN IDEA
FACTS
DETAILS
EXPLANATION
MAIN IDEA RESTATED

Here is an example of the Classic:

In my opinion, what dampens zeal for reading more than anything else is the fact that youngsters do not spend enough time reading. Social activities, movies, and television absorb a disproportionate amount of their time. Nothing succeeds like success, and in this matter of reading the enjoyment from books enhances and spurs on the desire for further reading experience. But the pleasure comes only from mastery, and mastery comes only through habit, and habit is formed in only one way; by repetition. One must read and read and read to generate a liking for reading, and a settled habit for reading.

This pattern makes life easy for the reader. It gives him two chances at the main idea. Even if he tried, he couldn't miss seeing the author's point.

COMPREHENSION: For each of the following statements and questions, select the option containing the most complete or most accurate answer.

1. Which of the following beverages can be seriously misleading?
(c)
   - ☐ a. Gin
   - ☐ b. Beer
   - ☐ c. Scotch
   - ☐ d. Coca-Cola

2. The martini luncheon is
(f)
   - ☐ a. a boon to the business executive.
   - ☐ b. a tradition among retired businessmen.
   - ☐ c. a proven obstacle to serious work.
   - ☐ d. a legitimate business deduction.

3. The problem drinker is
(g)
   - ☐ a. a threat to society.
   - ☐ b. his own best counsel.
   - ☐ c. a misunderstood person.
   - ☐ d. a victim of circumstances.

4. The tone of the selection is
(i)
   - ☐ a. sober.
   - ☐ b. snide.
   - ☐ c. unkind.
   - ☐ d. encouraging.

5. Considered from the author's point of view, alcohol is
(e)
   - ☐ a. a profitable industry.
   - ☐ b. a necessary evil.
   - ☐ c. a rare pleasure.
   - ☐ d. a costly commodity.

6. The alcoholic should be
(g)
   - ☐ a. imprisoned for his own safety.
   - ☐ b. given medical treatment.
   - ☐ c. publicly embarrassed.
   - ☐ d. institutionalized.

7. The prevention of alcoholism would be possible if
(c)
   - ☐ a. alcohol were priced beyond the means of the average person.
   - ☐ b. its treatment were preceded by public education.
   - ☐ c. more people were encouraged to take the pledge.
   - ☐ d. prohibition were strictly enforced by the government.

8. An alcoholic
(h)
   - ☐ a. must be willing to receive treatment.
   - ☐ b. has no will power.
   - ☐ c. can undergo a complete cure.
   - ☐ d. can never hope to control his drinking.

9. A person who generally looks forward to drinking cocktails
(h)
   - ☐ a. may have a potential drinking problem.
   - ☐ b. should be refused bar service.
   - ☐ c. has an acute alcoholic problem.
   - ☐ d. can be considered a safe drinker.

10. Medical authorities are mainly concerned with
(c)
   - ☐ a. the quantity of alcohol people take.
   - ☐ b. the families of alcoholics.
   - ☐ c. legal problems resulting from alcoholism.
   - ☐ d. the reasons which prompt people to drink.

Comprehension Skills: a—isolating details; b—recalling specific facts; c—retaining concepts; d—organizing facts; e—understanding the main idea; f—drawing a conclusion; g—making a judgment; h—making an inference; i—recognizing tone; j—understanding characters; k—appreciation of literary forms.

Atlantis: Legend Lives On

...And the Island of Atlantis in Like Manner Disappeared in the Depths of the Sea.

Arturo Gonzalez

"...There occurred violent earthquakes and floods, and in a single day and night of misfortune, all your warlike men in a body sank into the earth, and the island of Atlantis in like manner disappeared in the depths of the sea. For which reason the sea in those parts is impassable and impenetrable because there is a shoal of mud..."

These words, written by Plato centuries ago, have sent expedition after expedition chasing down the world's most fascinating and intellectual archeological detective story—what is the precise location of the lost land of Atlantis?

More than 5,000 books, and tens of thousands of magazine and newspaper articles have been written on the subject. At least one scientific party, headed 30 years ago by a certain Colonel Fawcett from Britain, went deep into the Amazon jungle in search of Atlantis and has never been heard from again.

Atlantis is a legend which dies far more slowly than the mythical country itself expired. A convention of British journalists recently ranked a verifiable re-emergence of Atlantis as one of the most important front-page stories newsmen could ever hope to write—far more compelling, in their professional opinion, than even the Second Coming of Christ. Such is the fascination of the unknown that in an era when hitting the moon with a manned expedition is a fait accompli, the thought of finding this lost land somewhere beneath the earth's endless ocean surface still captures our imagination with an intensity that few other concepts can match.

To study the alleged history of Atlantis is to journey back in time onto a magnificent continent of antiquity . . . to hear the cry of vendors in the crowded markets of the capital city . . . to listen to the clang of armor and weapons as imperial guards troop by . . . to see the glitter of royal crowns amidst thousands of cheering subjects. This is the vision of bygone beauty which has impelled countless scholars and scientists to turn their backs on the magnificence of their labs in modern New York, their libraries in Paris or colonnaded museums in Rome to devote a lifetime to the search for the dead, seaweed-encrusted remains of a lost, centuries-old continent—which indeed may never have existed.

These honest scientists are perhaps not the most fascinating Atlantis-seekers. Far more amusing are the theories of the man charlatans, cosmologists, faith healers and crackpots who over the years have seen Atlantis as a nondebatable historical proof for every variety of strange philosophy they may espouse. Atlantis attracts the kind of fanatics who spend their entire lives trying to prove that Bacon wrote Shakespeare's plays. The Atlantis theme has, over the years, been tied in a variety of ways to romanticism, racism, pacifism, theosophy, socialism, communism, and spiritualism. Crackpots have linked it with cannibalism, the Cyclops and flying saucers as well.

A Russian cosmologist named Velikovsky insisted that Jupiter erupted millennia ago and spewed up a fiery comet which sped past the earth in 1600 or 1500 B.C., swamping Atlantis in the same roaring tide which parted the Red Sea and conveniently allowed the children of Israel to pass into the Promised Land. He explains that historians make no record of this event with the convenient rationale that the human race suffers from "collective amnesia."

The most monumental Atlantis hoax was perpetrated by Herman Schleimann who, in 1912, conned the *New York American* into running a lengthy feature story entitled "How I Discovered Atlantis, the Source of All Civilization." This not only sold newspapers to impressed New Yorkers by the thousands, but so befuddled the academic world that many texts and source books on the Atlantis legend still list facts and figures from Schleimann's daring piece of science fiction.

Atlantis has never yet been absolutely identified or pinpointed on the earth's surface. Numerous scientists have periodically amassed mounds of conflicting evidence to "definitely and indisputably" locate the mysterious continent variously in South, West and North Africa, the Azores, the Canary Islands, the Caucasus, Ceylon, Spitsbergen, 13,000 feet up in the Andes and in the Baltic Sea. Racial experts have credited Atlantis with fathering both the Spanish and the Italian races, and one of Hitler's hack philosophers in the thirties actually tried to trace Aryan supremacy back to the glorious Atlantans, locating the island just a few miles off the Nazi coastline.

A few years ago no less than three costly expeditions were simultaneously exploring different world sites in a futile search for the remains of Atlantis. Depth charges and sonar were being bounced off the ocean bottom near the Azores; a descendant of Leon Trotsky was skin-diving off Bermuda in search of the lost country, while the *Discovery II*, a British research ship, charted the Galicia Bank, a steep-sided, 20-mile-long protuberance in the seabed 2,400 feet under the Atlantic's surface 30 miles off the coast of Spain, another alleged site of the lost continent.

Many experts insist on placing Atlantis midway in the Atlantic Ocean, claiming this location makes it a bridge between the Old World and the New and helps to explain some striking similarities between early Egyptian and American Indian cultures, as shown, for example, by the fondness each civilization had for pyramid-like structures.

But now, two scientists persuasively argue that Atlantis was not in the Atlantic at all, but was a Mediterranean island off the coast of Greece. In their new book *Atlantis, the Truth Behind the Legend,* A.G. Galanopoulos and Edward Bacon present convincing evidence that the original Atlantis is really the Island of Santorini, 78 miles northeast of Crete. Atlantis, they insist, was really a Mediterranean/Middle Eastern civilization—a culture mysteriously destroyed around 1500 B.C. They think they have even found a reason for its destruction: a massive volcanic eruption similar to the explosion which destroyed Krakatoa in Indonesia in 1883, which sent most of Santorini plunging under the sea and triggered huge tidal waves that swept up against Middle Eastern shorelines and through the Mediterranean, washing away life in the Minoan city of Knossos on Crete, just a little under 100 miles away.

There can be no doubt that Santorini was destroyed by a huge volcanic eruption in approximately 1450 B.C. Today, it remains as five islands, clearly composing the nearly perfectly circular walls and central cone of a volcano which has exploded and collapsed in on itself.

To understand how a single volcanic eruption could completely destroy a multi-island culture one has only to look at Krakatoa. When this volcano exploded in 1883, the explosion was heard 1,900 miles away and the sea was covered in pumice for more than 100 miles. So much ash went into the sky that sunsets around the world were extremely red for more than a year. It sent

out tidal waves so large that ships at anchor in South America broke their mooring chains.

Using this as a yardstick, it's interesting to note that the Santorini explosion would have been three times as large. The Krakatoa blast destroyed only nine square miles of land; the Santorini explosion would have blown up more than 31 square miles.

The huge tidal waves it caused started floods as far away as Egypt, according to the legends of Manetho, and may have been the reason why Noah took to his ark. Its waves could have even been the reason the Red Sea opened up for Moses, and the iron oxide fallout from its smoke might have been the reason that the Bible says the Nile ran red. The tidal wave it caused definitely dropped pumice on the Jaffa shoreline 562 miles away, some 16½ feet above sea level.

One definite result of the eruption: it buried sections of Santorini beneath 100 feet of ash. And under this ash has recently been discovered a buried Minoan town, similar to the sophisticated civilization found on Crete, and quite probably the remains of the city of Atlantis which so fascinated the Greeks because it was so civilized and then disappeared so completely. The city—called Thera—was found by an American, James W. Mavor, Jr. of the Woods Hole Oceanographic Institution. He helped build the Alvin, the mini-sub that recovered the lost H-bomb off Spain, and several years ago cruised Santorini's central bay in the research ship *Chain,* using sonar to map the bottom and bringing up evidence that there was a major community destroyed by the volcanic explosion below. Actually, researchers have known that there was a community under both the bay and the shoreline for more than a century; during the construction of the Suez Canal, builders found that the ash from Thera made a high-quality, waterproof cement and in digging it up, first evidences of a city under it all came to light.

Now the village looks very much as if it is becoming an Eastern Mediterranean Pompeii, an intact city of two- and three-story houses apparently still standing under the ash. As one researcher summed it up, "We had expected to find the ruins of a prehistoric town. What surprised us was that it was three-dimensional. In most finds, the ruins don't come up to your knee. . . ." Even the frescoes, usually just piles of plaster on the floor by the time the archeologists get to them, are beautifully preserved. The first nine trenches that were dug, yielded enough artifacts to load down 35 donkeys. The absence of skeletons and gold suggests that the ancient inhabitants had some disaster warning, escaping in their boats and leaving houses and furniture sealed under the preserving ash for the scientists to find. A volcano which smoked for a few days before blowing up would have been enough to drive the frightened citizens away. Some refugees almost certainly went to Lebanon and Syria; some of today's Middle Easterners are thus Atlantans by heritage.

Where precise details on the Plato story of Atlantis and the current Cretan theory don't match exactly, there is also an explanation. Plato, after all, picked up the story, secondhand, from Solon who, in turn, got it from Egyptian priests, who had been handing it down verbally for a thousand years. Possible translations and misinterpretations of the legend help to explain away the few incongruities and even the incongruities are under investigation. A small team of researchers sponsored by the government of Greece and the Boston Museum of Fine Arts is working steadily away and as recently as December a Professor Marinatos discovered some frescoes suggesting that the remains of a royal palace are not far off.

And so, the legend of Atlantis is moving from mystery to an Eastern Mediterranean fact. Now the big remaining, unsolved mystery is: whatever happened to Colonel Fawcett?

Starting Time: _____	Finishing Time: _____
Reading Time: _____	Reading Rate: _____
Comprehension: _____	Vocabulary: _____

VOCABULARY: The following words have been taken from the selection you have just read. Put an X in the box before the best meaning or synonym for the word as used in the selection.

1. **impelled**, page 103, column 1, paragraph 5
"This is the vision of bygone beauty which has impelled countless scholars and scientists..."
☐ a. repelled
☐ b. urged
☐ c. discouraged
☐ d. haunted

2. **espouse**, page 103, column 2, paragraph 2
"...every variety of strange philosophy they may espouse."
☐ a. encourage
☐ b. mention
☐ c. marry
☐ d. adopt

3. **perpetrated**, page 103, column 2, paragraph 4
"The most monumental Atlantis hoax was perpetrated by Herman Schleimann..."
☐ a. perpetuated
☐ b. carried out
☐ c. provoked
☐ d. almost discovered

4. **intact**, page 104, column 2, paragraph 5
"...it is becoming an Eastern Mediterranean Pompeii, an intact city of two- and three-story houses..."
☐ a. tacit
☐ b. well-preserved
☐ c. incomplete
☐ d. unusual

5. **incongruities**, page 105, column 1, paragraph 2
"...help to explain away the few incongruities..."
☐ a. illusions
☐ b. exaggerations
☐ c. impossibilities
☐ d. contradictions

EXPECTANCY CLUES

The most important aids to word recognition and, therefore, fluency in reading are meaning clues. Good readers use these clues effectively and automatically. Meaning clues permit the reader to anticipate words before actually reading them.

Expectancy clues refer to the sorts of words and concepts one might expect to encounter in a given subject. For example in a story about big city life, the reader should expect to meet words like *subway, traffic congestion, urban renewal, ghetto, high-rise apartments,* and so on. Anticipating these words enables the reader to move along the printed lines rapidly, with understanding.

The following words, except two, all appeared in a story about hospitals. Think first about the kinds of words you would find in such a story and then examine the words below. Underline the two words you would *not* expect to find in this story.

1. intern	5. out-patient	9. upholstery
2. emergency	6. defendant	10. examination
3. stethoscope	7. postoperative	11. suture
4. dressing	8. anesthetic	12. diagnostic

Which of the following phrases would you expect to read in a newspaper account of discrimination in housing? Put an *X* in the box before them.

☐ 1. covered wagons	☐ 11. violations of the code
☐ 2. department of urban affairs	☐ 12. rights of owners
	☐ 13. cutting metal pipe
☐ 3. unscrupulous realtors	☐ 14. racially-mixed neighborhoods
☐ 4. property values	
☐ 5. slum landlords	☐ 15. home to the suburbs
☐ 6. rubber-soled shoes	☐ 16. urban relocation
☐ 7. substandard conditions	☐ 17. necessary repair and maintenance
☐ 8. inadequate and unsafe	
☐ 9. neighborhood improvement association	☐ 18. hurricane barrier
	☐ 19. fair housing laws
☐ 10. add a column of figures	☐ 20. absentee ownership

THE THINKER PARAGRAPH

This pattern of paragraph development is truly different from any other because the main idea or generalization does not appear anywhere—it is not stated.

The Thinker paragraph seeks to create an impression in the reader's mind. The main idea is implied rather than stated.

Graphically the Thinker looks like this:

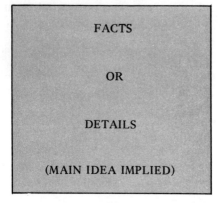

FACTS

OR

DETAILS

(MAIN IDEA IMPLIED)

Here is an example of the Thinker:

Then there are those persons who are temperamentally given to hesitancy of mind, to exaggerating difficulties, and to discounting everything that bears the semblance of truth. These temperamental skeptics come to prize their doubting as a sign of a nicely adjusted mentality. Indeed, after a while they regard any definite, positive statement as an evidence of coarseness of mind, as some departure from the neutrality of the wise spectator. They assume the aloofness of a detached observer, judging, examining, approving, condemning, but never yielding to the temptation of a determined choice.

In this example, there is no one statement inclusive or general enough to represent the thought of the entire paragraph. All of the sentences taken together contribute to the idea communicated by the author.

COMPREHENSION: For each of the following statements and questions, select the option containing the most complete or most accurate answer.

1. The reaction to Plato's account of the dis-
(f) appearance of Atlantis seems to justify the belief that it
- □ a. once existed.
- □ b. never existed.
- □ c. was destroyed by fire.
- □ d. was conquered by Greece.

2. The interest generated by the sunken city of
(a) Atlantis illustrates the public's
- □ a. fascination with the unknown.
- □ b. interest in Christ's Second Coming.
- □ c. interest in space exploration.
- □ d. concern for Colonel Fawcett.

3. Scholars and scientists who have searched for
(b) the lost city have been driven by
- □ a. the promise of wealth.
- □ b. creative genius.
- □ c. social pressures.
- □ d. a vision of beauty.

4. Atlantis, the legend, has generated
(g)
- □ a. scientific conclusions.
- □ b. international unrest.
- □ c. weird theories.
- □ d. new religions.

5. The most monumental Atlantis hoax was
(a) perpetrated by
- □ a. Velikovsky.
- □ b. Herman Schleimann.
- □ c. Colonel Fawcett.
- □ d. A.G. Galanopoulos.

6. The book, *Atlantis, The Truth Behind the*
(a) *Legend,* attributes the destruction of Atlantis to
- □ a. a tidal wave.
- □ b. a flood.
- □ c. a volcanic eruption.
- □ d. an invasion.

7. The author seems to support the theory that
(c) Atlantis is the sunken remains of
- □ a. Krakatoa.
- □ b. Pompeii.
- □ c. the Azores.
- □ d. Santorini.

8. The city buried under Santorini's central bay
(b) owes its remarkable preservation to
- □ a. archaeologists.
- □ b. volcanic ash.
- □ c. the Minoans.
- □ d. James W. Mavor, Jr.

9. The author's claim that some of today's Mid-
(g) dle Easterners have an Atlantan heritage
- □ a. seems quite reasonable.
- □ b. is contradicted by the facts.
- □ c. is filled with racial implications.
- □ d. contradicts Plato's theory.

10. The legend of the lost city of Atlantis may
(c) change someday from
- □ a. fact to fiction.
- □ b. the Atlantic to the Pacific.
- □ c. legend to fact.
- □ d. commonplace to exciting.

Comprehension Skills: a—isolating details; b—recalling specific facts; c—retaining concepts; d—organizing facts; e—understanding the main idea; f—drawing a conclusion; g—making a judgment; h—making an inference; i—recognizing tone; j—understanding characters; k—appreciation of literary forms.

New Use for Old Cars

A Rockerfeller Foundation Grant Encourages Innovative Approaches to Auto Recycling

Anthony Wolff

A defunct automobile, like a used paper towel or an empty pop bottle, is a disposable item in America. To the car's final owner, junking his old car may be a matter of less concern than finding an overnight parking place for his new one. But for a small group of metallurgists working under Dr. Monroe S. Wechsler at the University of Iowa in Ames, this year's junk could be the potential raw material for next year's model, and the derelict auto junkyard a rich lode of high-assay ore. Though Dr. Wechsler himself drives—gently—a vintage Volvo that shows no signs of decrepitude, he and his colleagues are out to rescue the cars that are rusting away on the scrapheap and recycle them into shiny new steel.

What Dr. Wechsler and his team are looking for is a metallurgical solution to an economic foul-up. Fifteen percent of the six to eight million cars junked in the United States each year are never reprocessed. They remain stalled forever in the junkyards, adding a million more useless hulks to an inventory that already totals 15 to 20 million. Weighing an average 1,400 pounds each, these car corpses represent hundreds of million of tons of ore laboriously torn from the earth, 10 to 14 million tons of metal exactingly processed and manufactured, and billions of dollars spent—all come to an economic dead-end. There is so little demand for auto scrap that an estimated 12 percent of all cars never even make it to the junkyard. Over 80,000 of them were simply abandoned on the streets of New York City alone last year, not worth the cost of towing. Untotaled thousands more mar the countryside across America.

Analyzing this junkyard traffic jam, the Ames researchers found there is a bottleneck between the auto wrecker, who strips the corpse of its radio, radiator and other salable parts, and the auto-scrap dealer, who buys the remaining steel carcass from him and processes it for resale. One major obstacle to this flow is that the wrecker cannot extract all the non-ferrous "contaminants"—especially copper, but also nickel, aluminum, and chromium—that are part of the auto body.

The steel industry has a limited appetite for contaminated scrap: as little as 0.3 percent copper, for instance—just four pounds in a 1,400-pound

auto hulk—may cause imperfections in their new product. So the scrap dealer can't buy all the auto-wrecker's dead bodies, and they pile up in roadside junkyards where they offend beauty-lovers and metallurgists alike.

As a professional soldier might measure a nation by its military strength, or a poet by its literary prowess, so Frederick Schmidt, the principal investigator on the auto-scrap project at Ames and a twenty-year-veteran metallurgist, believes with a mixture of faith and reason that "a country's strength depends on its ability to handle metals." From that creed, it is only a short logical jump to the corollary that a nation that squanders metal dissipates its strength. For Schmidt there's something immoral in that.

In his unglamorous, uncomfortable office, with its tabletops, shelves, and boxes crowded with bottled samples of his precious pure metals, Schmidt can chalktalk a layman through the ABC's of auto scrap, and at the same time persuade him that finding a way to recycle the stuff is "a way to do something for our country."

Schmidt has a point. The recycling of junked metal is *not* primarily a matter of aesthetics, but of conserving non-renewable resources of which steel mills devour terrifying quantities in relation to world supply.

At first, the Ames group concentrated on several ways of melting auto scrap in a vacuum to separate out the impurities. In one vacuum process, a bar of compacted scrap, identical in composition to auto scrap, is bombarded with electrons from a gun very much like the one at the rear of a TV tube, but many times more powerful and focused on a much smaller area. Visible only through a protective filter, the tip of the scrap "compact" glows red, then white, and eventually melts into a water-cooled mold below. In the molten puddle at the top of the mold, some of the heat-excited atoms of metal evaporate into the very thin air of the vacuum; condensing on the walls of the experimental chamber to await later recovery. The electron-beam-melting experiments succeed in removing 90 percent of the copper and tin from the scrap, while evaporating only 8 percent of the iron.

The rest hardens in the mold into an almost pure ingot, ready for re-use.

Although they yield promising results, the vacuum melting experiments also reveal some problems. Not the least of them is the vacuum itself, a difficult and expensive condition to maintain on an industrial scale. Also, it has been demonstrated that some significant impurities—chromium and nickel, for instance—cannot be separated from iron by vacuum melting because the iron evaporates before they do.

With their initial study already funded by the Environmental Protection Agency and under way, the Ames researchers' interest was drawn to an alternative process that involved neither evaporation nor a vacuum: this innovative line of research, called electroslag remelting, attracted the Rockefeller Foundation's interest. In the electroslag process, electricity flows directly through the scrap "compact" to the mold, passing through a layer of powdered vitreous material—called slag—in between. The slag's high resistance to electricity causes it to heat up, just like the heating element of an electric range. The slag melts; as its temperature rises it in turn melts the bar of scrap. "It's like lowering a wax candle into boiling water," says Schmidt. The slag is concocted with substances that combine readily with the impurities in the scrap: as the molten scrap sinks through the pool of slag, the impurities are filtered out, leaving pure iron.

The trick in the electroslag remelting process is to come up with a slag recipe that includes extractants for all the impurities in the scrap. In theory, according to Schmidt, it should be possible to get them all. The development of the electroslag process is currently proceeding under a new EPA grant, based on the hopeful results of the first year's research. According to the researchers' first-year report, "We believe that electroslag remelting is an extremely promising method for purifying not only auto scrap, but other types of scrap metal such as tin cans, appliances, and selected metal fractions from municipal refuse."

The ultimate proof of the process, of course, will come with its adoption by industry. However,

Dr. Wechsler does not anticipate any great enthusiasm from Big Steel for purified auto scrap, no matter how practical and economic the process. He points to the steel industry's huge investment in the "integrated" mills which include ore supplies, transportation and manufacture, and supply 92 percent of the nation's steel. Indeed, as one observer at Ames comments, "Our biggest enemy has been Big Steel. They pooh-poohed our proposal." Dr. Wechsler foresees that in the beginning his customers for recycled auto scrap are likely to be a growing number of smaller, local "mini-mills." To others, such as the RF's Dr. Ralph Richardson, who recommended the grant-in-aid to the Ames group, all technological innovation starts small, but, says Dr. Richardson, "I can foresee the day when Big Steel, as part of a new plant or in renovating an old one, might give this a try."

"In current terminology," says Dr. Wechsler, "auto scrap has been treated as an economic 'externality.' But as populations grow and the store of resources dwindles in our finite world, such externalities will become of central importance."

Starting Time: _____   Finishing Time: _____

Reading Time: _____   Reading Rate: _____

Comprehension: _____   Vocabulary: _____

VOCABULARY: The following words have been taken from the selection you have just read. Put an X in the box before the best meaning or synonym for the word as used in the selection.

1. **derelict**, page 108, column 1, paragraph 1
"...and the derelict auto junkyard..."
☐ a. delinquent
☐ b. deserted
☐ c. illegal
☐ d. abandoned

2. **vintage**, page 108, column 1, paragraph 1
"...a vintage Volvo that shows no signs of decrepitude, he and his colleagues..."
☐ a. outdated and old-fashioned
☐ b. inoperative
☐ c. unsafe
☐ d. old, but of high quality

3. **prowess**, page 108, column 2, paragraph 2
"...or a poet by its literary prowess, ..."
☐ a. reputation
☐ b. heroism
☐ c. pride
☐ d. style

4. **corollary**, page 108, column 2, paragraph 2
"...it is only a short logical jump to the corollary that a nation..."
☐ a. idea
☐ b. decision
☐ c. conclusion
☐ d. falsehood

5. **finite**, page 109, column 2, paragraph 2
"...and the store of resources dwindles in our finite world, ..."
☐ a. infinite
☐ b. conditional
☐ c. untamed
☐ d. limited

ROOTS

Many English words consist of a base or root word to which prefixes (beginnings) and suffixes (endings) have been added. To the root word **agree** (a verb) we can add both a prefix and a suffix to get **disagreeable** (an adjective) which has an opposite meaning.

Roots are Latin and Greek stems on which our English words are based. For example, **bio** (life) is a Greek root on which the word **biology** (the study of plant and animal life) is built.

Two Roots

1. **aud, audit** are variants of the Latin stem for **hear** or **listen**. The **audio** portion of the program is the part you hear.

2. **viv** is also Latin and it is the stem for **life** or **lively**. The **survivors** are those who remained alive.

In the following sentences these two roots have been left out. Space has been left indicating where the roots belong. Add one of these roots and write your word on the line following the sentence.

1. The —ience responded to the sensitive performances.

   _____

2. —isection is performed on living animals to study the function of certain parts.

   _____

3. His —id description brought strikingly real images to the mind.

   _____

4. An —orium was hired for the performance of the play.

   _____

5. —ions were held for the role of Othello.

   _____

6. Religious re—al meetings seek to restore life to the soul.

   _____

7. Oxygen was used to re—e the rescued swimmers.

   _____

8. The ear is responsive to —ory stimuli.

   _____

9. Students may —it certain classes without receiving credit.

   _____

10. A con—ial atmosphere is festive and lively.

    _____

THE ART OF WRITING, I

It seems that every new student hates to write and yet reading, writing, and speaking are the student's tools of learning. We all have good ideas—the trouble arises in *expressing* our ideas. It is the lack of organization which makes students fear writing. The student who can organize his approach to writing will find the experience at least rewarding (in higher grades) if not enjoyable.

Here are the steps to follow when preparing to write.

State a Subject

You must think first and carefully about your subject. It should not be just a one-word title; it should be a statement of the topic you plan to discuss and also what you plan to say about it. You should be able to state clearly in a sentence or two the views you wish to present relating to your subject. Many students fail right here before they begin by not determining what their views are. Obviously, you cannot write effectively if you don't know what you're going to say; yet, how many times have you attempted to do just this? Spend enough time forming your subject statement; it saves you time later.

Limit the Subject

You should know before you begin writing how long your paper will be, or how long you want it to be. This means that your subject will have to be limited to just those aspects that can be suitably reported in a paper of that length. Many students try to include too much in too little space. The result is that they have not really covered anything—their paper consists of a series of unrelated general facts with no real point or substance.

You must stop, think, and define the limitations of your subject. Decide exactly on the two or three points you want to consider and know before you write what you intend to say about them.

COMPREHENSION: For each of the following statements and questions, select the option containing the most complete or most accurate answer.

1. Doctor Wechsler and his team of metallurgists
(e) have devised a way
- [ ] a. to beautify the countryside.
- [ ] b. to decontaminate metal scrap.
- [ ] c. to prevent metal rust.
- [ ] d. to eliminate auto junkyards.

2. New ways must be found to recycle discarded
(c) metal because
- [ ] a. natural supplies are limited.
- [ ] b. the automobile industry is competitive.
- [ ] c. the general public is concerned.
- [ ] d. foreign competition makes it necessary.

3. The problem of abandoned cars and eyesore
(f) junkyards is really a problem of
- [ ] a. greed.
- [ ] b. apathy.
- [ ] c. economics.
- [ ] d. organization.

4. If the vacuum melting process were to be used
(b) on an industrial scale,
- [ ] a. the process would have to be supervised.
- [ ] b. heat-excited atoms would be difficult to control.
- [ ] c. the enforcement of safety procedures would create a problem.
- [ ] d. the vacuum would present a problem.

5. Frederick Schmidt is
(j)
- [ ] a. an organized man.
- [ ] b. a convincing person.
- [ ] c. a confused scientist.
- [ ] d. a boring person.

6. The most serious obstacle faced by the Ames
(b) group, according to Schmidt, is
- [ ] a. the automobile industry.
- [ ] b. the electroslag technique.
- [ ] c. the vacuum melting technique.
- [ ] d. Big Steel.

7. The vacuum and electroslag techniques
(g)
- [ ] a. depend heavily upon electric power.
- [ ] b. are equally preferred by scientists.
- [ ] c. create more problems than they solve.
- [ ] d. are inexpensive to implement.

8. The electroslag method of recycling scrap iron
(h)
- [ ] a. seems promising.
- [ ] b. baffles scientists.
- [ ] c. damages the environment.
- [ ] d. alarms the military.

9. It can be inferred from the selection that
(h)
- [ ] a. Big Steel is interested in conservation.
- [ ] b. the strength of a nation is measured by its literature.
- [ ] c. tomorrow's needs must be met today.
- [ ] d. natural resources will be available to satisfy demands.

10. The tone of the selection is
(i)
- [ ] a. factual.
- [ ] b. argumentative.
- [ ] c. conciliatory.
- [ ] d. dogmatic.

Comprehension Skills: a—isolating details; b—recalling specific facts; c—retaining concepts; d—organizing facts; e—understanding the main idea; f—drawing a conclusion; g—making a judgment; h—making an inference; i—recognizing tone; j—understanding characters; k—appreciation of literary forms.

Part Three
Selections 21-30

Topics
for the
Restless

The Interlopers

And If We Chose To Make Peace, There Is None Other To Interfere

Saki

In a forest of mixed growth somewhere on the eastern spurs of the Carpathians a man stood one winter night watching and listening, as though he waited for some beast of the woods to come within the range of his vision and, later, of his rifle. But the game for whose presence he kept so keen an outlook was none that figured in the sportsman's calendar as lawful and proper for the chase; Ulrich von Gradwitz patrolled the dark forest in quest of a human enemy.

The forest lands of Gradwitz were of wide extent and well stocked with game; the narrow strip of precipitous woodland that lay on its outskirt was not remarkable for the game it harbored or the shooting it afforded, but it was the most jealously guarded of all its owner's territorial possessions. A famous lawsuit in the days of his grandfather had wrested it from the illegal possession of a neighboring family of petty landowners; the dispossessed party had never acquiesced in the judgment of the courts, and a long series of poaching affrays and similar scandals had embittered the relationships between the families for three generations. The neighbor feud had grown into a personal one since Ulrich had come to be head of his family; if there was a man in the world whom he detested and wished ill to, it was Georg Znaeym, the inheritor of the quarrel and the tireless game-snatcher and raider of the disputed border-forest.

The feud might, perhaps, have died down or been compromised if the personal ill will of the two men had not stood in the way: as boys they had thirsted for one another's blood, as men each prayed that misfortune might fall on the other; and this wind-scourged winter night Ulrich had banded together his foresters to watch the dark forest, not in quest of four-footed quarry, but to keep a lookout for the prowling thieves whom he suspected of being afoot from across the land boundary. The roebuck, which usually kept in the sheltered hollows during a storm wind, were running like driven things tonight, and there was movement and unrest among the creatures that were wont to sleep through the dark hours. Assuredly there was a disturbing element in the forest, and Ulrich could guess the quarter from whence it came.

He strayed away by himself from the watchers whom he had placed in ambush on the crest of the hill, and wandered far down the steep slopes amid the wild tangle of undergrowth, peering through the tree trunks and listening through the whistling and skirling of the wind and the restless beating of the branches for sight or sound of the marauders. If only on this wild night, in this dark, lone spot, he might come across Georg Znaeym man to man, with none to witness—that was the wish that was uppermost in his thoughts.

And as he stepped round the trunk of a huge beech, he came face to face with the man he sought.

The two enemies stood glaring at one another for a long, silent moment. Each had a rifle in his hand; each had hate in his heart and murder uppermost in his mind. The chance had come to give full play to the passions of a lifetime. But a man who has been brought up under the code of a restraining civilization cannot easily nerve himself to shoot down his neighbor in cold blood and without word spoken, except for an offense against his hearth and honor. And before the moment of hesitation had given way to action, a deed of Nature's own violence overwhelmed them both.

A fierce shriek of the storm had been answered by a splitting crash over their heads, and ere they could leap aside, a mass of falling beech tree had thundered down on them. Ulrich von Gradwitz found himself stretched on the ground, one arm numb beneath him and the other held almost as helplessly in a tight tangle of forked branches, while both legs were pinned beneath the fallen mass. His heavy shooting boots had saved his feet from being crushed to pieces, but if his fractures were not as serious as they might have been, at least it was evident that he could not move from his present position till someone came to release him. The descending twigs had slashed the skin of his face, and he had to wink away some drops of blood from his eyelashes before he could take in a general view of the disaster. At his side, so near that under ordinary circumstances he could almost have touched him, lay Georg Znaeym, alive and struggling but obviously as helplessly pinioned down as himself. All round them lay a thick-strewn wreckage of splintered branches and broken twigs.

Relief at being alive and exasperation at his captive plight brought a strange medly of pious thank-offerings and sharp curses to Urich's lips.

Georg, who was nearly blinded with the blood which trickled across his eyes, stopped his struggling for a moment to listen, and then gave a short, snarling laugh. "So you're not killed, as you ought to be, but you're caught anyway," he cried, "caught fast! Ho, what a jest—Ulrich von Gradwitz snarled in his stolen forest. There's real justice for you!" And he laughed again, mockingly and savagely.

"I'm caught in my own forest land," retorted Ulrich. "When my men come to release us, you will wish, perhaps, that you were in a better plight than caught poaching on a neighbor's land—shame on you!"

Georg was silent for a moment; then he answered quietly: "Are you sure that your men will find much to release? I have men, too, in the forest tonight, close behind me, and *they* will be here first and do the releasing. When they drag me out from under these branches, it won't need much clumsiness on their part to roll this mass of trunk right over on the top of you. Your men will find you dead under a fallen beech tree. For form's sake I shall send my condolences to your family."

"It is a useful hint," said Ulrich fiercely. "My men had orders to follow in ten minutes' time—seven of which must have gone by already—and when they get me out, I will remember the hint. Only, as you will have met your death poaching on my lands, I don't think I can decently send any message of condolence to your family."

"Good," snarled Georg, "good. We fight this quarrel out to the death, you and I and our for-esters, with no cursed interlopers to come between us. Death and damnation to you, Ulrich von Gradwitz."

"The same to you, Georg Znaeym, forest-thief, game-snatcher."

Both men spoke with the bitterness of possible defeat before them, for each knew that it might be long before his men would seek him out or find him; it was a bare matter of chance which party would arrive first on the scene.

Both had now given up the useless struggle to free themselves from the mass of wood that held them down; Ulrich limited his endeavors to an effort to bring his one partially free arm near enough to his outer coat pocket to draw out his wine flask. Even when he had accomplished that operation, it was long before he could manage the unscrewing of the stopper or get any of the liquid down his throat. But what a heaven-sent draft it seemed! It was an open winter, and little snow had fallen as yet; hence the captives suffered less from the cold than might have been the case at that season of the year; nevertheless, the wine was warming and reviving to the wounded man, and he looked across with something like a throb of pity to where his enemy lay, just keeping the groans of pain and weariness from crossing his lips.

"Could you reach this flask if I threw it over to you?" asked Ulrich suddenly. "There is good wine in it, and one may as well be as comfortable as one can. Let us drink, even if tonight one of us dies."

"No, I can scarcely see anything, there is so much blood caked round my eyes," said George, "and in any case I don't drink wine with an enemy."

Ulrich was silent for a few minutes, and lay listening to the weary screeching of the wind. An idea was slowly forming and growing in his brain, an idea that gained strength every time that he looked across at the man who was fighting so grimly against pain and exhaustion. In the pain and languor that Ulrich himself was feeling, the old fierce hatred seemed to be dying down.

"Neighbor," he said presently, "do as you please if your men come first. It was a fair compact. But as for me, I've changed my mind. If my men are the first to come, you shall be the first to be helped, as though you were my guest. We have quarreled like devils all our lives over this stupid strip of forest, where the trees can't even stand upright in a breath of wind. Lying here tonight, thinking, I've come to think we've been rather fools; there are better things in life than getting the better of a boundary dispute. Neighbor, if you will help me to bury the old quarrel, I—I will ask you to be my friend."

Georg Znaeym was silent for so long that Ulrich thought perhaps he had fainted with the pain of his injuries. Then he spoke slowly and in jerks. "How the whole region would stare and gabble if we rode into the market square together. No one living can remember seeing a Znaeym and a von Gradwitz talking to one another in friendship. And what peace there would be among the forester folk if we ended our feud tonight. And if we chose to make peace among our people, there is none other to interfere, no interlopers from outside. You would come and keep the Sylvester night beneath my roof, and I would come and feast on some high day at your castle. I would never fire a shot on your land save when you invited me as a guest, and you should come and shoot with me down in the marshes where the wild-fowl are. In all the countryside there are none that could hinder if we willed to make peace. I never thought to have wanted to do other than hate you all my life, but I think I have changed my mind about things too this last half hour. And you offered me your wine flask. Ulrich von Gradwitz, I will be your friend."

For a space both men were silent, turning over in their minds the wonderful changes that this dramatic reconciliation would bring about. In the cold, gloomy forest, with the wind tearing in fitful gusts through the naked branches and whistling round the tree trunks, they lay and waited for the help that would now bring release and succor to both parties. And each prayed a private prayer that his men might be the first to arrive, so that he might be the first to show honorable attention to the enemy that had become a friend.

Presently, as the wind dropped for a moment, Ulrich broke silence. "Let's shout for help," he said. "In this lull our voices may carry a little way."

"They won't carry far through the trees and undergrowth," said Georg, "but we can try. Together, then."

The two raised their voices in a prolonged hunting call.

"Together again," said Ulrich a few minutes later, after listening in vain for an answering hallo. "I heard something that time, I think," said Ulrich.

"I heard nothing but the pestilential wind," said Georg hoarsely.

There was silence again for some minutes, and then Ulrich gave a joyful cry. "I can see figures coming through the wood. They are following in the way I came down the hillside."

Both men raised their voices in as a loud shout as they could muster.

"They hear us! They've stopped. Now they see us. They're running down the hill towards us," cried Ulrich.

"How many of them are there?" asked Georg.

"I can't see distinctly," said Ulrich. "Nine or ten."

"Then they are yours," said Georg. "I had only seven out with me."

"They are making all the speed they can, brave lads," said Ulrich gladly.

"Are they your men?" asked Georg. "Are they your men?" he repeated impatiently, as Ulrich did not answer.

"No," said Ulrich with a laugh, the idiotic chattering laugh of a man unstrung with hideous fear.

"Who are they?" asked Georg quickly, straining his eyes to see what the other would gladly not have seen.

"*Wolves*."

Starting Time: _____	Finishing Time: _____
Reading Time: _____	Reading Rate: _____
Comprehension: _____	Vocabulary: _____

VOCABULARY: The following words have been taken from the selection you have just read. Put an *X* in the box before the best meaning or synonym for the word as used in the selection.

1. **afforded**, page 115, column 1, paragraph 2
"...was not remarkable for the game it harbored or the shooting it afforded, ..."
☐ a. affected
☐ b. provided
☐ c. encouraged
☐ d. allowed

2. **acquiesced**, page 115, column 1, paragraph 2
"...the dispossessed party had never acquiesced in the judgment of the courts, ..."
☐ a. protested
☐ b. acquired
☐ c. submitted
☐ d. taken over

3. **wont**, page 115, column 1, last paragraph
"...the creatures that were wont to sleep through the dark hours."
☐ a. in need of
☐ b. anxious
☐ c. accustomed
☐ d. reluctant

4. **languor**, page 116, column 2, paragraph 4
"In the pain and languor that Ulrich himself was feeling, ..."
☐ a. feebleness
☐ b. tenderness
☐ c. heartlessness
☐ d. vitality

5. **succor**, page 117, column 1, paragraph 2
"...help that would bring release and succor to both parties."
☐ a. success
☐ b. assistance
☐ c. encouragement
☐ d. revenge

CONTEXTUAL AIDS: APPOSITIVES

Studies of good readers show that they are aware of the context of what they are reading. This means that they are anticipating what is coming next by what has gone before.

The many ways in which context functions to help the reader recognize words are called contextual aids.

Contextual Aid. A word can be understood through another word or phrase used in apposition to it. An appositive is a word or phrase which explains the word it is placed next to. Appositives give the reader a clue to the meaning of the unknown word. In the sentence, **He wanted to be _____, the elected head of the state,** the appositive phrase, **elected head of the state,** tells the reader that the missing word has to be **governor.**

In the following sentences, similar contextual aids have been used in apposition to nonsense words. Underline the nonsense word and write the correct word on the line.

1. A cromp, or survey, was conducted to determine the favorite.

   _____

2. Lapostomy, the science of living things, is studied by every college freshman.

   _____

3. Drindels, specially trained underwater demolition experts, mined the harbor entrance.

   _____

4. The malsered buston, or prairie schooner, was used by pioneers to cross the prairies.

   _____

5. He aspired to the endostrocy, the highest office of the land.

   _____

6. The probent, a self-propelled projectile, is designed to intercept approaching aircraft.

   _____

7. Huddenpats, jokingly called "head-shrinkers," are licensed doctors.

   _____

8. The aircraft was towed to the sendron, a garage for airplanes.

   _____

9. The weatherman predicted banfaps, brief periods of rain.

   _____

10. The kitchen drint, now called a range, has been improved over the years.

    _____

THE ART OF WRITING, II

We have said that the first two tasks for the writer are 1) Select a Subject, and 2) Limit the Subject. Here are the next steps for the student to take.

Clarify the Purpose

Every student has a purpose in mind when he is writing. It may be the purpose assigned by his instructor or, too often, it may be some vague, poorly defined idea of what he hopes to accomplish.

Words should convey the exact meaning intended by the writer. This presupposes that the writer knows which exact meanings he wants to convey. This must be part of his plan; he must know clearly what his prupose in writing is: he must take a position regarding his subject and defend or support it. Purposeless writing is ineffective writing. Unless your reader knows where you are leading him, your writing will not make sense. Aimless writing creates aimless and dull reading. Be sure of your stand before you start.

Support the Ideas

Every paper, essay, or theme must do more than merely present facts: the facts must be supported. You cannot expect your reader to accept your position unless it is properly presented and clearly defined.

This does not mean that everything you write has to take a stand on some controversial issue — it means that, whatever your subject and purpose, your writing must include the facts, details, illustrations which make your ideas reasonable and acceptable to the reader.

We have been discussing the various patterns of development used by authors. Get ideas from these. Employ the different techniques shown in these patterns in your writing. Observe how skilled writers flood the reader with all kinds of support for their generalizations and main ideas.

COMPREHENSION: For each of the following statements and questions, select the option containing the most complete or most accurate answer.

1. The narrow strip of woodland on the out-
(c) skirts of Gradwitz's property was

  ☐ a. a popular hunting area.
  ☐ b. an old bone of contention.
  ☐ c. off limits to von Gradwitz.
  ☐ d. well stocked with game.

2. The activity of the roebuck on this windy
(h) winter night suggests the

  ☐ a. start of the mating season.
  ☐ b. abundance of small game.
  ☐ c. threat of a fire.
  ☐ d. presence of intruders.

3. The two men did not shoot each other in
(c) cold blood because they

  ☐ a. were too cowardly to carry out a de-
    cision each had made in the past.
  ☐ b. preferred to reach an agreement.
  ☐ c. were the products of the civilizing ef-
    fects of a structured society.
  ☐ d. were alone and needed witnesses.

4. Helpless and seriously hurt himself, Georg
(i) Znaeym's reaction to von Gradwitz's plight was

  ☐ a. bitter and sarcastic.
  ☐ b. conciliatory.
  ☐ c. quick and unexpected.
  ☐ d. terrified.

5. The two trapped men knew that the outcome
(h) of their predicament would be

  ☐ a. a foregone conclusion.
  ☐ b. a beginning of peace.
  ☐ c. a one-sided development.
  ☐ d. a race for time.

6. The first indication of a change in von Grad-
(d) witz's attitude toward Znaeym occurred

  ☐ a. when the tree fell.
  ☐ b. after he drank from his flask.
  ☐ c. when he offered his flask.
  ☐ d. after Znaeym fainted.

7. The hatred two people have for each other
(f)
  ☐ a. causes others to respect them.
  ☐ b. sours their lives and affects others.
  ☐ c. encourages others to cheat and steal.
  ☐ d. is usually turned to friendship.

8. The dramatic reconciliation was prompted by
(g)
  ☐ a. financial reasons.
  ☐ b. the fear of death.
  ☐ c. a shared disaster.
  ☐ d. religious consideration.

9. The story ends on a note of
(i)
  ☐ a. terror.
  ☐ b. bravery.
  ☐ c. relief.
  ☐ d. friendship.

10. Another title for this selection could be
(e)
  ☐ a. The Revenge.
  ☐ b. The Storm.
  ☐ c. The Hunt.
  ☐ d. The Encounter.

Comprehension Skills: a—isolating details; b—recalling specific facts; c—retaining concepts; d—organizing facts; e—understanding the main idea; f—drawing a conclusion; g—making a judgment; h—making an inference; i—recognizing tone; j—understanding characters; k—appreciation of literary forms.

Beyond Freedom and Dignity

Almost All Living Things Act To Free Themselves from Harmful Contacts

B.F. Skinner

Freedom

Almost all living things act to free themselves from harmful contacts. A kind of freedom is achieved by the relatively simple forms of behavior called reflexes. A person sneezes and frees his respiratory passages from irritating substances. He vomits and frees his stomach from indigestible or poisonous food. He pulls back his hand and frees it from a sharp or hot object. More elaborate forms of behavior have similar effects. When confined, people struggle ("in rage") and break free. When in danger they flee from or attack its source. Behavior of this kind presumably evolved because of its survival value; it is as much a part of what we call the human genetic endowment as breathing, sweating, or digesting food. And through conditioning similar behavior may be acquired with respect to novel objects which could have played no role in evolution. These are no doubt minor instances of the struggle to be free, but they are significant. We do not attribute them to any love of freedom; they are simply forms of behavior which have proved useful in reducing various threats to the individual and hence to the species in the course of evolution. A much more important role is played by behavior which weakens harmful stimuli in another way. It is not acquired in the form of conditioned reflexes, but as the product of a different process called operant conditioning. When a bit of behavior is followed by a certain kind of consequence, it is more likely to occur again, and a consequence having this effect is called a reinforcer. Food, for example, is a reinforcer to a hungry organism; anything the organism does that is followed by the receipt of food is more likely to be done again whenever the organism is hungry. Some stimuli are called negative reinforcers; any response which reduces the intensity of such a stimulus—or ends it—is more likely to be emitted when the stimulus recurs. Thus, if a person escapes from a hot sun when he moves under cover, he is more likely to move under cover when the sun is again hot. The reduction in temperature reinforces the behavior it is "contingent upon"—that is, the behavior it follows. Operant conditioning also occurs when a person simply avoids a hot sun—when, roughly speaking, he escapes from the threat of a hot sun.

Negative reinforcers are called aversive in the sense that they are the things organisms "turn away from." The term suggests a spatial separation—moving or running away from something—but the essential relation is temporal. In a standard apparatus used to study the process in the laboratory, an arbitrary response simply weakens an aversive stimulus or brings it to an end. A great deal of physical technology is the result of this kind of struggle for freedom. Over the centuries, in erratic ways, men have constructed a world in which they are relatively free of many kinds of threatening or harmful stimuli—extremes of temperature, sources of infection, hard labor, danger, and even those minor aversive stimuli called discomfort.

Escape and avoidance play a much more important role in the struggle for freedom when the aversive conditions are generated by other people. Other people can be aversive without, so to speak, trying: they can be rude, dangerous, contagious, or annoying, and one escapes from them or avoids them accordingly. They may also be "intentionally" aversive—that is, they may treat other people aversively because of what follows. Thus, a slave driver induces a slave to work by whipping him when he stops; by resuming work the slave escapes from the whipping (and incidentally reinforces the slave driver's behavior in using the whip). A parent nags a child until the child performs a task; by performing the task the child escapes nagging (and reinforces the parent's behavior). The blackmailer threatens exposure unless the victim pays; by paying, the victim escapes from the threat (and reinforces the practice). A teacher threatens corporal punishment or failure until his students pay attention; by paying attention the students escape from the threat of punishment (and reinforce the teacher for threatening it). In one form or another intentional aversive control is the pattern of most social coordination—in ethics, religion, government, economics, education, psychotherapy, and family life.

A person escapes from or avoids aversive treatment by behaving in ways which reinforce those who treated him aversively until he did so, but he may escape in other ways. For example, he may simply move out of range. A person may escape from slavery, emigrate or defect from a government, desert from an army, become an apostate from a religion, play truant, leave home, or drop out of a culture as a hobo, hermit, or hippie. Such behavior is as much a product of the aversive conditions as the behavior the conditions were designed to evoke. The latter can be guaranteed only by sharpening the contingencies or by using stronger aversive stimuli.

Another anomalous mode of escape is to attack those who arrange aversive conditions and weaken or destroy their power. We may attack those who crowd us or annoy us, as we attack the weeds in our garden, but again the struggle for freedom is mainly directed toward intentional controllers—toward those who treat others aversively in order to induce them to behave in particular ways. Thus, a child may stand up to his parents, a citizen may overthrow a government, a communicant may reform a religion, a student may attack a teacher or vandalize a school, and a dropout may work to destroy a culture.

It is possible that man's genetic endowment supports this kind of struggle for freedom: when treated aversively people tend to act aggressively or to be reinforced by signs of having worked aggressive damage. Both tendencies should have had evolutionary advantages, and they can easily be demonstrated. If two organisms which have been coexisting peacefully receive painful shocks, they immediately exhibit characteristic patterns of aggression toward each other. The aggressive behavior is not necessarily directed toward the actual source of stimulation; it may be "displaced" toward any convenient person or object. Vandalism and riots are often forms of undirected or misdirected aggression. An organism which has received a painful shock will also, if possible, act to gain access to another organism toward which it can act aggressively. The extent to which human aggression exemplifies innate tendencies is not clear, and many of the ways in which people

attack and thus weaken or destroy the power of intentional controllers are quite obviously learned.

What we may call the "literature of freedom" has been designed to induce people to escape from or attack those who act to control them aversively. The content of the literature is the philosophy of freedom, but philosophies are among those inner causes which need to be scrutinized. We say that a person behaves in a given way because he possesses a philosophy, but we infer the philosophy from the behavior and therefore cannot use it in any satisfactory way as an explanation, at least until it is in turn explained. The literature of freedom, on the other hand, has a simple objective status. It consists of books, pamphlets, manifestoes, speeches, and other verbal products, designed to induce people to act to free themselves from various kinds of intentional control. It does not impart a philosophy of freedom; it induces people to act.

The literature often emphasizes the aversive conditions under which people live, perhaps by contrasting them with conditions in a freer world. It thus makes the conditions more aversive, "increasing the misery" of those it is trying to rescue. It also identifies those from whom one is to escape or those whose power is to be weakened through attack. Characteristic villains of the literature are tyrants, priests, generals, capitalists, martinet teachers, and domineering parents.

The literature also prescribed modes of action. It has not been much concerned with escape, possibly because advice has not been needed; instead, it has emphasized how controlling power may be weakened or destroyed. Tyrants are to be overthrown, ostracized, or assassinated. The legitimacy of a government is to be questioned. The ability of a religious agency to mediate supernatural sanctions is to be challenged. Strikes and boycotts are to be organized to weaken the economic power which supports aversive practices. The argument is further strengthened by exhorting people to act, describing likely results, reviewing successful instances on the model of the advertising testimonial, and so on.

The would-be controllers do not, of course, remain inactive. Governments make escape impossible by banning travel or severely punishing or incarcerating defectors. They keep weapons and other sources of power out of the hands of revolutionaries. They destroy the written literature of freedom and imprison or kill those who carry it orally. If the struggle for freedom is to succeed, it must then be intensified.

The importance of the literature of freedom can scarcely be questioned. Without help or guidance people submit to aversive conditions in the most surprising way. This is true even when the aversive conditions are part of the natural environment. Darwin observed, for example, that the Fuegians seemed to make no effort to protect themselves from the cold; they wore only scant clothing and made little use of it against the weather. And one of the most striking things about the struggle for freedom from intentional control is how often it has been lacking. Many people have submitted to the most obvious religious, governmental, and economic controls for centuries, striking for freedom only sporadically, if at all. The literature of freedom has made an essential contribution to the elimination of many aversive practices in government, religion, education, family life, and the production of goods.

The contributions of the literature of freedom, however, are not usually described in these terms. Some traditional theories could conceivably be said to define freedom as the absence of aversive control, but the emphasis has been on how that condition *feels.* Other traditional theories could conceivably be said to define freedom as a person's condition when he is behaving under nonaversive control, but the emphasis has been upon a state of mind associated with doing what one wants. According to John Stuart Mill, "Liberty consists in doing what one desires." The literature of freedom has been important in changing practice (it has changed practices whenever it has had any effect whatsoever), but it has nevertheless defined its task as the changing of states of mind and feelings. Freedom is a "possession." A person escapes from or destroys the power of a controller in order to feel free, and once he feels free and can do what he desires, no further action is recommended and none is prescribed by the literature of freedom, except perhaps eternal vigilance lest control be resumed.

Starting Time: _____	Finishing Time: _____
Reading Time: _____	Reading Rate: _____
Comprehension: _____	Vocabulary: _____

VOCABULARY: The following words have been taken from the selection you have just read. Put an *X* in the box before the best meaning or synonym for the word as used in the selection.

1. **aversive**, page 120, column 2, paragraph 2
   "Negative reinforcers are called aversive in the sense that..."
   ☐ a. subversive
   ☐ b. repugnant
   ☐ c. negative
   ☐ d. physical

2. **innate**, page 121, column 1, last paragraph
   "The extent to which human aggression exemplifies innate tendencies is not clear, ..."
   ☐ a. native
   ☐ b. personal
   ☐ c. learned
   ☐ d. unusual

3. **scrutinized**, page 121, column 2, paragraph 2
   "...are among those inner causes which need to be scrutinized."
   ☐ a. found
   ☐ b. controlled
   ☐ c. studied
   ☐ d. eliminated

4. **sporadically**, page 122, column 1, paragraph 2
   "...striking for freedom only sporadically, if at all."
   ☐ a. impulsively
   ☐ b. regularly
   ☐ c. occasionally
   ☐ d. frequently

5. **vigilance**, page 122, column 2, last sentence
   "...except perhaps eternal vigilance lest control be resumed."
   ☐ a. sleeplessness
   ☐ b. vigor
   ☐ c. struggle
   ☐ d. watchfulness

ROOTS

Many English words consist of a base or root word to which prefixes (beginnings) and suffixes (endings) have been added. To the root word **agree** (a verb) we can add both a prefix and a suffix to get **disagreeable** (an adjective) which has an opposite meaning.

Roots are Latin and Greek stems on which our English words are based. For example, **bio** (life) is a Greek root on which our word **biology** (the study of plant and animal life) is built.

Two Roots

1. **vid, vis** are variants of the Latin root for **see**. The **video** portion of the television program is the part we see.

2. **vac** is also Latin and it is the root for **empty** or **free**. An **evacuated** city has been emptied of people.

In the following sentences, these two roots have been left out. Space has been left indicating where the roots belong. Add one of these roots and write your word on the line following the sentence.

1. Try to —ualize this; form a mental image.

   _____

2. Because of his idealistic ideas and dreams, he was regarded as a —ionary.

   _____

3. Try to free yourself from work and take a —ation.

   _____

4. Due to prevailing weather conditions —ibility is limited to 300 yards.

   _____

5. It was a —uous argument — it showed no thought at all.

   _____

6. There were three applications for each —ancy at the plant.

   _____

7. A government appointee will occupy the —ant post.

   _____

8. It was obvious he was overworking; he was —ibly tired.

   _____

9. A —it from our friends gives us an opportunity to see them.

   _____

10. In physics a totally empty space is labeled a —uum.

   _____

THE ART OF WRITING, III

The first four steps taken by the student in organizing his writing are: 1) State a Subject, 2) Limit the Subject, 3) Clarify the Purpose, and 4) Support the Ideas. The next steps are these.

Distinguish Fact from Opinion

In every essay or theme, the writer presents both facts and opinions regarding his subject. A student whose approach is disorganized frequently fails to identify for his reader which of his ideas are facts and which are opinions. As you would expect, this leaves the reader hanging and confused — uncertain as to the validity of your conclusions.

Present the facts clearly for your reader to see and understand. Then state opinions based on those facts for him to appraise and evaluate. The reader can decide intelligently to agree or disagree with you. This is an instance of effective communication at work.

Structure the Presentation

Your organization must be clear to the reader; he must be able to see how your theme or essay is structured. Unstructured writing is disorganized—the reader does not know where you are leading him and he is unable to see the logic of your discussion. The reader needs to be aware of the divisions of your subject—when you have completed discussion of one aspect and moved on to the next. He needs to be aware of the transitions you make in presenting your case. Only then can he put the pieces together intelligently.

Justify the Conclusions

A sign of the inexperienced writer is his statement of a conclusion not justified or supported by the evidence. Your conclusion may be obvious to you because of your research into the subject. The reader, however, cannot be expected to "buy" your conclusion unless you give him all the facts supporting it.

COMPREHENSION: For each of the following statements and questions, select the option containing the most complete or most accurate answer.

1. The more simple form of behavior, called
(g) reflexes, are

☐ a. premeditative.
☐ b. voluntary.
☐ c. instinctive.
☐ d. harmful.

2. Human reflexes play an important role in
(c) an individual's

☐ a. preservation and survival.
☐ b. love of freedom.
☐ c. operant conditioning.
☐ d. breathing and sweating.

3. Compared to human reflexes, operant con-
(g) ditioning is

☐ a. automatic.
☐ b. beneficial.
☐ c. voluntary.
☐ d. natural.

4. An individual's tendency to turn away from
(c) negative reinforcers has

☐ a. played an important role in shaping his environment.
☐ b. a disastrous influence on his personality.
☐ c. had a negative effect on his expected life span.
☐ d. developed a tendency which is both harmful and antisocial.

5. A person who resorts to aversive control
(f)

☐ a. respects the individuality of others.
☐ b. forces other people to submit to his will.
☐ c. earns the respect and admiration of others in his group.
☐ d. engages in a rarely used form of control.

6. Many social, political, religious, and educa-
(f) tional problems are the direct result of

☐ a. instinctive reflexes.
☐ b. aversive control.
☐ c. operant conditioning.
☐ d. negative reinforcers.

7. The selection attempts
(e)

☐ a. to encourage people to revolt.
☐ b. to explain the causes of human conflict.
☐ c. to discourage human aspirations.
☐ d. to condemn anti-social behavior.

8. The intentional controller is
(h)

☐ a. respected by everyone.
☐ b. respectful of liberty.
☐ c. never justified.
☐ d. open to attack.

9. The literature of freedom is
(g)

☐ a. a threat to the establishment.
☐ b. a part of the natural environment.
☐ c. a bonanza to law and order.
☐ d. a danger to the economy.

10. The literature of freedom
(c)

☐ a. seeks to destroy society.
☐ b. is communist inspired.
☐ c. has a limited objective.
☐ d. is not taken seriously.

> Comprehension Skills: a—isolating details; b—recalling specific facts; c—retaining concepts; d—organizing facts; e—understanding the main idea; f—drawing a conclusion; g—making a judgment; h—making an inference; i—recognizing tone; j—understanding characters; k—appreciation of literary forms.

Organic Gardening in Perspective

Organic Matter Has Many Values, but Not a Special Health Magic

Dr. Milton Salomon

It has only been about a century since the introduction of commercial chemical fertilizers. Since that time, they have become the major source of plant food. Previously, the maintenance of soil fertility depended on the use of animal manures, composts and crop rotation.

This does not mean that chemical fertilizers are better than applications of manures, but rather they have become a recognized and tested means of filling new and special demands upon the land. This need was associated with expanding populations, an industrial revolution, and an amazing growth of cities.

The values of organic matter have not decreased, but its major values are for quite different reasons than many organic gardeners believe.

Through the years, there has emerged an understandable yet almost mystical devotion to the idea that only by a system of natural organic, non-chemical or biodynamic farming would it be possible to maintain a bountiful, healthy agriculture. Traditionally, the adherents of this concept have been a rather small group, mainly middle-aged, who honestly thought this was the only route to take.

Over the past decade, however, the idea has caught the imagination of a broad segment of the youth culture. Generally this group consists of well educated, affluent, middle class children whose experiences and backgrounds are found in the cities and suburbs. They are a rather unusual segment of the population and no one denies they have made an impact upon our attitudes and values. Their interest in agriculture from a special viewpoint is well worth looking at.

One of the most fascinating by-products of the search by the young for a new identity and meaning in life has been a growing awareness and sensitivity to the natural world and a spiritual awakening of the deeper senses. Evidence of this may be found in a strong yearning for the land, a return to simple values and communal living, a questioning of the establishment, and a revolt against the dehumanizing effects of massive technology. The commitment in many runs very deep and is often accompanied by turning inward, self-denial, asceticism and, in the extreme, to practices of ancient religious forms associated with the East.

Outwardly, there has evolved a new life style in dress and manners. More complete involvement often includes a desire for special natural foods and diets. Natural, organic, "macrobiotic," and other health food stores and outlets that cater to these tastes have mushroomed across the country. Briefly, it is generally accepted by their customers that foods produced and marketed without the use of chemicals (fertilizers, pesticides, additives) are superior to those grown by modern farm management practices. Crops grown solely by use of animal manures, composts and such natural untreated products as ground limestone and rock are believed to be healthier, taste better, and have greater nutritive and life-giving properties.

It is generally accepted by these people that agricultural chemicals are poisonous and deleterious to health and should be avoided. In a broad sense, adherents to this idea are committed to a system of organic or "biodynamic" gardening rather than the commonly recommended practices of modern mechanized agriculture, which includes the use of chemicals. There is much appeal to this concept and many young people (and old) have flocked to the practice and have accepted the whole picture without carefully analyzing some of the claims and accusations.

There is little question that the careless use of pesticides and injudicious additions of certain food preservatives can produce toxic effects in animals and humans. As examples, dieldrin, a pesticide, can cause death in fish, and excess amounts of sodium nitrate, a food additive, can be toxic to very young children.

But government agencies such as the Food and Drug Administration and others continually monitor food products shipped to markets. Allowable residues of chemicals, which are set by law at very low and non-toxic levels, are carefully checked and when there is any doubt about their safety they are withdrawn from sale. The record in this respect, considering the huge quantity and variety of foods reaching the consumer, is very good.

Certainly there must be continuing vigilance in seeing that chemicals used in the production, processing and preserving of foods have no long- or short-term ill effects on the health of the consumer. However, there is little doubt these chemicals have been most useful in assuring and maintaining high quality foods in this country.

I believe it important that organic gardeners and special natural diet advocates distinguish between pesticides, food additives, chemical fertilizers, and organic matter. Their composition, method of application, reasons for usage, and fate in the environment are not the same.

In most instances, pesticides are synthetic chemical compounds not found naturally in the environment. They are used to kill or discourage insects, disease and weeds. Food additives are normally simpler materials, many occur naturally and are used as preservatives, emulsifiers, coloring agents, and so on. Both pesticides and additives are usually added directly to the plant, animal or food and may or may not remain as residues on the product. They may or may not be toxic.

The more intriguing story emerges when we compare organic materials with chemical fertilizers and analyze their role and place in the growth of plants and their effects upon the soil and food. When man discovered that he could use inorganic, mineral fertilizers to substitute and augment organic manures, he was merely imitating nature.

When organic matter breaks down in the soil, mineral fertilizer elements such as nitrates, phosphates, calcium and others are released to the soil solution for subsequent uptake by plants. When chemical fertilizers are added to soils, the same elements are made soluble rather quickly and they, too, are then absorbed by plant roots. The plant does not and cannot distinguish, for example, nitrate from a compost pile from that coming from an inorganic chemical source. They are the same chemical and once in the plant enter into the life activity with no "memory" or special distinguishing attributes.

The plant plays the near-miraculous role of coordinating the processes of mineral uptake with photosynthesis to form its own organic matter. And it is precisely this organic matter, that is, food, which finds its way back to manure piles, compost heaps or the supermarket to be reused again in the release of chemical mineral elements to the soil or directly to man. This is the greatest recycling operation of all. I see nothing magical, special or healthier in foods grown only with organic fertilizers.

There are, however, a number of compelling reasons why we should use as much organic materials as we reasonably and economically can. Certainly, they should not be wasted. Many benefits are derived from manure and composts that cannot be duplicated by chemical fertilizers alone.

Manure and composts store and slowly release nutrients and minor elements to the soil solution; they affect the release of nutrients from inorganic fertilizer sources; they are a source of energy and nutrients for soil organisms; they encourage good soil structure and water movement; they help conserve moisture; they assist the exchange of nutrients from soil colloids, such as clay, to soil solution for plant absorption; they increase carbon dioxide content of the soil; and some manures and composts have inherent growth regulating and antibiotic effects on living things.

TOPICS FOR THE RESTLESS

On the other hand, there have been fears that continuous use of chemical fertilizers deteriorates the soil, is poisonous to plants and domestic animals and may result in inferior, poor quality foods. These claims are not supported by careful experimentation and observation performed over the last century. Overwhelming evidence is to the contrary.

Perhaps we should look upon the use of fertilizers as a device created by man to assist nature. Remember that agriculture is for man's purpose and is in effect a diversion and disruption of the balance in nature. When one considers that the practice of agriculture has gone on for several thousand years, the record of the farmer as an environmentalist has not been too bad, relative to some other industries.

We should not forget that man and domestic animals are voracious users and converters of organic compounds into energy. In this sense, they may seriously interrupt the normal organic cycle. The loss of nutrients, for example, through city sewage and garbage disposal, can only partially be reclaimed and this only by the expenditure of great effort and resources, let alone commitment.

It makes very good sense to re-use as much of our waste products as possible. This is a problem that must be faced now. However, based on my experience, I do not believe that for the foreseeable future we can generate and reclaim enough organic residues to be delivered at the right places, at the right time and in the right condition to feed even our present size and distribution of population.

Additions of chemical fertilizers complement in a very flexible and economical way the benefits derived from organic matter. Chemical fertilizers are a safe, logical way of building and maintaining our soils and agriculture.

VOCABULARY: The following words have been taken from the selection you have just read. Put an *X* in the box before the best meaning or synonym for the word as used in the selection.

1. **adherents**, page 125, column 1, paragraph 4
"...the adherents of this concept have been a rather small group, ..."
□ a. enemies
□ b. supporters
□ c. advisers
□ d. originators

2. **deleterious**, page 125, column 2, paragraph 3
"...agricultural chemicals are poisonous and deleterious to health..."
□ a. harmful
□ b. beneficial
□ c. necessary
□ d. delectable

3. **augment**, page 126, column 1, paragraph 5
"...mineral fertilizers to substitute and augment organic manures, ..."
□ a. auger
□ b. double
□ c. control
□ d. increase

4. **inherent**, page 126, column 2, paragraph 2
"...some manures and composts have inherent growth regulating and antibiotic effects..."
□ a. deterrent
□ b. unusual
□ c. mysterious
□ d. built-in

5. **voracious**, page 127, column 1, paragraph 3
"...man and domestic animals are voracious users and converters of..."
□ a. cruel
□ b. wasteful
□ c. generous
□ d. insatiable

SYLLABICATION

Knowing how to reduce words to their syllables aids both reading and spelling. Frequently a long word can be recognized and understood if pronounced by syllables. And in spelling, of course, knowledge of syllables contributes to accuracy.

There are rules or generalizations which we can follow when dividing words. One such rule tells us that when a word ends in **le**, preceded by a consonant, the word is divided before that consonant. For example, the word **simple** is divided into **sim** and **ple** — the word is divided before the consonant in front of **le**. An exception to this rule are words ending in **ckle**. The **ck** acts as a single letter—it cannot be split—so the word must be divided after the **k**. An example is **pickle**, which is divided into **pick** and **le** because of the **ck** combination.

The following sentences contain words of both types. In each sentence divide the word in bold print according to the rule or the exception. Write the word on the line to the right using hyphens (-) to separate the syllables.

1. **Freckles** are beauty marks. _____

2. This dance is for **couples** only. _____

3. **Double** your money. _____

4. A tear **trickled** down. _____

5. He's **able** and willing. _____

6. **Angle** for a better view. _____

7. Read the **title** page. _____

8. The grass was **trampled**. _____

9. A **triple** play resulted. _____

10. He **dabbled** in stocks. _____

11. The audience **chuckled**. _____

12. **Fiddles** played. _____

13. **Fickle** friends move on. _____

14. Use **hackle** flies for bait. _____

15. His suit was **wrinkled**. _____

16. Live the **simple** life. _____

17. Carry the **bundles** carefully. _____

18. **Knuckle** down to work. _____

EDITING THE THEME, I

After you finish writing a theme, essay, or paper, it needs to be read, edited, and revised. This is the time to polish your writing, smooth out the rough spots, and correct any errors.

It is a mistake to believe that a satisfactory work can result from just one writing. Everyone needs to work from a rough draft, polishing and editing to arrive at a finished product. Skilled writers revise several times because they have learned that each editing produces an improved version. Your writing too can profit from many revisions, but at least one is essential to make a paper acceptable. When proofing and editing your first copy, follow these steps.

Reread

After you have finished writing your paper, read it again to get the effect. This time read it aloud. Listen to see if the words create the effect you intended. Does it sound the way you want it? Certain errors of agreement and usage will be obvious when heard. Generally, though, you are listening for impact—to determine if your paper makes the presentation of ideas in the way you intended.

Review Sentence Structure

Check first for incomplete thoughts (fragments) or run-on thoughts (comma splices). Each sentence should express a complete thought. Long, involved sentences can confuse your reader. Search for a more accurate way to express your ideas. Look for ways to combine thoughts — connect sentences which are related. Check each sentence carefully. It is generally here where themes first tend to break down.

Check Punctuation

Punctuation is intended to help the reader understand your writing; it is a way of showing on paper the pauses and inflections we make when we speak. Use the proper mark of punctuation. Consult your dictionary or guide for assistance.

COMPREHENSION: For each of the following statements and questions, select the option containing the most complete or most accurate answer.

1. Chemical fertilizers were introduced on the
(c) commercial market
  - ☐ a. to meet the needs of the times.
  - ☐ b. to replace organic matter.
  - ☐ c. to protect the health of the nation.
  - ☐ d. to increase the nutritional value of food.

2. Biodynamic farming
(f)
  - ☐ a. contributes to better health.
  - ☐ b. does not contaminate the soil.
  - ☐ c. increases productivity.
  - ☐ d. none of the above.

3. The new youth culture has identified itself with
(c)
  - ☐ a. ancient religions.
  - ☐ b. dehumanizing life styles.
  - ☐ c. honest values.
  - ☐ d. overthrowing the establishment.

4. People who patronize health food stores do so
(d) under the assumption that
  - ☐ a. organically grown food is unhealthy.
  - ☐ b. natural foods have life-giving properties.
  - ☐ c. health foods cost less.
  - ☐ d. chemically grown food is sanitary.

5. The selection attempts to present
(k)
  - ☐ a. a biased argument.
  - ☐ b. an undocumented theory.
  - ☐ c. an alarming idea.
  - ☐ d. a balanced viewpoint.

6. The safe use of agricultural chemicals de-
(c) pends on
  - ☐ a. control.
  - ☐ b. profits.
  - ☐ c. economy.
  - ☐ d. irrigation.

7. The author states that the effect of inorganic
(c) and organic fertilizers is
  - ☐ a. questionable.
  - ☐ b. difficult to analyze.
  - ☐ c. essentially the same.
  - ☐ d. dangerous.

8. Everything else being equal, farmers should
(f)
  - ☐ a. use chemical fertilizers.
  - ☐ b. use organic fertilizers.
  - ☐ c. practice crop rotation.
  - ☐ d. use modern machinery.

9. Which of the following industries has the best
(a) environmental record?
  - ☐ a. Lumber
  - ☐ b. Fishing
  - ☐ c. Agriculture
  - ☐ d. Advertising

10. The author
(e)
  - ☐ a. laments the abuses of agriculture.
  - ☐ b. is preoccupied with public apathy.
  - ☐ c. is sympathetic to big business.
  - ☐ d. defends the use of chemical fertilizers.

Comprehension Skills: a—isolating details; b—recalling specific facts; c—retaining concepts; d—organizing facts; e—understanding the main idea; f—drawing a conclusion; g—making a judgment; h—making an inference; i—recognizing tone; j—understanding characters; k—appreciation of literary forms.

Federal Jobs

How Jobs Are Filled and Conditions of Employment

Overseas

United States citizens are employed by the Federal Government in Alaska, Hawaii, United States territories, and in foreign countries. They are found in almost every occupational field. They are construction and maintenance workers, doctors, nurses, teachers, technical experts, mining engineers, meteorologists, clerks, stenographers, typists, geologists, skilled tradesmen, social workers, agricultural marketing specialists, and agricultural and other economists.

Current needs of agencies with jobs to fill are generally limited to highly qualified and hard-to-find professional personnel, skilled technicians, and, in some cases, stenographers and clerical and administrative personnel. A few agencies are seeking experienced teachers, librarians, nurses, and medical personnel. However, a few vacancies occur in most fields from time to time because of normal turnover in personnel.

How Jobs Are Filled

In Alaska, Hawaii, and United States territories, most vacancies are filled by the appointment of local eligibles who qualify in competitive civil-service examinations which are announced and held in the local area. Normally, there is a sufficient local labor market to fill the needs and examinations are not publicized outside the local areas. Some positions, however, may be filled by transferring career Government employees from the United States mainland.

When a vacancy is to be filled in a foreign country, determination is made whether to recruit from among persons in the area where the job is located or to seek qualified applicants residing in the United States. If the position is to be filled locally, the appointee may be a United States citizen residing or traveling in the area, the wife or dependent of a citizen employed or stationed in the area, or a foreign national.

In most instances where United States installations are established in foreign countries, either formal or informal agreements have been drawn up assuring the host government that local nationals will be employed wherever possible in order to be of maximum assistance to the economy of that country. Furthermore, it is almost always to the economic advantage of the United States to employ foreign nationals at local pay rates without responsibility for travel costs and overseas cost-of-living allowances. Positions held by foreign nationals are in the excepted service and are not subject to the competitive requirements of the Civil Service Act and rules.

However, there are many thousands of technical, administrative, and supervisory positions in which United States citizens are employed in foreign countries. These positions are usually in the competitive service, and as vacancies occur they are filled in most cases by transferring career Government employees from the United States. This is the case in the Department of Defense, the largest employer of overseas personnel, and in most other agencies having overseas positions. When Government employees are not available for transfer overseas, and qualified United States citizens cannot be recruited locally, these vacancies are filled through the regular competitive examining process.

Approximately 60 examinations now open on a nationwide basis are being used, as recruiting needs require, to fill overseas positions. The examinations cover a variety of business and economics, engineering and scientific, medical, social and educational, and trades positions. Qualified persons interested in overseas assignments in these fields should file for appropriate examinations. Copies of the examination announcements, containing full information on how and where to apply, and application forms, can be obtained from the U.S. Civil Service Commission, Washington, D.C., 20415.

Some positions are excepted from the competitive requirements of the civil-service rules and regulations. Included in this group are positions in the Foreign Service of the Department of State, dependents' school teachers, positions in the attaché offices, and most positions of clerk-translator, translator, and interpreter. Applications for these positions should be made directly to the agency in which employment is desired.

Conditions of Employment

Age. The minimum age for overseas appointments made in the United States is generally 21. In most cases, there is no maximum age limit.

Physical Requirements. Applicants for most overseas positions must be able to pass rigid physical examinations since employees may be required to serve under extremely difficult living conditions and, in some areas, at posts where complete medical facilities are not available. Physical standards are applied which are suitable for the location and occupation involved, and may include standards of mental and emotional stability and maturity.

Any physical defect which would make the employee a hazard to himself or to others, or prevent efficient performance of the duties of the positions is disqualifying. Conditions which require periodic medical care, hospitalization, special foods or medicine may be disqualifying for some areas.

Accompanying dependents may also be required to pass rigid physical examinations.

Tour of Duty. Individuals selected in the United States for overseas employment generally are required to sign a transportation agreement for a definite period of service, which is usually for a minimum of 36 months. In certain areas the minimum period is 12 or 24 months.

Investigation. All appointments are subject to satisfactory security, character, and suitability investigations. Applicants considered for appointment are carefully screened, and only those possessing suitable qualifications are selected for overseas employment.

General Information

Qualifications. Generally, the qualification requirements are the same as those established for like positions in the United States. Applicants may, however, be required to meet certain additional or higher standards. A foreign language capability, while not required in all, or even most, Federal jobs overseas, would obviously be a valuable qualification.

Dependents. For middle and upper-level positions in what may be broadly termed "professional occupations," most agencies permit employees to take their families with them. In certain other job categories, and in accordance with an established system of priorities, it is usually possible to arrange for dependents to follow from several months to a year after the employee has arrived at the overseas post.

For most clerical and secretarial positions abroad, agencies prefer single persons without dependents.

Appointments of both husband and wife are very infrequent, since there rarely are simultaneous vacancies in which their qualifications could be appropriately utilized at the same post. However, in foreign countries with a large American presence, both governmental and private-industrial, qualified U.S. citizens are in demand for a wide variety of job openings. In the majority of cases, dependents of U.S. Government employees overseas are given priority consideration for such employment.

Salary. Generally, overseas white-collar workers are paid the same base salaries as Federal employees in the United States occupying similar positions. In addition, where warranted by conditions at the post, they receive a post differential or cost-of-living allowance. In foreign areas, the wages of blue-collar workers are based upon continental United States rates plus, in some cases, a post differential or cost-of-living allowance; in United States areas overseas, their wages may be set in a similar way or they may be based on local rates.

Quarters Allowances. In foreign areas, employees are sometimes housed in Government quarters. If Government housing is not provided, a quarters allowance is paid which covers in large part the cost of rent and utilities. In most United States areas, Government quarters are not provided and no quarters allowance is paid.

Federal Employment Benefits. In general, Federal employees are entitled to such liberal benefits as paid vacations, sick leave with pay, and retirement coverage. They are eligible for life insurance and health benefits partially financed by the Government. Employees serving overseas also normally receive special benefits such as free travel for themselves and their dependents, free transportation or storage for their household goods, and additional paid vacations with free travel to their homes in the United States between tours of duty. Also, the United States Government operates dependents' schools in many areas and provides educational opportunities for children which are comparable to those offered in the better schools in the United States.

Federal Job Information Centers

The Civil Service Commission offers Federal employment information through a nationwide network of Federal job information centers. For an answer to your questions about Federal employment call, visit, or write the information center located in your city. If you are located outside the local dialing area, you can dial a toll-free "800-number" when one is listed for the State in which you are dialing.

The Civil Service Commission invites you to call and talk with an information specialist before writing a letter or filling out an application. Information specialists can mail you appropriate job announcements, application forms, and pamphlets. A call can save you valuable time and unnecessary effort.

Starting Time: _____	Finishing Time: _____
Reading Time: _____	Reading Rate: _____
Comprehension: _____	Vocabulary: _____

VOCABULARY: The following words have been taken from the selection you have just read. Put an X in the box before the best meaning or synonym for the word as used in the selection.

1. **recruit**, page 130, column 1, paragraph 4
"...determination is made whether to recruit from among persons in the area..."
☐ a. select
☐ b. repair
☐ c. pursue
☐ d. advertise

2. **stability**, page 131, column 1, paragraph 2
"...may include standards of mental and emotional stability..."
☐ a. constancy
☐ b. character
☐ c. strain
☐ d. requirements

3. **screened**, page 131, column 1, paragraph 6
"Applicants considered for appointment are carefully screened, ..."
☐ a. rejected
☐ b. protected
☐ c. defended
☐ d. considered

4. **utilized**, page 131, column 2, paragraph 3
"...in which their qualifications could be appropriately utilized..."
☐ a. appreciated
☐ b. put to use
☐ c. bargained for
☐ d. organized

5. **warranted**, page 131, column 2, paragraph 4
"...where warranted by conditions at the post, ..."
☐ a. encouraged
☐ b. guaranteed
☐ c. justified
☐ d. authorized

TOPICS FOR THE RESTLESS

ROOTS

Many English words consist of a base or root word to which prefixes (beginnings) and suffixes (endings) have been added. To the root word **agree** (a verb) we can add both a prefix and a suffix to get **disagreeable** (an adjective) which has an opposite meaning.

Roots are Latin and Greek stems on which our English words are based. For example, **bio** (life) is a Greek root on which the word **biology** (the study of plant and animal life) is built.

Two Roots

1. spec, spic are variants of the Latin root for **look** or **see**. **Spectators** come to see.

2. prim is the Latin root for **first**. **Prime** beef is first quality.

In the following sentences these two roots have been left out. Space has been left indicating where the roots belong. Add one of these roots and write your word on the line following the sentence.

1. —e the surface with an undercoat before painting.

_____

2. The **pro—ts** for his release are quite promising.

_____

3. This —itive art dates from earliest man.

_____

4. The principal woman singer in an opera is the —a donna.

_____

5. With all those colors, the billboard was certainly **con—uous**.

_____

6. Children's first reading books were called —ers.

_____

7. A —imen for us to examine is coming by mail.

_____

8. The —ary instincts of man are those relating to food and shelter.

_____

9. The exhibition of the unique animals created quite a —tacle.

_____

10. —tacular is the word to describe his amazing performance on the high wire.

_____

11. The barracks are ready for **in—tion**.

_____

We have discussed the first three steps to follow when editing and revising your paper: 1) Reread Aloud, 2) Review Sentence Structure, and 3) Check Punctuation. Here are the other items to consider.

Check Antecedents

Pronouns, as you know, replace nouns. The antecedent of every pronoun must be clear to your reader—there must be no doubt. Check, too, to be sure that each pronoun agrees with it's antecedent in person and number. A frequent student error is to use a plural pronoun (these, they) to replace a singular noun. Errors like these will be apparent when you review.

Improve Nouns and Verbs

We all tend to use the same nouns and verbs over and over. This makes our writing dull and unimaginative. Try to replace with a more specific and image-provoking word each noun and verb of importance in your paper. Help the reader see and feel your thoughts through the use of descriptive and accurate nouns and verbs.

Add Adjectives

Every sentence you write can be improved by adding a colorful adjective. Try it; it works. Practice this with simple sentences and see how interesting they become. The skilled writer excels in the images he creates in his readers' minds. This one technique alone can double the effectiveness of your writing.

Use Appropriate Language

There are, as you know, levels of usage—formal occasions demand formal language, but conversations with friends permit the use of fragmented or informal speech. The usage which you employ in your writing must be appropriate for your subject, your purpose, and your reader. The level of language you use is determined on the basis of these considerations.

COMPREHENSION: For each of the following statements and questions, select the option containing the most complete or most accurate answer.

1. The federal government can be considered
(c)
   ☐ a. an employment service.
   ☐ b. a major employer.
   ☐ c. a social agency.
   ☐ d. a professional clearinghouse.

2. Current needs of agencies with jobs to fill are
(f)
   ☐ a. general.
   ☐ b. negligible.
   ☐ c. urgent.
   ☐ d. specialized.

3. The policy followed in selecting applicants to
(g) fill government vacancies seems
   ☐ a. just and competitive.
   ☐ b. irresponsible and arbitrary.
   ☐ c. generous and patriotic.
   ☐ d. lax and political.

4. The largest employer of overseas personnel is
(a)
   ☐ a. the U.S. Civil Service Commission.
   ☐ b. the Foreign Service.
   ☐ c. the Department of Transportation.
   ☐ d. the Department of Defense.

5. The selection is
(k)
   ☐ a. scientific.
   ☐ b. literary.
   ☐ c. informational.
   ☐ d. propagandistic.

6. The strict health and physical requirements
(g) demanded of candidates for overseas positions are made
   ☐ a. to protect the nationals from disease.
   ☐ b. to eliminate undesirable applicants.
   ☐ c. to safeguard the interests of applicants.
   ☐ d. to discriminate against women.

7. The dependents of overseas employees
(c)
   ☐ a. can find suitable employment abroad.
   ☐ b. can easily become a government liability.
   ☐ c. are encouraged to remain in the U.S.
   ☐ d. are a big drain on the host country's economy.

8. In certain cases, overseas employees do better
(f) financially than
   ☐ a. the heads of their delegations.
   ☐ b. their stateside counterparts.
   ☐ c. professionals in private industry.
   ☐ d. most Americans abroad.

9. It can be inferred from the selection that a
(h) career in the Foreign Service is
   ☐ a. too demanding.
   ☐ b. dangerous.
   ☐ c. uncommon.
   ☐ d. desirable.

10. The tone of the selection is
(i)
   ☐ a. hostile.
   ☐ b. factual.
   ☐ c. negative.
   ☐ d. stimulating.

Comprehension Skills: a—isolating details; b—recalling specific facts; c—retaining concepts; d—organizing facts; e—understanding the main idea; f—drawing a conclusion; g—making a judgment; h—making an inference; i—recognizing tone; j—understanding characters; k—appreciation of literary forms.

TOPICS FOR THE RESTLESS

Natural Steam

Natural Geysers: A Potential Source of Commercial Energy

for Power

With increasing population and industrial expansion, domestic requirements for electric power have been doubling about every ten years. To meet these growing needs, government and industry are vigorously investigating and rapidly developing new sources of energy. Among the possible new sources, atomic energy probably has the largest potential, but geothermal energy—a previously little explored source—may prove to be most important in many areas.

For years man has viewed with awe the spectacular bursts of natural steam from volcanoes, geysers, and boiling springs. Although the use of hot springs for baths dates to ancient times, the use of natural steam for the manufacture of electric power did not begin until 1905. That year the first geothermal power station was built at Larderello, Italy. For the next several decades, there were no other major developments in the field, and even now Italy leads the world in power production from natural steam. New Zealand began major exploration of hot spring and geyser areas in 1950, and successful results there proved that commercial steam can be developed from areas containing very hot water rather than steam at depth. Today, the United States, Japan, and the Soviet Union are also producing power from geothermal sources, and Iceland uses hot water from geyser fields for space heating. Many other countries have geothermal energy potential, and several are now conducting exploration for sources to be developed.

In the United States, the first commercial geothermal power plant was built by the Pacific Gas and Electric Co., in 1960 at "The Geysers," California.

Sites for Geothermal Exploration

Most of the promising areas for geothermal power development are within belts of volcanic activity. A major belt called "the ring of fire," surrounds the Pacific Ocean. The "hot spots" favorable for geothermal energy are related to volcanic activity in the present and the not-too-distant past. In the western United States, particularly along the Pacific Coast, widespread and intense volcanic activity has occurred during the past ten million years. The record of volcanism in our western states, therefore, holds promise for geothermal power development. Currently, exploration for power sites is focused in California, Nevada, Oregon, and New Mexico, with some interest being displayed in the whole region from the Rocky Mountains to the Pacific Ocean.

Sources for Commercial Steam

Volcanoes produce the most dramatic displays of natural steam. Water that comes into contact with molten lava (temperatures of 2000 degrees Fahrenheit and higher) near the earth's surface can exist only as steam. Rapid expansion of steam and other gases below the surface causes some of nature's most violent and explosive eruptions.

Almost all active volcanoes have fumaroles, or vents, that discharge steam and other hot gases. But, despite the large quantities of steam discharged during active volcanism, the energy cannot be harnessed as a dependable source of power. In some areas the emission of steam cannot be controlled, and in other areas the costs of controlling the steam would exceed the value of the power obtained.

More promising sources for commercial steam are certain other subsurface hot spots or geothermal reservoirs that are generally found in areas of volcanism. These reservoirs contain larger and more dependable volumes of steam or hot water. Wells are drilled into the reservoirs to tap the naturally hot fluids that may drive power generators.

Most known geothermal reservoirs contain hot water, rather than steam. Water at depth and under high pressure remains liquid at temperatures far above 212 degrees Fahrenheit, the boiling point of water at sea level. When this water is tapped by drilled wells and rises to the surface, the pressure falls. As the pressure decreases, the water boils, perhaps violently, and the resulting steam is separated from the remaining liquid water. Because the well itself acts as a continuously erupting geyser, the expanding steam propels the liquid water to the surface and pumping costs are nil.

Why Do Hot Spots Exist?

Mineral exploration over the world has shown that temperatures in deep mines and oil wells usually rise with increasing depth below the surface. One popular explanation assumes that our planet has a fiery origin and that a shallow crustal layer encases a large molten core. Most geologists, however, now believe that our planet was not hot when it first formed. The weight of the evidence suggests instead that a natural radioactivity, present in small amounts in all rocks, has gradually heated the earth, and that heat is still being produced. Geophysical studies also indicate that the molten core is much smaller than was once supposed, and that it is not, in itself, a source of the heat in the earth's crust. The reasons for the existence and specific location of the earth's volcanic belts are still subjects of vigorous scientific study and controversy, but the energy from natural radioactivity in rocks of the earth's crust and upper mantle is the fundamental cause of heat within the earth.

Types of Geothermal Fields

In a general way, geothermal fields are either hot spring systems or deep insulated reservoirs that have little leakage of heated fluids to the surface. Yellowstone National Park and Wairakei, New Zealand are examples of large hot spring systems. Larderello in Italy and the Salton Sea area of California are examples of insulated reservoirs.

Hot springs have a plumbing system of interconnected channels within rocks. Water from rain or snow seeps underground. If the water reaches a local region of greater heat it expands and rises, being pushed onward by the pressure from new cold and heavy water that is just entering the system. The hot water is discharged as hot springs or geysers.

Deep reservoirs with little surface area have porous rocks (like those in a petroleum reservoir) capped by rocks such as clays and shales that prevent the free upward escape of water and heat. Larderello, Italy, and the Salton Sea area of California are examples of this type. Both reservoirs have feeble thermal springs coming to the surface, but there may be undiscovered areas that have no leakages.

Hot Water and Dry Steam Systems

Because of the pressures at great depths, water can be entirely liquid rather than steam deep in hot spring and insulated reservoir systems, even at very high temperatures. Steam forms in these systems if the hot water rises to levels where the pressure drops to the point where water can boil. This flashing of steam from liquid water is the major potential source of geothermal energy for commercial use because natural hot water systems are relatively abundant.

However, in a few explored systems the heat supply is so high and the rate of discharge of water is so low that steam forms deep in the system. Larderello in Italy and "The Geysers" in California are examples of the less common reservoirs of dry natural steam.

Characteristics Favorable for Geothermal Reservoirs

The most favorable geologic factors for a geothermal reservoir of commercial value include:

1. A potent source of heat, such as a large chamber of molten magma. The chamber should be deep enough to insure adequate pressure and a slow rate of cooling, and yet not too deep for natural circulation of water and effective transfer of heat to the circulating water. Magma chambers of this type are most likely to occur in regions of recent volcanism, such as the Rocky Mountain and Pacific States.

2. Large and porous reservoirs with channels connected to the heat source, near which water can circulate and then be stored in the reservoir. Even in areas of slight rainfall, enough water may percolate underground to sustain the reservoir.

3. Capping rocks of low permeability that inhibit the flow of water and heat to the surface. In very favorable circumstances, cap rocks are not essential for a commercial field. However, a deep and well-insulated reservoir is likely to have much more stored energy than an otherwise similar but shallow and uninsulated reservoir.

The Potential of Geothermal Power

It is too early to judge whether natural steam has the potential to satisfy an important part of the world's requirements for electric power, but in locally favorable areas it is already an attractive source for cheap power. Current exploration, based upon geologic and geophysical methods, is likely to develop presently undiscovered fields. The recent discovery of a new field at Monte Amiata, Italy—where there are only meager surface manifestations of abnormal geothermal energy—was based in part on the use of such methods. These are now well enough developed to support exploration for wholly concealed reservoirs.

All natural geyser areas of the world are potential sites for commercial geothermal energy, yet it is to be remembered that development of these areas for the recovery of steam may destroy the geysers themselves. Although the need to develop new sources of energy may become urgent, still every effort must be made to protect these scenic wonders of nature.

Starting Time: _____ Finishing Time: _____

Reading Time: _____ Reading Rate: _____

Comprehension: _____ Vocabulary: _____

VOCABULARY: The following words have been taken from the selection you have just read. Put an *X* in the box before the best meaning or synonym for the word as used in the selection.

1. **nil**, page 135, column 2, paragraph 5
"...pumping costs are nil."
☐ a. minimal
☐ b. moderate
☐ c. nonexistent
☐ d. high

2. **controversy**, page 136, column 1, paragraph 1
"...are still subjects of vigorous scientific study and controversy, ..."
☐ a. violence
☐ b. investigation
☐ c. disagreement
☐ d. conversation

3. **insulated**, page 136, column 1, paragraph 2
"...deep insulated reservoirs that have little leakage of heated fluids to the surface."
☐ a. isolated
☐ b. unconnected
☐ c. uncovered
☐ d. protected

4. **potent**, page 137, column 1, paragraph 1
"A potent source of heat, such as a large chamber of molten magma."
☐ a. powerful
☐ b. persuasive
☐ c. ineffectual
☐ d. potential

5. **meager**, page 137, column 2, paragraph 1
"...where there are only meager surface manifestations of abnormal geothermal energy—"
☐ a. obvious
☐ b. poor
☐ c. hidden
☐ d. scanty

CONTEXTUAL AIDS: CAUSE AND EFFECT

Studies of good readers show that they are aware of the context of what they are reading. This means that they are anticipating what is coming next by what has gone before.

The many ways in which context functions to help the reader recognize words are called contextual aids.

Contextual Aid. Words can be understood through a cause and effect relationship between the unknown word and other words in the sentence. The reader's understanding of the cause-effect pattern offers a clue to the meaning of the unknown word. In the sentence, **Because of the heavy traffic, he arrived _____**, the reader who understands the effects of traffic congestion surmises that the missing word is **late.**

In the following sentences, similar cause and effect patterns have been employed to help you determine the meaning of nonsense words. Underline the nonsense word and write the correct word on the line following each sentence.

1. He took aspirin to help relieve his drespan.

   _____

2. Because they ate just before swimming, most of the team suffered brills.

   _____

3. If you break the law, you can expect to be selteped.

   _____

4. She did well on the examination because she felmanced the previous night.

   _____

5. After the liner struck the iceberg, the manblats were lowered.

   _____

6. Upon completion of four years of high school, he was awarded a sapenter.

   _____

7. He was suspended from school for merting a rule.

   _____

8. He suffered blescromp because he had forgotten his gloves.

   _____

9. There was not sufficient capital to keep the company from going repstelpt.

   _____

10. Heat the water until it trins.

    _____

REVIEWING FOR EXAMINATIONS

Every student knows that the best way to prepare for final examinations is to study during the semester. Most students do not do this, however, and find it necessary to cram for examinations on the night before.

During the semester you should plan to outline the course as you go along and relate what you learn from lectures with what you learn from your reading.

During the final week here's what you should do.

Outline the Course

Use your lecture notes and chapter headings and questions to prepare a two or three page outline (definitely not longer) of the entire course. Your instructor may do this for you by summarizing and indicating the main points and major divisions of the subject.

Fill in the Outline

Using pencil and paper, or mentally, if you trust yourself, complete your outline by filling in all the details you can remember. If you do this on paper, you'll be able to see what's been omitted when you compare it with your text and notes. Using the text, your lecture notes, and questions following each chapter, fill in the gaps in your information. You have a week, so segment the project, doing some each day. Save two days at the end for the final review.

Question Yourself

Every student knows some of the questions that will be included on the examination. Give yourself an examination based on these questions and others you suspect may be asked. Your written answers will reveal what you have forgotten or failed to learn.

Review Everything

On the eve of the examination, recite your answers. See if you can produce all of the information you have been studying.

COMPREHENSION: For each of the following statements and questions, select the option containing the most complete or most accurate answer.

1. The increasing demands for power are re-
(c) lated to
   - ☐ a. decreasing world supplies.
   - ☐ b. people and their needs.
   - ☐ c. new scientific exploration.
   - ☐ d. wasteful use of energy.

2. Which of the following sources of energy
(b) seems to have the greatest potential?
   - ☐ a. Atomic power
   - ☐ b. Natural steam
   - ☐ c. Natural gas
   - ☐ d. Oil shale

3. Which of the following best expresses the
(e) main idea of the selection?
   - ☐ a. Population Explosion
   - ☐ b. Natural Wonders
   - ☐ c. Use and Abuse
   - ☐ d. Search and Development

4. Cheap and abundant sources of natural steam
(b) energy are likely to be found in areas of
   - ☐ a. intense volcanic activity.
   - ☐ b. high radioactivity.
   - ☐ c. dense population.
   - ☐ d. scientific exploration.

5. Active volcanoes are not dependable sources
(g) of power because their
   - ☐ a. life span is too short.
   - ☐ b. locations are inaccessible.
   - ☐ c. activity is unpredictable.
   - ☐ d. use has never been considered.

6. The physical law which explains why water at
(c) great depths does not boil at temperatures above 212 degrees Fahrenheit is
   - ☐ a. acceleration.
   - ☐ b. buoyancy.
   - ☐ c. pressure.
   - ☐ d. gravity.

7. Which of the following best explains the origin
(b) of the earth's source of heat?
   - ☐ a. The molten core theory
   - ☐ b. The natural radioactivity theory
   - ☐ c. The fiery origin theory
   - ☐ d. The relativity theory

8. As opposed to hot spring systems, deep insu-
(f) lated reservoirs
   - ☐ a. must be vented.
   - ☐ b. have less potential.
   - ☐ c. have less pressure.
   - ☐ d. must be drilled.

9. Hot spring systems are
(h)
   - ☐ a. fed from the surface.
   - ☐ b. deep and tightly insulated.
   - ☐ c. rare and difficult to find.
   - ☐ d. relatively inexpensive to develop.

10. Geothermal power can contribute to
(g)
   - ☐ a. a stable economy.
   - ☐ b. nuclear development.
   - ☐ c. a better environment.
   - ☐ d. political unrest.

Comprehension Skills: a—isolating details; b—recalling specific facts; c—retaining concepts; d—organizing facts; e—understanding the main idea; f—drawing a conclusion; g—making a judgment; h—making an inference; i—recognizing tone; j—understanding characters; k—appreciation of literary forms.

Dying, One Day at a Time, I

The Plight of Our Prisons and Prisoners

Robert Lionel

In our contemporary "free" society, there are today in American prisons and correctional institutions more than 500,000 people to whom the concept of "freedom" is a hollow mockery. They have been stored away by their peers for transgressions against the open society; they have forfeited, for a time, their birthright to pursue their individual happiness under an aura of liberty. Many of these men and women, classified as felons, are biding away years of their lives in institutions designated as penitentiaries; an archaic assumption that time thus spent will result in their becoming "penitent." There is little supportive evidence that anything like that desired self-assessment ever truly takes place. Most emerge, at the end of their sentences, not with an internalized new strength toward self-redirection to better goals—but with a festering bitterness that now it is society who owes *them* a debt! Attempts to collect on that debt, among a society in which they are now twice-watched, contributes to the failure (or recidivist) statistics which prove that nearly two out of every three ex-convicts will return to prison! It is perhaps remarkable that the one out of three manages to stay out, considering the occupational barriers we construct against reintegration into our midst with respectable, competitively paying jobs.

The Cost In Souls and Dollars

The half-a-million convicts mentioned at the start of this article pass their tedious days in more than 200 federal and state prisons dotting this land like so many eyeless silos of despair. Together, their sentences comprise more than three million years—ten times longer than man himself has occupied the earth. Today, approximately 5000 new convicts are incarcerated each year.

The cost to society to maintain the system runs to more than a billion dollars a year. New correctional facilities alone require annual expenditures in excess of $45 million. In 1965, we spent over $800 million to sustain our prison populations. This averaged out to $2000 for each felon, $1000 for each misdemeanant, and $3600 for each juvenile delinquent, the latter figure being higher based on the theory that we should spend more in an effort to rehabilitate our youthful offenders. Additionally, taxpayers forked over another $196 million to cover the costs of parole for 850,000 ex-convicts.

But what about the inmates themselves? Has all this coin purchased us a "better" convict, a greater respect for society? Not if we believe the statistics just cited on recidivism—that two out of three return to life in the Big House.

As we will see in this article, money unto itself is not the answer to our penal woes. Only the commitment of a society which truly believes that a life is worth saving—worth "rehabilitating"—can spell the difference between a man or woman making it on the outside, or returning quickly to prison.

Our thinking *must* change. We must realize that a society which allows half-a-million souls to stagnate behind bars can never call itself wholly "free." To do so makes an obscenity of the word.

We do not advocate that all prisons be abolished, but we do advocate that once a man has "paid his debt to society," his time of punishment must end. The man must have a true chance to prove himself, or else we must build bigger prisons from which only death can serve as the ultimate rehabilitation. We must become a *part* of rehabilitation, or a part of the imprisonment. We cannot have it both ways. We cannot release a man and then say to him, "You are yet a criminal in our eyes, and we expect the worst of you. Do not disappoint us." Instead we must say, "We will watch you closely for a while because we know your past, but we will help you to a full, lasting life if that is now your true goal." A man must first be taken at his word—and then his deed. If his words are those of honesty, then we must provide him with the opportunities to turn those words into deeds. We will know his genuine intent soon enough.

I do not believe that most ex-convicts want to return to a life of crime immediately upon release. They want a job commensurate with their pre-criminal abilities. They want the love of a family, the warmth of a woman. They want to feel the starch in a fresh shirt, the privacy of a bathroom, the pleasures of a bedroom. In short, they want all those things—more desperately than we can ever imagine—which were denied them so long.

But what do they find? Hostility. Suspicion. Fear. But, most horrible of all, they find apathy. They emerge from prison shedding the walled cocoon of their incarcerated lives only to find higher walls of public scorn and disinterest. Soon, they give up. They then go to those people who will not stare at them, nor run from them babbling syrupy platitudes. They go to their most recent friends—the friends they made in prison. And from those meetings, it is a oneway street back to the cement courtyards.

We can blame a man when he commits a crime—and we can fit a punishment to suit that crime. But we cannot blame a man when he comes out. If he fails during those first few days, or weeks, or months, the blame most usually falls upon us all, we free men of the free society. We who carry the theory of equal opportunity within our troubled consciences like so many pennies in a rich man's suit. We of the American Dream.

The Theory of Rehabilitation

A tenet of rehabilitation of the alcoholic begins with self-acknowledgment that one *has the problem.* Only then can help have a chance for success. Can this rubric not be extended to apply to the felon? Until he can accept the immorality of his act, there is little room to move him toward an internalized and subjective goal of redirected, socially-constructive, positive behavior.

If an ex-convict perceives that society will never help him, be assured he will feel little compunction, and few uneasy twinges, when the opportunity to offend that society again presents itself. Our help should not spring from this fear, but from the highest philosophic or religious ethics our reason and civilization have developed—those traits which have hopefully set us above the other animals.

Present-day criminologists, average men, and thinkers and philosophers centuries before Christ have agonized about the management of those who offend and assault and prey upon their contemporary societies—yet few writers have undertaken to bring these ideas together for examination.

In 1748, the great French philosopher, Rousseau, made the observation that "frequent punishments are always a sign of weaknesses or remissness on the part of government." On the point of rehabilitation, he observed "there is not a single ill-doer who could not be turned to some good." On capital punishment, his comment was to the effect that the state "has no right to put to death, even for the sake of making an example, anyone whom it can leave alive without danger." On the subject of pardon, or exempting the guilty from a penalty imposed by the law and pronounced by the judge, he felt that this right belongs "only to an authority which is superior to both judge and law." This he defined as the sovereign. In a well-governed state, he observed there are few punishments. Not because there are many pardons, but because criminals are rare. It is when a state is in decay, so Rousseau believed, that the multitude of crime grows out of proportion.

As early as 334 B.C., in his *Nicomachean Ethics,* Aristotle observed that "man commits unjust actions voluntarily and, by taking the initiative, reveals that he acted by his own choice." He went on to say, "This injustice amounts to an inequality which the judge tries to equalize—by means of the penalty, the judge takes away from the gain of the offender." By gain he meant not only gains such as by stealing, but he extended this even to the inflicting of a wound. The wound is a "loss" to the sufferer even though there has been no real "gain" to the criminal. Moreover, in his essay on politics written about the same time, Aristotle conceptualized the need for the separation of the duties of judges and jailors. He saw the judicial process as odious at best, but "a double odium is incurred when the judges who have passed also executed the sentence, and if they are also the executioners, they will be the enemies of all." In a lecture to the people of Athens, he spoke of the separate functions of a jailor, and wondered if some device could not be arrived at to render the office less unpopular. He felt jailors are "as necessary as executioners, but good men do all they can to avoid either position." He felt worthless persons could not be safely trusted with being jailors, for "many themselves require a guard, and are not fit to guard others."

In Biblical times, justice apparently was swift and personal and final. It may be we have come full circle and justice and punishment are being once again seen as one and the same, and the element of personal vengeance cannot be separated out. Indeed, a frightened populace and its media may be in concert to form a symbiotic relationship with a demand that an impersonal crime be punished personally and publically, as witness the many recent suggestions offered as suitable punishment for skyjackers, not the least of which is public execution.

Starting Time:	_____	Finishing Time:	_____
Reading Time:	_____	Reading Rate:	_____
Comprehension:	_____	Vocabulary:	_____

VOCABULARY: The following words have been taken from the selection you have just read. Put an X in the box before the best meaning or synonym for the word as used in the selection.

1. **transgressions**, page 140, column 1, paragraph 1
"They have been stored away by their peers for transgressions against the open society; ..."
☐ a. disobediences
☐ b. encroachments
☐ c. offences
☐ d. regressions

2. **stagnate**, page 140, column 2, paragraph 4
"...a society which allows half-a-million souls to stagnate behind bars..."
☐ a. progress
☐ b. stand still
☐ c. stagger
☐ d. make noise

3. **commensurate**, page 140, column 2, paragraph 6
"They want a job commensurate with their pre-criminal abilities."
☐ a. commemorative
☐ b. equal
☐ c. superior
☐ d. subordinate

4. **tenet**, page 141, column 1, paragraph 4
"A tenet of rehabilitation of the alcoholic begins with self-acknowledgment..."
☐ a. test
☐ b. tenant
☐ c. remedy
☐ d. principle

5. **compunction**, page 141, column 1, paragraph 5
"...he will feel little compunction, and few uneasy twinges, ..."
☐ a. regret
☐ b. compulsion
☐ c. satisfaction
☐ d. understanding

ROOTS

Many English words consist of a base word or root word to which prefixes (beginnings) and suffixes (endings) have been added. To the root word **agree** (a verb) we can add both a prefix and a suffix to get **disagreeable** (an adjective) which has an opposite meaning.

Roots are Latin and Greek stems on which our English words are based. For example, **bio** (life) is a Greek root on which the word **biology** (the study of plant and animal life) is built.

Two Roots

1. magni is a Latin root which means **large** or **great**. A **magnifying** lens enlarges.

2. scrib, script is also Latin and it is the root for **write**. The **scriptures** are believed to be sacred writings.

In the following sentences these two roots have been left out. Space has been left indicating where the roots belong. Add one of these roots and write your word on the line following the sentence.

1. Refusing to seek help only **−fied** her problems.

   _____

2. The **in−ion** on the stone was weathered and impossible to read.

   _____

3. His bombastic speech could be described as **−loquent**.

   _____

4. **Tran−e** your shorthand notes and type two copies for me.

   _____

5. A **de−ion** of the man was circulated throughout the neighborhood following the robbery.

   _____

6. The notes were **−bled** on the back of an envelope.

   _____

7. Have you seen the **−ficent** painting by this artist on display in the museum?

   _____

8. You must **sub−e** each year if you wish to receive the magazine.

   _____

9. A **−fication** of the image failed to make it readable.

   _____

10. The **−tude** of the crime shocked the community.

   _____

TAKING OBJECTIVE EXAMS

Objective-type examinations consist of multiple-choice, matching, fill-in, and similar type questions. Answering questions on objective examinations will produce better results if you follow these rules and steps.

Rule 1. Answer all the questions. Even when you are penalized for wrong answers, your chances of scoring higher are better if you follow a hunch rather than leave the question unanswered.

Rule 2. Do not change an answer unless you know for sure that it is incorrect. Sometimes, a later question may reveal that one of your earlier responses was wrong. Otherwise, go with your first choice.

Rule 3. Use all the time. Do not be tempted to finish early. Give yourself every advantage. Take every bit of the time scheduled for the examination.

Keeping these three rules in mind, follow these procedures when you answer the questions.

Answer Easy Questions

Divide the examination period into three equal parts. During the first period, read all of the questions. Answer those that are easy and whose answers you know immediately. If you must stop to think over a response, go on to the next. Doing the easy ones first helps to settle you down. We all tend to be anxious and seeing the questions eliminates uncertainty about what to expect; and answering the easy ones gets us off to a secure start.

Answer Less Difficult Questions

During the second period, read all of the unanswered questions. If after a brief pause, you can supply an answer, mark it and go on. Follow your hunches now. Mark all of those you think you know. Leave the most difficult blank.

Answer Difficult Questions

During the third round you will have more time to spend answering the difficult questions. Take your time and choose the best or most likely answer. Answer all the questions this time.

COMPREHENSION: For each of the following statements and questions, select the option containing the most complete or most accurate answer.

1. In the opening paragraph, the author supports
(c) which of the following positions?
   - ☐ a. Society should keep a closer watch on ex-convicts.
   - ☐ b. Prisoners should not be denied their right to freedom and happiness.
   - ☐ c. In general, prisoners have a poor record of rehabilitation.
   - ☐ d. The judicial system is responsible for bitterness felt by ex-convicts.

2. The expression, "...like so many eyeless silos
(k) of despair," is an example of
   - ☐ a. a personification.
   - ☐ b. a simile.
   - ☐ c. a metaphor.
   - ☐ d. an alliteration.

3. The author is a firm believer that recidivism
(e) can be reduced if
   - ☐ a. ex-convicts cooperate with society.
   - ☐ b. society undergoes a change of attitude.
   - ☐ c. prison conditions are made less attractive.
   - ☐ d. society agrees to spend more money.

4. The author's attitude toward rehabilitation is
(g)
   - ☐ a. positive.
   - ☐ b. unrealistic.
   - ☐ c. negative.
   - ☐ d. dangerous.

5. Which of the following conclusions can be
(f) drawn from the selection?
   - ☐ a. Juvenile delinquents should not be given special treatment.
   - ☐ b. The American public is sensitive to the plight of ex-convicts.
   - ☐ c. Human nature is constant and will never change.
   - ☐ d. The free society must reconsider its attitudes toward prisms.

6. The criminal mind cannot undergo a basic
(h) transformation unless it
   - ☐ a. understands the folly of crime.
   - ☐ b. fears the possibility of punishment.
   - ☐ c. accepts psychiatric help.
   - ☐ d. accepts moral values.

7. The French philosopher Rousseau believed in
(f)
   - ☐ a. the perfectibility of man.
   - ☐ b. the need for frequent punishment.
   - ☐ c. the need for a strong government.
   - ☐ d. the inevitability of crime.

8. Rosseau's social and political philosophy was
(g)
   - ☐ a. popular.
   - ☐ b. archaic.
   - ☐ c. enlightened.
   - ☐ d. traditional.

9. The author would most probably agree with
(f) which of the following statements?
   - ☐ a. Impersonal crimes should not be punished by imprisonment.
   - ☐ b. Prison officials should be blamed for the high crime rate.
   - ☐ c. Prison guards should be good, well-trained men.
   - ☐ d. The opinions of Aristotle and Rousseau are a threat to public safety.

10. Justice and punishment should be
(h)
   - ☐ a. personal and final.
   - ☐ b. kept separate.
   - ☐ c. administered swiftly.
   - ☐ d. slow and deliberate.

Comprehension Skills: a—isolating details; b—recalling specific facts; c—retaining concepts; d—organizing facts; e—understanding the main idea; f—drawing a conclusion; g—making a judgment; h—making an inference; i—recognizing tone; j—understanding characters; k—appreciation of literary forms.

Dying, One Day at a Time, II

While Punishment Is the Right of Society, Rehabilitation Is the Responsibility of That Society

Robert Lionel

The earliest function of jails in Anglo-Saxon society, from which we derive most of our social institutions, was to safely keep accused persons to be sure they were on hand to stand trial when the King's traveling judges came around. This responsibility dates back to the 10th Century and it was several centuries later before jails also became places of punishment for petty offenders, vagrants and debtors.

It is natural that the colonists who came to America set up local jails to serve as British counterparts in the new country. Later, when Quaker humane influence turned the new country against the barbarous forms of corporal punishment that had been inflicted upon more serious offenders, imprisonment for long periods of time became the general practice and a new kind of institution called the penitentiary came into being. Customarily, these facilities have been administered by the states and, later, by the federal government.

The jails, keeping their time-honored functions of detaining accused persons and offenders serving short sentences, remained under local control. At the same time, probably because of their accessibility, they were used to deal with other kinds of problem people, including the insane, children who could not be controlled elsewhere, alcoholics, and men who would not support their families. In short, jails have tended to become convenient repositories for all kinds of misfits for whom society has not made more adequate provision.

Given the limitations of local financing, absence of essential programming, resources, and the impossibly diverse problems heaped upon them, it is little wonder that local jails have been in disrepute for their archaic methods of operation. Many harsh words have been directed toward the jails and the people who run them, but few systematic attempts have been made to correct the sources of their long-standing evils.

Today, there are new trends along the whole range of correctional thinking and practice which forecast the possibility of new and more constructive uses of local jails. These trends must be taken into account in planning new or remodeled local correctional facilities both for these reasons and for the added likelihood that other program developments and procedural changes may well have an effect on the number and kinds of our jail populations.

Rehabilitation: It Can Work

Theoretically, rehabilitation is a primary objective of imprisonment, but in practice it is subordinated to the intended deterrent effects of tight custody, regimentation, and a climate of repression. The "good prisoner" is one who seems subdued in that environment—a serious drawback to successful social adjustment after release. Prison systems range in quality from marginal acceptability in those of a few states and the federal government, down to the medieval level of some state and local systems. Facilities are severely overcrowded and are generally below acceptable physical standards; narcotics traffic and sexual abuses thrive.

The failure rate is very high: 63 percent of federal parolees released in 1963 were rearrested within six years, as were 76 percent of those given mandatory releases. Such information as is available indicates that experience with state prison releases is comparable. The appalling fact is that firm statistical data on recidivism is practically nonexistent at state and local levels. Only occasional spot studies have been made and coordination of records from the many state, local, and federal institutions has not been attempted.

Rehabilitative efforts vary, but few teachers, psychologists or psychiatrists are found on prison staffs. Many inmates have no work assignments; idleness is the chief prison occupation. Custodial restraints then breed resentment. The work that is available rarely fosters skills useful after discharge. Experience in producing license plates or mail bags has slight value on the outside labor market.

Every objective study of American prisons has called attention to the low qualifications of prison guards, and to their lack of intensive training. Both the nature of their work and compensation scales are unattractive. The usual disciplinary emphasis encourages brutalization, greatly worsened where guards collude in the drug traffic or overlook inmate violence extending to homosexual assaults. Lives of prisoners are endangered by racial violence and other forms of hostility. In many prisons, moreover, tensions between all-white staffs and prison populations dominated by militant blacks have reached explosive levels. Prisoners usually lack avenues of complaint and are denied access to legal counsel or other protections of due process; they are made to feel subhuman.

Before rehabilitation can be truly effective, a change must come about in the minds of men. Society must realize that building penal facilities is not the only answer. Not all criminals are locked up for life. They serve their sentence and are released. They come back into society more hardened than before. They have had time to think and plan their method by which they can "get even" with the society who put them behind bars.

Not until the offender can "believe in" the society of which he has never before been a part, can genuine rehabilitation work. But first, a "rehabilitation" in thinking must take place within the public at large.

It's Up to Us

We need action. We need a public which admits and understands that jail as punishment is not effective. The concept has failed; vengeance purely and simply dehumanizes both the convicted prisoners and society itself.

We need a public that is willing to accept some of the new ideas which correction authorities are talking about at this time. These are not the wild ideas of "do-gooders." They are the result of years of planning and consideration by concerned penologists, psychologists, and sociologists who have worked out new programs: Programs in which the convict leaves prison during the day to work and returns to prison at night; programs of regulated conjugal visits for long-term prisoners so the prisoner, once released, still has a family to go home to, (or don't we believe that families are stabilizing influences and that these men need as much stability as society can give them?) We need programs that include training for skilled jobs; after-care programs to get a released felon past that crucial first three months of freedom, something to bridge the gap between the closed society of prison and the sudden variety of choices confronting the "free" man; programs that pay for the jobs performed within prisons at a decent pay level so the convict, once released, is not obliged as the first order of business to stick up a store in order to get money to eat.

Law enforcement is everybody's business. Not only the police, but the "correctional" systems as well. The average law-abiding citizen is satisfied to confine the criminal in a maximum security prison far from the community, and this is exactly what we have been doing. It has not worked.

But rehabilitation *does* work. The establishment of halfway houses—places located within the community where ex-convicts can receive counseling and make a gradual re-entry into society—demonstrate that ex-convicts so maintained suffer a great deal less recidivism than those convicts released directly from prisons. Additionally, such laudable programs as The United States Jaycees "Project Re-Con," plus the establishment of in-prison Jaycee chapters, reduce the recidivistic rate tremendously. It has been demonstrated that convicts who become Jaycees while in prison have a return rate after release of only 15 to 20 percent!

The single major problem faced by rehabilitation is the apathy of the general citizenry. We just don't want to get involved. Even concerned social action groups, such as the Jaycees, find it difficult to enlist the wholehearted support of their membership. The groups will tackle willingly such immense problems as VD, drugs, and alcoholism, but they shy away frequently from active work in criminal rehabilitation programs. Similarly, Congress and state legislatures get very nervous when asked for additional sums to undertake sweeping programs of penal reform. However, thanks in a very sick way to such horrors as the Attica riot and the Arkansas prison scandals, hopes are higher now that legislative bodies are becoming more responsive to the conditions of the United States prison system, both on the federal and local level.

While punishment is the *right* of society, rehabilitation is the *responsibility* of that society. No nation can afford to waste the human potential inherent in millions of lives. Criminal rehabilitation is the one hope we have in reclaiming a majority of that potential. The stakes are too high to pull out of the game. The time is growing too short to look the other way. We, the citizens, must make a decision: Do we now practice what we preach—that man is noble and life sacred—or do we turn our backs and forever throw the keys of hope down the gutter of despair?

Starting Time: _____	Finishing Time: _____
Reading Time: _____	Reading Rate: _____
Comprehension: _____	Vocabulary: _____

VOCABULARY: The following words have been taken from the selection you have just read. Put an X in the box before the best meaning or synonym for the word as used in the selection.

1. **provision,** page 145, column 1, paragraph 3
"...jails have tended to become convenient repositories for all kinds of misfits for whom society has not made more adequate provision."
- ☐ a. plans
- ☐ b. supplies
- ☐ c. decisions
- ☐ d. reservations

2. **disrepute,** page 145, column 1, paragraph 4
"...it is little wonder that local jails have been in disrepute for their archaic methods of operation."
- ☐ a. dispute
- ☐ b. disregard
- ☐ c. disfavor
- ☐ d. disruption

3. **collude,** page 146, column 1, paragraph 1
"...where guards collude in the drug traffic or overlook inmate violence..."
- ☐ a. collide
- ☐ b. inspire
- ☐ c. conspire
- ☐ d. resist

4. **laudable,** page 146, column 2, paragraph 2
"...such laudable programs as The United States Jaycees 'Project Re-Con,'..."
- ☐ a. loud
- ☐ b. extraordinary
- ☐ c. discriminating
- ☐ d. praiseworthy

5. **apathy,** page 146, column 2, paragraph 3
"The single major problem faced by rehabilitation is the apathy of the general citizenry."
- ☐ a. interest
- ☐ b. indifference
- ☐ c. concern
- ☐ d. attitude

SYLLABICATION

Knowing how to reduce words to their syllables aids both reading and spelling. Frequently a long word can be recognized and understood if pronounced by syllables. And in spelling, of course, knowledge of syllables contributes to accuracy.

There are rules or generalizations which we can follow when dividing words. One such rule tells us that a suffix is usually regarded as a separate syllable. Thus the word **hunter** is divided into **hunt** and **er** because **er** is a suffix added to the base word **hunt**.

The following sentences contain similar words. Find them and write them on the lines to the right separating the base words from the suffixes with hyphens (-).

1. Arsonists burned the barn. _____

2. She's a patroness of the Arts. _____

3. The lioness hunts for food. _____

4. He's a Brooklynite. _____

5. The lecturer spoke well. _____

6. Isolationists favor the old policy. _____

7. Merriment prevailed. _____

8. It was a pointless talk. _____

9. Observers watched from a distance. _____

10. Endorse it to the payee. _____

11. He's an adventurer. _____

12. Advertisers pay for space. _____

13. Don't be an alarmist. _____

14. They sat on bleachers. _____

15. Fill the container. _____

16. Buy a basketful of fruit. _____

17. Signs of boredom appeared. _____

18. Hold the package up. _____

19. The man had an owlish look. _____

20. Avoid wordly goods. _____

21. The singer bowed. _____

TAKING ESSAY EXAMINATIONS

Following certain rules and using certain techniques when taking examinations can result in higher grades. Procedures which organize and improve your performance permit you to use your knowledge of the subject to best advantage.

Another type of examination is the essay or composition type. This requires the student to compose responses to several questions. Many students dislike this type, preferring objective-type questions. Yet knowing how to handle the written examination produces better results.

Outline Answers

Outline the answers to all questions before doing any writing. Confine your outline to main headings only. Include a subhead only if you feel you may forget it.

Balance Outlines

Look over all of your outlines. Some will be complete; others will be weak. Transfer some of the headings from the strong answers to the weak ones. This will give you confidence in answering because you will know something about all of them. The questions are all on the same subject so a little deliberation will indicate how you can transfer headings and make them applicable to the new questions.

Apportion Time

Divide your time proportionately. Base your time allotments on the credit value of the questions—spend more time on those that are worth more. If all of the questions are of equal value, devote equal time to each answer. This permits you to make your answers of generally similar length, concealing any weaknesses in your answers. A too-short answer signals the instructor that your knowledge on a certain question is lacking. Avoid giving such signals.

Write Legibly

Even if your answers must be shorter, take the time to make your handwriting clear and readable.

COMPREHENSION: For each of the following statements and questions, select the option containing the most complete or most accurate answer.

1. Most of our present-day social institutions are
(b) derived from

☐ a. Anglo-Saxon society.
☐ b. the Quaker philosophy.
☐ c. British institutions.
☐ d. the Dark Ages.

2. The development of prisons over the centuries
(c) has been

☐ a. humane.
☐ b. necessary and expensive.
☐ c. enlightened.
☐ d. gradual and expanding.

3. The selection is written in the form of
(k)
☐ a. a debate.
☐ b. a short story.
☐ c. a news report.
☐ d. an exposition.

4. The author concludes that jails presently con-
(f) tain a variety of misfits because

☐ a. society prefers easy solutions.
☐ b. crime is out of control.
☐ c. doctors are in short supply.
☐ d. society must be protected.

5. The reasons which help explain the state of
(g) penal institutions are

☐ a. oversimplified.
☐ b. complex.
☐ c. questionable.
☐ d. financial.

6. Modern trends in correctional thinking and
(f) practices may

☐ a. result in better rehabilitation.
☐ b. encourage the courts to be lenient.
☐ c. endanger the lives of citizens.
☐ d. bankrupt the American taxpayer.

7. The "good prisoner" is
(h)
☐ a. a rehabilitated prisoner.
☐ b. an innocent person.
☐ c. a disadvantaged person.
☐ d. a prison informer.

8. The average prison in the United States is
(g) oriented toward

☐ a. rehabilitation.
☐ b. occupational therapy.
☐ c. physical fitness.
☐ d. security and restraint.

9. American penal institutions
(e)
☐ a. require minor improvements.
☐ b. operate at maximum efficiency.
☐ c. reflect society's apathy.
☐ d. conform to basic standards.

10. If permanent criminal rehabilitation is to
(f) be achieved

☐ a. prisons must be built in isolated areas.
☐ b. freed prisoners must be financed publicly.
☐ c. society must be willing to take risks.
☐ d. religious groups must become involved.

Comprehension Skills: a—isolating details; b—recalling specific facts; c—retaining concepts; d—organizing facts; e—understanding the main idea; f—drawing a conclusion; g—making a judgment; h—making an inference; i—recognizing tone; j—understanding characters; k—appreciation of literary forms.

Textbooks and the Invisible Woman

Textbook Treatment of Women Reflects Cultural Ideas of Female Inferiority

Janice Law Trecker

Within the last half dozen years, there has been an increasing interest in women's history and women's studies on the college and university level. The resulting new scholarship and material have, however, barely penetrated the secondary level. Despite such promising developments as new supplementary texts on women's history, new resource and audio-visual materials and a growing concern about the quality of education for women and girls, the amount of women's history taught on the secondary level remains extremely small.

American history textbooks reflect a mythic rather than an historical view of women. Their basic assumption is that history is masculine, and their characteristic belief that society, culture, politics, art, science and economics are all male domains leads to the wholesale omission of women and to the distortion and minimization of those females who do appear. The clearest evidence for this viewpoint is the fact that 51 percent of the population is usually "covered" by about one page of text.

Of course, the typical textbook is not totally devoid of women's names. There are always a few women too important or too unique to be completely excluded. Harriet Beecher Stowe, Harriet Tubman, Sacajawea, Phillis Wheatley, Clara Barton, Dorothea Dix and Susan B. Anthony are among the small and exclusive circle of women who are found deserving of a sentence or two.

While there has been a recent noticeable shift to include some history of minorities, the pattern of excluding minority women is evident and what is presented is still a male-only view. Women like Sojourner Truth, the founders of Black educational institutions like Lucy Laney and Mary Bethune, and Fannie Lou Hamer, a founder of the Mississippi Freedom Democratic Party, are never included. Pocahantas is almost always noted (after all, she saved a white male), but the vital and complex role the Clan Mothers in the Hou-den-no-shaun-nee (People of the Longhouse), or as the French called it, the Iroquois Confederacy, is rarely mentioned. Gertrudis Bocanegra, "the Joan of Arc of Mexico," and Mariana Bracetti, the Puerto Rican leader in the El Grito de Lares revolutionary movement—

who usually is credited only for sewing its first flag—are invisible heroines in our texts marred by sexism and racism. Lola Rodriguez de Tió, the nineteenth-century feminist, and Juana Colon, the twentieth-century union organizer of women laborers, are but a few examples of the serious omissions that continue to scar our history textbooks.

Their presence, however, only points up the deficiencies in the overall conception of women's place in history. A few "great names" accompanied by a factual statement—without explanation or any analysis—would never qualify as a proper historical treatment for any but "women's issues."

Tokenism is the rule

Tokenism is the rule in the texts' treatment of women, because only females who distinguish themselves in a masculine hierarchy are considered bona fide historical characters. Women who act outside the normal male channels of power—or most of the significant women in America before the twentieth century—are automatically suspect. If they are controversial, they are simply ignored along with whatever cause they may have championed, as are women like Margaret Sanger, Emma Goldman, Ida B. Wells, Mother Jones, Alice Paul and Rosa Parks.

If, however, it appears to masculine sensibilities that a woman was simply eccentric, she is sure to be included. Providing comic relief is the function of at least half of all so-called women's history in these books. The need for a few light touches insures that hatchet-wielding Carrie Nation will be preferred to the brilliant and influential organizer Frances Willard in discussing temperance, and that the Gibson Girl and the Flapper will displace the social reformer or feminist in tracing the evolution of the modern woman. By and large, authors prefer to write sparkling discussions of skirt lengths and hair styles rather than to dig into such serious topics as the exploitation of female labor, the treatment of women in slavery, or women's role in mass education. A little wit, so conspicuously absent in the other 99 percent of the average school history, is seen as the best way to avoid sticky questions like women and sex mores, or the long and disgraceful history of organized religious opposition to women's rights and opportunities.

Yet nothing more clearly illustrates the paucity of research and information that typify these texts than discussions which take the upper class Victorian matron (or the Gibson Girl or the Flapper) as *the* American woman of her time. While a minority may have sipped tea and embroidered flowers, the majority of American women toiled on the nation's farms or in the textile plants. Immigrant women wore out their lives in domestic service or in sweatshop tenements; slave women worked like cattle to bring in the cotton, rice and indigo of the Old South. Chivalry, decorum and all the trappings of the familiar "pedestal" of the nineteenth-century lady were no part of their lives. But their history, touching as it does on the heart of the country's economic, social and cultural life, is omitted in favor of a few platitudes or silence.

The Housework Fallacy

Textbooks' treatment of women reflects cultural ideas of female inferiority as well as the notion that women's lives and interests are basically dependent upon those of some favored male. The implication is that women have never had any activities of interest or importance outside of traditional male preoccupations; within the male hierarchy, they have, of course, occupied mostly inferior positions.

There is a basic problem with this assumption: it is incorrect.

To illustrate this, let me select one area—some aspects of American economic history—and point out some of the facts, issues and events ignored by the current population of textbook authors.

If you were to ask students what most American women have done during our history, I suspect that the answer would be "housework." That would be correct, yet what we today consider housework bears little resemblance in either extent or importance to the multitude of tasks performed by the colonial and frontier housewife, and indeed by the rural woman well into the twentieth century. In the colonies, on the frontier and for the earlier part of the nineteenth century, most Americans lived on subsistence farms. Their families made almost everything they needed, and in the usual division of labor, the women of the family were responsible for the manifold manufacturing processes needed to turn all raw materials of the farm into useable goods. This included everything from turning raw flax into clothes, processing all foods (including making butter, cheese, sausages and preserving meats) to soap and

candle making. The kitchen garden and livestock were also their responsibility. When this work was added to the laborious routine of cleaning, washing and cooking, and to the burdens of maternity, nursing and general child care, it is easy to see women's economic importance. It is also easy to see why numbers of women were prepared to farm and homestead independently. According to historian Robert Smuts, probably the largest group of nineteenth-century female proprietors were women who claimed and worked their own land in the West.

The economic importance of the American woman was altered by the developments of the industrial revolution. The mechanization of home processes in the clothing industry, and later in baking, canning and cooking, led to the devaluation of a woman's labor. Housework was suddenly worthless, and women and their children followed "woman's work" out of the home and into the mills and factories.

Fragility and the 14-hour Day

There the "weak and fragile" creatures of Victorian sentiment were worked as long as 14 hours a day in cold, ill ventilated, unhealthy barns, foul with dust, fibers and chemicals. The old ideas of female inferiority now justified the lower wages of women operatives, with the result that they undercut men's wages, as their own were undermined by the pitiful salaries of the factory children. The availability of women and children for factory work was one of the important stimuli for industrialization in the East, and low wages and the long hours demanded of these operatives in effect subsidized the early industrial revolution in America.

The impact of the change in the locus of female labor, the conditions of the early industrial revolution, the rationale for employing female and child labor and the efforts of women as well as men to humanize the industrial system are all topics of real historical relevance. Yet if these changes receive as much as a paragraph, the author has been atypically generous.

Much of the widespread ignorance about the modern economic position of women may be traced to a similar disinterest in the later history of women in the labor force. Such changes as the rapid increase of women employed outside the home in the twentieth century, the mobilization of female labor during both world wars, and the beginnings of ideas about economic equality for women have had a vast impact on our economic structure. The history of women and work, including the trade union movement, and the social and cultural consequences of the American habit of using women as a pool of cheap expendable labor are certainly subjects properly in history texts and in materials prepared for social studies programs.

The economic aspect is not the only neglected facet of women's history. It is hard to get a complete picture of *any* topic in our history when half of the population is omitted from discussion. In addition to disregarding economic issues concerning women, the historical omissions and inaccuracies of the history textbooks usually encompass women's legal history; female contributions to art, science and culture; ideas and theories about women; the women's movement; and birth control and changing sexual standards. While serious from an historical point of view, these distortions and omissions have another, perhaps even more important, impact upon students' views of women. It is a striking illustration of assumptions of female inferiority when publishers, writers, teachers and parents accept materials that downgrade or ignore half or more of the consumers of text materials.

The treatment of American women in history texts is only one small facet in a pattern of sexism and racism. However, the history texts might make a real contribution to changing the image of American women and to improving the self image of female students. It is hard to see how one can accept the idea that women are weak and frivolous after learning about the suffrage movement, the role of women in the industrial revolution, the tasks of frontier women or the development of education for women of all races. It is very hard to see how women can be labeled "uncreative" and intellectually dependent after learning about the evolution of modern dance or of women's contributions to the performing and the visual arts. It is hard to imagine that students would uncritically accept the myths about women's intellectual capacities or personality after studying the pseudo-scientific theories marshalled to support them or the social, cultural and religious prejudices which sustained the inferiority of women. If demanding that the nation's textbooks stop purveying myths and stereotypes in place of history cannot, by itself, alter ideas about women, at least textbook changes could prevent the transmission of blatant sexism and racism to another generation of American young people.

Starting Time: _____		Finishing Time: _____	
Reading Time: _____		Reading Rate: _____	
Comprehension: _____		Vocabulary: _____	

VOCABULARY: The following words have been taken from the selection you have just read. Put an *X* in the box before the best meaning or synonym for the word as used in the selection.

1. **paucity,** page 151, column 1, paragraph 2
   "Yet nothing more clearly illustrates the paucity of research..."
   ☐ a. quality
   ☐ b. scarcity
   ☐ c. pattern
   ☐ d. dishonesty

2. **manifold,** page 151, column 1, paragraph 6
   "...the women of the family were responsible for the manifold manufacturing processes..."
   ☐ a. manifest
   ☐ b. simple
   ☐ c. complex
   ☐ d. numerous

3. **subsidized,** page 151, column 2, paragraph 3
   "...these operatives in effect subsidized the early industrial revolution..."
   ☐ a. made possible
   ☐ b. supplied
   ☐ c. substituted
   ☐ d. hindered

4. **marshalled,** page 152, column 2, paragraph 1
   "...the pseudoscientific theories marshalled to support them..."
   ☐ a. presented
   ☐ b. ushered
   ☐ c. scattered
   ☐ d. ordered

5. **purveying,** page 152, column 2, paragraph 1
   "...the nation's textbooks stop purveying myths and stereotypes..."
   ☐ a. surveying
   ☐ b. inventing
   ☐ c. demanding
   ☐ d. providing

TOPICS FOR THE RESTLESS

EXPECTANCY CLUES

The most important aids to word recognition and, therefore, fluency in reading are meaning clues. Good readers use these clues effectively and automatically. Meaning clues permit the reader to anticipate words before actually reading them.

Expectancy clues refer to the sorts of words and concepts one might expect to encounter in a given subject. For example, in a story about big city life, the reader should expect to meet words like *subway, traffic congestion, urban renewal, ghetto, high-rise apartments,* and so on. Anticipating these words enables the reader to move along the printed lines rapidly, with understanding.

The following words, except two, were all taken from a story about air pollution. Think first about the kinds of words you would find in such a story and then examine the words below. Underline the two words you would *not* expect to find in this story.

1. industrial	5. contaminate	9. particles
2. pollutants	6. carbon	10. furnace
3. smog	7. smoke	11. typewriter
4. haze	8. factories	12. asparagus

Which of the following phrases would you expect to read in a newspaper account of a courtroom trial? Put an *X* in the box before them.

☐ 1. counsel for the defense

☐ 2. testimony of witnesses

☐ 3. testifying under oath

☐ 4. cross examination

☐ 5. adhering to the surface

☐ 6. turned state's evidence

☐ 7. thirty pounds of pressure per tire

☐ 8. inadmissible as evidence

☐ 9. purchased on sale

☐ 10. pending in this case

☐ 11. foreman of the jury

☐ 12. fasten the ends together

☐ 13. approach the bench

☐ 14. penalty for perjury

☐ 15. refuse to incriminate

☐ 16. objections by the defense

☐ 17. minimum and maximum penalties

☐ 18. in a rocking chair

☐ 19. custody of the county

☐ 20. precedent for this action

SELECTION 28

READING THE NEWSPAPER, I

As a means of communication, the newspaper is unique—it overcomes all the disadvantages of radio and television. For example, newspaper coverage of an event is much more thorough and complete. It is also permanent—we can refer to last week's news. The newspaper is portable, it is everywhere, and it is cheap. Also the newspaper offers the reader the widest choice of news; there is something for everyone: world and national events, local happenings, sports news, women's page, classified ads, and so on. Finally, the newspaper is current; it comes out each day with a new edition. No wonder everyone reads the newspaper.

Lead Paragraph

The lead paragraph is intended to give the main points of the article; it contains the five *w's* of news reporting: *who, what, where, when,* and *why*. The reporter's task is to give the reader the essentials of the story in one or two well-constructed sentences. Ideally, the reader should be able to get a capsule version of the story from the lead paragraph.

Here are the different kinds of lead paragraphs you can expect to find in a daily newspaper.

Digest Lead

This is the most popular one; it is used for most news reporting. In a Digest Lead, the important facts of the story are clearly and plainly summarized for the reader.

Personal Appeal Lead

This opening paragraph speaks directly to the reader; frequently it asks a question. The personal approach is designed to arouse the reader's interest —give him a personal reason for reading the article.

Circumstantial Lead

This opening paragraph describes the circumstances under which an event occurred. It sets the stage for the reader, gives him the background he needs.

COMPREHENSION: For each of the following statements and questions, select the option containing the most complete or most accurate answer.

1. The position women occupy in society is
(e) clearly related to
  - ☐ a. the level of education they achieve as a group.
  - ☐ b. the decisions handed down by the Supreme Court.
  - ☐ c. the role they have played in history.
  - ☐ d. the treatment given them in textbooks.

2. The statement, "Harriet Beecher Stowe, Har-
(i) riet Tubman...are among the small and exclusive circle of women who are found deserving of a sentence or two," is
  - ☐ a. sarcastic.
  - ☐ b. humorous.
  - ☐ c. inflammatory.
  - ☐ d. pious.

3. To the general public, the contributions of
(g) the women listed in the selection
  - ☐ a. do not ring true.
  - ☐ b. have always been known.
  - ☐ c. confirm its suspicions.
  - ☐ d. come as a surprise.

4. Traditionally, American history textbooks
(b) have reflected
  - ☐ a. a cultural historical view of women.
  - ☐ b. an accurate view of women.
  - ☐ c. a mythic historical view of women.
  - ☐ d. a revolutionary view of women.

5. Those women who have earned a legitimate
(c) place in history have had
  - ☐ a. to lower their standards.
  - ☐ b. to meet masculine standards.
  - ☐ c. to champion controversial causes.
  - ☐ d. to provide comic relief.

6. In their treatment of women, historians have
(f) preferred for the most part
  - ☐ a. to ignore them completely.
  - ☐ b. to stress detail rather than substance.
  - ☐ c. to insist on their religious contributions.
  - ☐ d. to defend their right to be heard.

7. Considering the subhuman existence of the
(g) majority of women in early America, it is understandable that
  - ☐ a. the male establishment found it expedient to ignore them.
  - ☐ b. they were not allowed the right to vote.
  - ☐ c. they were not considered ready for secondary education.
  - ☐ d. they worked hard for social justice.

8. The developments of the industrial revolution
(c)
  - ☐ a. liberated women from their homes.
  - ☐ b. made women financially independent.
  - ☐ c. changed the form of female subjugation.
  - ☐ d. contributed to equalizing the sexes.

9. Which of the following can exert positive in-
(h) fluence toward changing the image of women in printed materials?
  - ☐ a. politicians
  - ☐ b. publishers
  - ☐ c. writers
  - ☐ d. the general public

10. The traditional ideas concerning women are
(g)
  - ☐ a. difficult to disprove.
  - ☐ b. accepted by women in general.
  - ☐ c. substantiated by historical events.
  - ☐ d. disproved by observable facts.

Comprehension Skills: a—isolating details; b—recalling specific facts; c—retaining concepts; d—organizing facts; e—understanding the main idea; f—drawing a conclusion; g—making a judgment; h—making an inference; i—recognizing tone; j—understanding characters; k—appreciation of literary forms.

The Assault on Privacy

The Rise, Fall, and Resurrection of the National Data Center

Arthur R. Miller

The federal government long has been the nation's primary user of data-processing equipment; in fact, it was a government agency—the Bureau of the Census—that purchased the first commercially available computer following the Second World War. Reliance on electronic data-processing is a natural response to the proliferation of citizen reports and governmental information activities that are the by-products of today's pervasive federal involvements. The social security and income tax programs alone produce more than six hundred million annual reports. In addition, statistics are becoming increasingly crucial as a foundation for the social and economic research, policy-making, and environmental planning that go into the administration of federal programs. In these contexts, the computer's ability to manipulate huge bodies of detailed information concerning a large number of potentially relevant variables that may pertain to events occurring over long periods of time permits the testing of hypotheses in ways that have never been feasible. Without modern electronics, planners might wander aimlessly in the federal government's paperwork jungle.

But even with the computer, the government's information activities seem to lack coherence and direction. All too often the gathering of reports and compilation of statistics only beget additional gathering of reports and compilation of statistics. Viewed from the outside, the over-all effect appears to be an unrelenting flow of data that is generated and consumed by some diabolical Sorcerer's Apprentice. Nonetheless, the experts tell us that even the federal government's vast information activities and technological resources are no match for the data gathering and processing tasks that must precede rational decision making.

Perhaps part of the reason is that as federal agency functions currently are arranged, only one government organization, the Census Bureau, has the collection and analysis of statistics as its principal goal. The other agencies generate statistics only incidentally to their operations, and occasionally have failed to preserve data that might prove valuable to numerous other governmental or private organizations. Furthermore, really effective inter-agency utilization of information is prevented because some agencies, such as the National Aeronautics and Space Administration and the Atomic Energy Commission, operate under stringent confidentiality requirements that preclude the general release or exchange of data. But because of the existing decentralized character of federal records, even collections of data that are intended to be open to the public frequently are almost impossible to locate, are arranged inconveniently for access and analytical purposes, or are difficult to compare or correlate with other information because of differences in agency information handling procedures. With the possible exception of the Committee on Scientific and Technical Information (COSATI) of the Federal Council of Science and Technology, there is no government organization that can provide a reference guide to the kinds and the location of information being collected at the national level.

These deficiencies in the federal government's information practices have several deleterious side-effects. First, the effort and time wasted in locating data and transposing them into a form that is functional for second and subsequent users reduces the over-all efficiency of governmental operations and increases their cost. Second, duplication in the information collected often means an unnecessarily high and repetitious reporting burden on private individuals and institutions. Third, large quantities of useful data never see the light of day and thus do not reach many of the users who might profit by the ready availability of the federal government's vast storehouse of information, much of which relates to a variety of important contemporary issues such as consumer and environmental protection.

All things considered, therefore, it was eminently logical for the Bureau of the Budget (absorbed in 1970 by the Office of Management and Budget) in the mid-1960s to attempt to take a step toward reforming the federal government's information activities by proposing the creation of a single federal statistical center—called the National Data Center. The effect of the Bureau's plan would have been to relieve the operating agencies of many data processing burdens and to centralize the

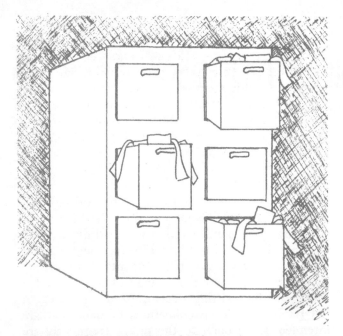

existing diffused bodies of information. Advocates of the center thought it would: 1) make more data available for researchers, both inside and outside the government; 2) reduce the unit cost of data; 3) enable larger and more effective samples to be taken; 4) facilitate the canvassing of wider ranges of variables; 5) reduce duplication in the government's data collection activities; 6) promote greater standardization of techniques among the agencies; 7) make research efforts easier to verify; and 8) provide a data processing pool for all the information handling agencies.

From the perspective of individual privacy, the original proposal seemed harmless enough; all that was being suggested was the creation of a *statistical* center that would compile and process information from governmental files on an aggregate basis. The possibility that an individualized intelligence or surveillance center was in the offing was ridiculed by the center's proponents. But the proposal had touched a raw nerve. Questions were raised concerning whether the dichotomy between statistical and intelligence work was tenable in the context of computerized data. Moreover, little in the way of privacy guarantees and protections was offered by the center's sponsors. Advocates of the center offered only a few platitudinous remarks about "appropriate" hardware and software controls, but they never provided details to allay the apprehensions of the questioners.

Not surprisingly, the National Data Center proposal became a lightning rod for the vague feelings of discontent generated by the computer revolution. Members of Congress, then newspapers and magazines, and finally several legal periodicals took turns castigating the idea, often in emotive or highly symbolic terms. To a degree, the clamor

was justifiable. The original proposals were incredibly myopic in their obsession with efficiency. None of the three reports recommending establishment of a central data bank gave the problem of privacy more than token attention. They focused almost exclusively on procuring "maximum information" and organizing to insure "maximum legitimate accessibility, for both governmental agencies and other users." In addition, despite early protestations to the contrary, proponents of the data center admitted that individual identification would have to be linked to some of the data in the center—an admission that immediately raised serious doubts about the level of protection that would be given to privacy. One of the chief advocates of the center subsequently conceded that the failure of his cohorts to come to grips with the privacy question was "a gigantic oversight."

Nonetheless, that failure does not necessarily represent a disregard of human values or indicate bureaucratic bad faith as some have suggested. The original Bureau of the Budget proposal was limited in scope. Putting to one side the long-range possibility of the center's expanding and individualizing its files, reasonable people might well view its threat to individual privacy as a relatively remote one. As a pragmatic matter, detailed consideration of the privacy question at the time the first proposals were advanced might have been premature. Until the contours of the center and its activities were more sharply delineated, the nature of the threat to privacy would remain obscure, making it difficult to formulate precise proposals for protection. But even when the situation is viewed most charitably, it still is shocking that high ranking government officials and prominent behavioral scientists were so preoccupied with the quantity of information and the data processing capabilities the center would put at their disposal, that they were virtually insensitive to the privacy question.

Ironically, it became clear in the course of the congressional debate that the existing decentralized nature of the federal reporting system, which the statisticians and social scientists derisively characterized as inefficient, actually serves as a safeguard against the compilation of extensive government dossiers on every citizen. And, although proponents of the data center properly pointed to the excellent record of protecting sensitive information compiled by some federal agencies, most notably the Census Bureau, the dialogue also revealed that several other agencies and bureaus had a less exemplary history in the privacy arena. To make matters worse, it became apparent that the information that ultimately would find its way into the proposed data bank would be "orders of magnitude more sensitive than those now at the Bureau of the Census," which meant that any failure of security was likely to be "many times more destructive to an individual."

Chastened by the public outcry, the statisticians and administrators retreated to reconsider their proposal and to investigate more carefully the safeguards necessary to render a National Data Center more palatable to Congress and the public. Subsequently, the House Committee on Government Operations recommended that "no work be done to establish the national data bank until privacy protection is explored fully and guaranteed to the greatest extent possible to the citizens whose personal records would form its information base." Taking the public statements emanating from both the Executive Branch and the Congress at face value, it seems safe to conclude that there currently is no "fully developed plan for a National Data Center."

The apparent victory against the National Data Center by the defenders of privacy is largely a Pyrrhic one, however. Information collected for statistical purposes, which was the focal point of the Bureau's proposal and bore the brunt of the outcry, comprises only about one-fifth to one-third of the reports and questionnaires pertaining to citizens generated by the government. Moreover, statistical studies generally do not contain sensitive data of the type that is attractive to snoopers and are somewhat easier to protect against intrusion than investigative or surveillance files, although the claimed distinction between the two types of systems certainly will become less valid with the passage of time. As a result, the public debate over the National Data Center never really reached the question of preserving the integrity of the bulk of sensitive data gathered by the government or the fundamental policy issue of how to curtail the government's increasing penchant for information collection.

Starting Time: _____	Finishing Time: _____
Reading Time: _____	Reading Rate: _____
Comprehension: _____	Vocabulary: _____

VOCABULARY: The following words have been taken from the selection you have just read. Put an *X* in the box before the best meaning or synonym for the word as used in the selection.

1. feasible, page 155, column 1, paragraph 1
"...permits the testing of hypotheses in ways that have never been feasible."
  □ a. enforceable
  □ b. impractical
  □ c. probable
  □ d. possible

2. stringent, page 155, column 2, paragraph 1
"...operate under stringent confidentiality requirements that preclude the general release or exchange of data."
  □ a. strict
  □ b. flexible
  □ c. urgent
  □ d. structured

3. deleterious, page 155, column 2, paragraph 2
"These deficiencies in the federal government's information practices have several deleterious side-effects."
  □ a. harmful
  □ b. delirious
  □ c. beneficial
  □ d. unhealthy

4. eminently, page 155, column 2, paragraph 3
"All things considered, therefore, it was eminently logical for the Bureau of the Budget..."
  □ a. famously
  □ b. unknowingly
  □ c. highly
  □ d. imminently

5. emanating, page 157, column 1, paragraph 2
"Taking the public statements emanating from both the Executive Branch and the Congress..."
  □ a. being covered up
  □ b. eliminating
  □ c. being leaked
  □ d. coming

CONTEXTUAL AIDS: CAUSE AND EFFECT

Studies of good readers show that they are aware of the context of what they are reading. This means that they are anticipating what is coming next by what has gone before.

The many ways in which context functions to help the reader recognize words are called contextual aids.

Contextual Aid. Words can be understood through a cause and effect relationship between the unknown word and other words in the sentence. The reader's understanding of the cause-effect pattern offers a clue to the meaning of the unknown word. In the sentence, **Because of the heavy traffic, he arrived _____**, the reader who understands the effects of traffic congestion surmises that the missing word is **late**.

In the following sentences similar cause and effect patterns have been employed to help you determine the meaning of nonsense words. Underline the nonsense word and write the correct word on the line following each sentence.

1. Don't stay out in the sun too long; you'll suffer heat drelt.

   _____

2. Along the Mississippi the rainy season brings grumping.

   _____

3. The speaker who spoke for over an hour only succeeded in nexing his listeners.

   _____

4. Drive carefully on ice or you'll drien.

   _____

5. He filled the balloon too full of air and it krelsched.

   _____

6. At the high altitude his pen leaked and got lemp all over his shirt.

   _____

7. He had never handled a rifle before and he sud himself.

   _____

8. Because he was late five days in a row, he was blebbed from his job.

   _____

9. The pollutants in the lake caused many fish to len.

   _____

10. When the electricity failed, all the meat in the freezer bloomed.

    _____

READING THE NEWSPAPER, II

In our discussion of the newspaper, we have pointed out the many advantages it enjoys over other news media. We saw too how special paragraphs are used in news reporting (containing the *who, what, where, when,* and *why*) to lead the reader into the article. The first three types of these lead paragraphs were called the Digest, Personal Appeal, and Circumstantial. Here are the others.

Quotation Lead

As you would expect this opening paragraph uses a direct quote, normally from someone well known to the reader, to start off the story. The statement often expresses one of the key points of the article.

Interest Lead

This type of lead paragraph is designed to tease or arouse the reader's interest. Bits and pieces of information are used as "bait" to leave the reader's curiosity aroused but not satisfied.

Tabulated Lead

This is the other popular lead paragraph used in news reporting. In this opening paragraph, the reader is given the facts sequentially; the order of occurrence of major events is reported to the reader. Presumably this article presents news of interest to most readers and this type of lead brings them quickly up to date on events which have occurred.

Stunt Lead

This type of opening paragraph is used for novelty or feature news. Some unusual event is reported first to surprise, astonish, or startle the reader, thus gaining his interest and attention.

In most news stories, the rest of the article reports the events or occurrences in the order of their importance, gradually expanding the coverage and giving more details. The most important facts are given first, followed by those of lesser importance, and ending with facts of least importance to the reader.

COMPREHENSION: For each of the following statements and questions, select the option containing the most complete or most accurate answer.

1. The federal government has come to rely on
(c) electronic data processing because it

☐ a. has an abundance of trained specialists.
☐ b. requires easily retrievable information.
☐ c. encourages research in this area.
☐ d. has important foreign commitments.

2. Government planners
(g)
☐ a. perform a questionable service.
☐ b. could not function without computers.
☐ c. operate with a skeletal staff.
☐ d. are controlled by electronic machines.

3. The government's computers
(c)
☐ a. cannot keep up with demand.
☐ b. require better trained technicians.
☐ c. operate at reduced efficiency.
☐ d. produce order from chaos.

4. Which of the following is a fair criticism of
(f) the data processing system?

☐ a. It does not enjoy public support.
☐ b. The electronic equipment is dated.
☐ c. The system is too expensive to operate.
☐ d. It seems to encourage a useless duplication of effort.

5. The planners of the National Data Center
(c) wanted it to be

☐ a. a clearing house of information.
☐ b. an expensive research center.
☐ c. a center for the training of computer operators.
☐ d. privately operated information center.

6. It is feared that the National Data Center
(e) could pose a serious threat to

☐ a. the balance of payments.
☐ b. international stability.
☐ c. individual income.
☐ d. personal privacy.

7. The opposition to the National Data Center
(b) was focused on

☐ a. cost.
☐ b. efficiency.
☐ c. privacy.
☐ d. personnel.

8. A system similar to the National Data Center
(g)
☐ a. would be impossible to organize and staff efficiently.
☐ b. could be a dangerous weapon in the hands of the wrong people.
☐ c. must depend entirely on the support of private funds.
☐ d. would weaken the executive branch of government.

9. The author's treatment of the issues raised
(k) in this selection is

☐ a. biased.
☐ b. confusing.
☐ c. balanced.
☐ d. superficial.

10. The victory against the National Data Center is
(h)
☐ a. temporary.
☐ b. final.
☐ c. useless.
☐ d. academic.

Comprehension Skills: a—isolating details; b—recalling specific facts; c—retaining concepts; d—organizing facts; e—understanding the main idea; f—drawing a conclusion; g—making a judgment; h—making an inference; i—recognizing tone; j—understanding characters; k—appreciation of literary forms.

Delinquency

Frequently, Delinquency Is Determined by the Acceptance—or Lack of Acceptance—of Certain Behavior

Today

Today, as in the past, juvenile delinquency rates are highest in the cities, lower in the suburbs, and lowest of all in the rural areas—at least as far as official police cases are concerned.

Regardless of which particular ethnic or racial group happens to be living there at any given time, big city slums disproportionately produce the largest number of juvenile and youthful offenders. In short, *where* he lives is usually far more crucial than whether a youth comes from a broken home, or whether his family is poor or socially deprived.

Over the years, delinquency in all communities appears to have shown a dramatic rise. In part, this rise is the result of better statistical reporting systems. In part, it also stems from increases in the number and proportion of the national population under 18 years of age.

Significantly, however, the increase in arrests of juveniles has outstripped the growth in the general child population, aged 10 through 17. Additionally, the rapid expansion of metropolitan areas almost certainly will continue to contribute to the growing rate of delinquency.

At present, it is predicted that one out of every six boys will end up in court for other than a traffic offense sometime before his 18th birthday, the upper limit of most juvenile court jurisdictions. When boys and girls are considered together, the ratio is likely to be one in nine.

Boys are most often sent to juvenile court for committing larceny, burglary, and motor vehicle theft. But a significant number are referred for truancy, ungovernable behavior, and similar offenses which would not be considered criminal acts if committed by adults. Girls are most often sent to juvenile court for running away, ungovernability, larceny, and sex offenses.

Various studies indicate that the actual rate of delinquency is much greater than that suggested by the reported figures. It is estimated that upwards of 90 percent of all youth commit acts for which they might be brought to court if apprehended.

Even among those who are apprehended, many may not be brought to court but may be dealt with by other means. Often, such youngsters are referred to a public or private social agency when such resources are available. Often, too, their cases are adjusted informally—after their parents have been notified—by the police or by the school.

The fact remains, then, that it is often only in the poorest residential areas, with the fewest social welfare resources, that the police are forced to send children to the court because no other realistic alternatives are available.

Thus, when the official enforcement pattern is examined, it becomes clear that slum-dwelling adolescents are more likely to be charged and adjudicated than are youth from more prosperous neighborhoods. They are also more frequently committed to large, overcrowded public institutions, and less often referred to mental health clinics, placed on probation, or otherwise provided with the best of contemporary correctional care.

Public Attitudes Toward Delinquency

Perspectives about delinquency are constantly shifting as new ideas and facts gradually replace older ones. But one thing seems clear: as the volume of delinquency increases, so does public concern about the problem.

Since the 1930s, many of the principles for dealing with the emotionally disturbed have been gradually adapted for use in programs designed to rehabilitate delinquent youth.

Thus, today, it is quite common to have psychiatrists, psychologists, and social caseworkers staffing such agencies as large city juvenile courts and residential treatment centers. In fact, these professionals have become identified as those best suited to do the job required—that is, diagnosing and treating the problems of individual delinquents.

Immediately prior to World War II, the delinquency field was greatly influenced by the writings and work of psychiatrists, psychologists, and social caseworkers. Since the 1950s, the field has been increasingly influenced by social scientists and social workers in community organizations.

The earlier researchers and practitioners focused on the individual delinquent and his family and stressed the need for changes in personal attitudes, values, and emotional adjustment. The more recent investigators and specialists emphasize the broader environmental aspects affecting delinquency and advocate changes in education, employment, and in various other social, political, and economic conditions prevailing in slum neighborhoods.

Today, the great challenge in the field is to merge these two viewpoints so that programs aimed at preventing and controlling delinquency can relate *both* to the individual and to his environment.

Juvenile Justice System

The juvenile justice system in recent years has also come under close scrutiny.

Increasingly, it is charged that the enforcement of the law works more hardships on some categories of juveniles than on others. Critics contend "there is one law for the poor, another for the rich."

These charges are not without merit.

Numerous studies have shown there *is* differential handling of youthful offenders, based on neighborhood and economic circumstances.

As previously noted, ghetto youth, primarily members of minority groups, are more likely to be involved in the juvenile justice system—from being charged by the police, to being processed and adjudicated by the courts. In contrast, youth from advantaged neighborhoods are more likely to be handled informally by the police, and thereby escape the stigma of being officially labeled delinquent.

Thus, for some youth, the juvenile courts have become a kind of dumping ground.

The Juvenile Courts

No single institution in the juvenile justice system in recent years has undergone as much change as the juvenile court.

Historically, the juvenile court has differed in both philosophy and jurisdiction from the adult criminal court. Unlike the adversary proceedings in adult courts, juvenile court hearings are based on procedural informality.

Traditionally, a major goal of the juvenile court has been to protect and rehabilitate problem youth. Within this context, its mandate extends beyond delinquency to include neglect and dependency cases.

But studies, such as those conducted by the President's Commission on Law Enforcement and Administration of Justice, have concluded that the juvenile courts have often fallen short of this goal.

In part, this failure stems from the fact that the juvenile courts frequently do not have available to them the necessary resources to handle their caseloads.

While the disposition of juvenile court cases supposedly relies on such considerations as a thorough investigation of a youth's background, the fact is many courts lack enough probation officers, psychiatrists, and other personnel to effectively carry out these functions. Even the personnel who are available, including many juvenile court judges themselves, often do not have the necessary experience and training. Recent surveys have shown, for example, that half of all juvenile court judges had no undergraduate degree, a fifth had not attended college, and another fifth had no law degree.

Still another problem faced by juvenile courts is the shortage of effective dispositional alternatives. Lacking sufficient probation services and community treatment centers, judges too often must commit youth to large, overcrowded residential correctional facilities.

And finally, questions have been raised about what many consider to be the failure of the juvenile courts to safeguard the rights of youth.

Denials of such basic rights as confrontation, cross-examination, representation by counsel, and notice of charges—denials which have traditionally characterized juvenile court proceedings—have resulted in a series of United States Supreme Court decisions which are producing the most significant changes in the juvenile court system since its establishment in the late 1890s.

Beyond this, legal experts and others are recommending the narrowing of the jurisdictional range of the juvenile court to include only the more serious cases. Those who advocate such change argue that the juvenile court should be used only as a last resort and that cases of a less serious nature be handled by non-judicial community agencies.

Coping with Delinquency Today

The gap between what *is* being done and what *might* be done to curb delinquency and youth crime is complicated today by new types of delinquent behavior which began to emerge during the mid- and late-1960s.

Ghetto riots of massive proportions have erupted in city after city. To a very considerable extent, the participants have been young male ghetto residents who were *not* among the most poorly educated or grossly unemployed in their neighborhoods.

Campus disturbances have also precipitated crises —some sustained and some transitory. Such outbreaks have involved not only blacks and other minority group students, but also whites, many of whom were *not* poor or culturally deprived.

In the wake of these new phenomena has come a public outcry for what is popularly called a "hard line" with its insistence that order be restored, limits be set, and sanctions be imposed.

The demand for increased police protection for ghetto areas and other parts of the inner-city, and for harsher penalties for muggers, drug addicts, and drug peddlers—as well as other law offenders—is well known to recent observers of urban life.

Although in many cities the offenders involved are Negroes, Puerto Ricans, or members of other minority groups, the issue is not drawn strictly along racial lines. Both black and white spokesmen urge rigorous law enforcement on the streets of their communities, regardless of whether the offenders involved are white, black, or brown.

A similar position is taken by many about campus disturbances—including parents, state legislators, university trustees, administrators, faculty members, and some students themselves.

But the demand for firm law enforcement is not universal. There is support and sympathy, among many blacks and whites alike, for the actions and goals of ghetto rioters and campus militants.

Still others suggest that those responsible for ghetto and campus disorders need psychiatric care and treatment.

In almost classic fashion, the newest forms of youthful waywardness are being greeted by the same reactions as were the older forms of deviancy. Thus, the controversy between the "punishment" and the "treatment" schools of thought in handling crime problems appears to be a permanent fixture of public debate in the delinquency field.

Starting Time:	_____	Finishing Time:	_____
Reading Time:	_____	Reading Rate:	_____
Comprehension:	_____	Vocabulary:	_____

VOCABULARY: The following words have been taken from the selection you have just read. Put an *X* in the box before the best meaning or synonym for the word as used in the selection.

1. **apprehended**, page 160, column 1, paragraph 7
"...commit acts for which they might be brought to court if apprehended."
☐ a. understood
☐ b. anticipated
☐ c. arrested
☐ d. comprehended

2. **adjudicated**, page 160, column 2, paragraph 3
"...slum-dwelling adolescents are more likely to be charged and adjudicated..."
☐ a. judged
☐ b. arrested
☐ c. jailed
☐ d. adjourned

3. **prevailing**, page 161, column 1, paragraph 1
"...social, political, and economic conditions prevailing in slum neighborhoods."
☐ a. effective
☐ b. predominant
☐ c. rare
☐ d. preventative

4. **stigma**, page 161, column 1, paragraph 7
"...escape the stigma of being officially labeled delinquent."
☐ a. danger
☐ b. distinction
☐ c. disgrace
☐ d. stickler

5. **mandate**, page 161, column 1, paragraph 11
"...its mandate extends beyond delinquency to include neglect and dependency cases."
☐ a. commission
☐ b. appeal
☐ c. mandarin
☐ d. authority

CONTEXTUAL AIDS: ASSOCIATION

Studies of good readers show that they are aware of the context of what they are reading. This means that they are anticipating what is coming next by what has gone before.

The many ways in which context functions to help the reader recognize words are called contextual aids.

Contextual Aid 8. Certain words bring associations to the mind of the reader, which in turn serve as an aid in recognizing an unfamiliar word. In the example, **The symphony was _____ for the first time by the orchestra,** the reader can guess that the missing word is **played** because this is what we associate with **symphony** and **orchestra.**

In the following sentences association clues have been provided to help you interpret nonsense words. Underline the nonsense word and write the correct word on the line following each sentence.

1. He closed the door, buckled his seat belt, and dramed off.

   _____

2. The children smiled and posed while I took their dralpoor.

   _____

3. For breakfast she cooked ham and werts and made coffee.

   _____

4. He lifted the dobberham and dialed the number of the office.

   _____

5. Because his eyesight was poor, he wore strumgers.

   _____

6. Taking his umbrella, he walked out in the tamp.

   _____

7. The dealer shuffled and dealt the blurbs.

   _____

8. Opening the letter, he mirued it carefully.

   _____

9. Dropping off one fare, the lap picked up another.

   _____

10. When the bell rang, the students filed into drall.

   _____

11. Wear your gloves and scarf; it's mord outside.

   _____

12. The room was dark until a wesp was turned on.

   _____

PARAGRAPHS OF CONCLUSION

We have been discussing the different ways which authors use paragraphs in presenting their subject and how the wise reader profits from recognizing these functions.

The function of the closing paragraph is obvious—to give the reader the author's concluding remarks or final words on the subject. The author may do this in one of several ways.

First, although this is quire rare, he may draw a conclusion based on the information contained in the lesson or chapter. Authors are reluctant to do this because conclusions based on an entire chapter are much too important to be mentioned just once at the end. We can expect to find the conclusion given early in the chapter and the facts supporting it to follow. It is likely, though, that such an important conclusion would be repeated or restated in the final paragraph.

Second, the author may use his final paragraph to summarize. Here is his opportunity to give the reader the points made during his presentation for one last time. In effect the author is saying, "Above all, remember this. This is what it's all been about." These summarizing remarks are most valuable to the learner and a definite aid in reviewing.

Last, the author may choose to leave his readers with one final thought —the central, all-inclusive idea around which the chapter was developed.

You recall that when we were discussing the paragraph of introduction, we mentioned that in a sense the writer is like a speaker—he uses some of the same techniques in addressing his audience. Occasionally you'll find an anecdote, story, or moral used at the end as a cap to the discussion.

This is the author's last chance to reach his audience. If he wants to leave his readers one last thought, here is where it'll be.

COMPREHENSION: For each of the following statements and questions, select the option containing the most complete or most accurate answer.

1. The high incidence of juvenile delinquency is
(c) related directly to
   - ☐ a. ethnic background.
   - ☐ b. racial group.
   - ☐ c. environment.
   - ☐ d. financial status.

2. The single most significant trend which will
(e) contribute to increased juvenile delinquency is the
   - ☐ a. rapid expansion of metropolitan areas.
   - ☐ b. growth in the general child population.
   - ☐ c. increased arrests of juveniles.
   - ☐ d. better statistical reporting systems.

3. The number of offenses committed by boys
(h) as opposed to the number of offenses committed by girls is
   - ☐ a. significantly lower.
   - ☐ b. substantially the same.
   - ☐ c. presently unknown.
   - ☐ d. significantly greater.

4. The author concludes that slum-dwelling de-
(f) linquents are more likely to be tried in court than delinquents of better neighborhoods because
   - ☐ a. wealthy parents can settle their problems out of court.
   - ☐ b. society has given up on these adolescents.
   - ☐ c. courts follow a double standard system.
   - ☐ d. better neighborhoods have other alternatives for their youthful offenders.

5. Public concern about the rising volume of
(g) juvenile delinquency has influenced the creation of attitudes and programs which
   - ☐ a. condemn violence.
   - ☐ b. encourage delinquency.
   - ☐ c. stress rehabilitation.
   - ☐ d. emphasize correction.

6. Research seems to indicate that a proportion
(h) of today's delinquents
   - ☐ a. resent those who offer help.
   - ☐ b. suffer from emotional problems.
   - ☐ c. should be kept in detention.
   - ☐ d. are beyond help.

7. The thinking of earlier researchers and prac-
(g) titioners is to the thinking of more recent investigators as
   - ☐ a. progressive is to radical.
   - ☐ b. narrow is to broad.
   - ☐ c. enlightened is to traditional.
   - ☐ d. good is to bad.

8. The author's opinion of the juvenile justice
(h) system is
   - ☐ a. complimentary.
   - ☐ b. encouraging.
   - ☐ c. unfair.
   - ☐ d. critical.

9. The results of the recent surveys made con-
(g) cerning the qualifications of juvenile court judges are
   - ☐ a. shocking.
   - ☐ b. encouraging.
   - ☐ c. normal.
   - ☐ d. surprising.

10. The author concludes by saying that so-
(h) cial attitudes
   - ☐ a. remain basically the same.
   - ☐ b. encourage youthful waywardness.
   - ☐ c. should be made public.
   - ☐ d. favor enlightened rehabilitation.

Comprehension Skills: a—isolating details; b—recalling specific facts; c—retaining concepts; d—organizing facts; e—understanding the main idea; f—drawing a conclusion; g—making a judgment; h—making an inference; i—recognizing tone; j—understanding characters; k—appreciation of literary forms.

Answer
Key

Topics for the Restless

ACKNOWLEDGMENTS

"Are You Really Ready for the Highways." Reprinted from the *Marathon World*, published by the Marathon Oil Company.

"The 1972 World Chess Tournament." Reprinted from *Mankind* magazine, Volume III, Number XI.

"Toward Understanding." Reprinted from the *Marathon World*, published by the Marathon Oil Company.

"The New York Subway System" by John Palcewski. Reprinted from *Olin Magazine*, Olin Corporation.

"The Duck Man of Venice." Reprinted with the permission of the author and from *The National Humane Review*, copyright 1972, The American Humane Association.

"The Selling of the Flesh." Reprinted from *Future Magazine*, The Official Publication of The United States Jaycees.

"Dr. Batman." Reprinted from *Saturday Review-World* February 1974 by permission of the author.

"Sickle Cell Anemia." Reprinted from *Future Magazine*, The Official Publication of The United States Jaycees.

"Police Brutality: Answers to Key Questions." Published by permission of Transaction, Inc., from *Transaction*, Vol. 5, No. 5. Copyright © 1968 by Transaction, Inc.

"Women of Lesbos" by Martha Shelley. From *Up Against the Wall, Mother* by Adams and Briscoe. Copyright by Martha Shelley.

"The Plight of the Porpoise." Reprinted with permission of the author and *The National Humane Review*, copyright 1973, The American Humane Association.

"Mononucleosis: The Overtreated Disease." From *McCall's Magazine*. Reprinted by permission of the author's agent, Lurton Blassingame. Copyright © 1974, The McCall Publishing Company.

"The Anatomy of Drink." Reprinted from *Future Magazine*, The Official Publication of The United States Jaycees.

"Atlantis: Legend Lives On." Reprinted from *Aramco World Magazine*, magazine of the Arabian American Oil Company.

"New Use for Old Cars." Reprinted with the permission of Anthony Wolff, the author.

"The Interlopers." From *The Complete Short Stories of Saki* (H.H. Munro) All rights reserved. Reprinted by permission of The Viking Press, Inc.

"Beyond Freedom and Dignity." *From Beyond Freedom and Dignity*, by B. F. Skinner. Copyright © 1971 by B.F. Skinner. Reprinted by permission of Alfred A. Knopf, Inc.

"Dying, One Day at a Time." Reprinted from *Future Magazine*, The Official Publication of The United States Jaycees.

"Textbooks and the Invisible Woman." Reprinted from the Council on Interracial Books for Children, Inc.'s Bulletin with the permission of the author.

"The Assault on Privacy." Reprinted from *The Assault On Privacy* by Arthur R. Miller. Reprinted with the permission of The University of Michigan Press. Copyright © 1971.

Minutes and Seconds Elapsed

Selection	Number of Words	15:00	14:40	14:20	14:00	13:40	13:20	13:00	12:40	12:20	12:00	11:40	11:20	11:00	10:40	10:20	10:00	9:40	9:20	9:00	8:40	8:20	8:00	7:40	7:20	7:00	6:40	6:20	6:00	5:40	5:20	5:00	4:40	4:20	4:00	3:40	3:20	3:00	2:40	2:20	2:00	1:40	1:20
1	1680	110	115	115	120	125	125	130	135	135	140	145	150	155	160	165	170	175	180	185	195	200	210	220	230	240	250	265	280	295	315	335	360	390	420	460	505	560	630	720	840	1010	1265
2	1610	105	110	110	115	120	120	125	125	130	135	140	140	145	150	155	160	165	175	180	185	195	200	210	220	230	240	255	270	285	300	320	345	370	405	440	485	535	605	690	805	970	1210
3	1715	115	115	120	125	125	130	130	135	140	145	145	150	155	160	165	170	175	185	190	200	205	215	225	235	245	255	270	285	305	320	345	370	395	430	470	515	570	645	735	860	1035	1290
4	1250	85	85	85	90	90	95	95	100	100	105	105	110	115	115	120	125	130	135	140	145	150	155	165	170	180	190	195	210	220	235	250	270	290	315	340	375	415	470	535	625	755	940
5	1210	80	85	85	85	90	90	95	95	100	100	105	105	110	115	115	120	125	130	135	140	145	150	160	165	175	180	190	200	215	225	240	260	280	305	330	365	405	455	520	605	730	910
6	1775	120	120	125	125	130	135	135	140	145	150	150	155	160	165	170	180	185	190	195	205	215	220	230	240	255	265	280	295	315	335	355	380	410	445	485	535	590	665	760	890	1070	1335
7	1435	95	100	100	105	105	110	110	115	115	120	125	125	130	135	140	145	150	155	160	165	170	180	185	195	205	215	225	240	255	270	285	310	330	360	390	430	480	540	615	720	865	1080
8	1520	100	105	105	110	110	115	115	120	125	125	130	135	140	145	145	150	155	165	170	175	180	190	200	205	215	230	240	255	270	285	305	325	350	380	415	455	505	570	650	760	915	1145
9	1460	95	100	100	105	105	110	110	115	120	120	125	130	135	135	140	145	150	155	160	170	175	185	190	200	210	220	230	245	260	275	290	315	335	365	400	440	485	550	625	730	880	1100
10	1375	90	95	95	100	100	105	105	110	110	115	120	120	125	130	135	140	140	145	155	160	165	170	180	190	195	205	215	230	245	260	275	295	315	345	375	415	460	515	590	690	830	1035
11	1360	90	95	95	95	100	100	105	105	110	115	115	120	125	130	130	135	140	145	150	155	165	170	175	185	195	205	215	225	240	255	270	290	315	340	370	410	455	510	585	680	820	1025
12	1230	80	85	85	90	90	90	95	95	100	105	105	110	110	115	120	125	125	130	135	140	150	155	160	170	175	185	195	205	215	230	245	265	285	310	335	370	410	460	525	615	740	925
13	2200	145	150	155	155	160	165	170	175	180	185	190	195	200	205	215	220	230	235	245	255	265	275	285	300	315	330	345	365	390	415	440	470	510	550	600	660	735	825	945	1100	1325	1655
14	1775	120	120	125	125	130	135	135	140	145	150	150	155	160	165	170	180	185	190	195	205	215	220	230	240	255	265	280	295	315	335	355	380	410	445	485	535	590	665	760	890	1070	1335
15	1560	105	105	110	110	115	115	120	125	125	130	135	135	140	145	150	155	160	165	175	180	185	195	205	215	225	235	245	260	275	295	310	335	360	390	425	470	520	585	670	780	940	1175
16	1310	85	90	90	95	95	100	100	105	105	110	110	115	120	125	125	130	135	140	145	150	155	165	170	180	185	195	205	220	230	245	260	280	300	330	355	395	435	490	560	655	790	985
17	1650	110	115	115	120	120	125	125	130	135	140	140	145	150	155	160	165	170	175	185	190	200	205	215	225	235	250	260	275	290	310	330	355	380	415	450	495	550	620	705	825	995	1240
18	1590	105	110	110	115	115	120	120	125	130	135	135	140	145	150	155	160	165	170	175	185	190	200	205	215	225	240	250	265	280	300	320	340	365	400	435	475	530	595	680	795	960	1195
19	1800	120	125	125	130	130	135	140	140	145	150	155	160	165	170	175	180	185	195	200	210	215	225	235	245	255	270	285	300	320	340	360	385	415	450	490	540	600	675	770	900	1085	1355
20	1290	85	90	90	90	95	95	100	100	105	110	110	115	115	120	125	130	135	140	145	150	155	160	170	175	185	195	205	215	230	240	260	275	295	325	350	385	430	485	555	645	775	970
21	2160	145	145	150	155	160	160	165	170	175	180	185	190	195	205	210	215	225	230	240	250	260	270	280	295	310	325	340	360	380	405	430	465	500	540	590	650	720	810	925	1080	1300	1625
22	1805	120	125	125	130	130	135	140	145	145	150	155	160	165	170	175	180	185	195	200	210	215	225	235	245	260	270	285	300	320	340	360	385	415	450	490	540	600	675	775	905	1085	1355
23	1510	100	105	105	110	110	115	115	120	120	125	130	135	135	140	145	150	155	160	170	175	180	190	195	205	215	225	240	250	265	285	300	325	350	380	410	455	505	565	645	755	910	1135
24	1410	95	95	100	100	105	105	110	110	115	120	120	125	130	130	135	140	145	150	155	165	170	175	185	190	200	210	225	235	250	265	280	300	325	355	385	425	470	530	605	705	850	1060
25	1440	95	100	100	105	105	110	110	115	115	120	125	125	130	135	140	145	150	155	160	165	175	180	190	195	205	215	225	240	255	270	290	310	330	360	395	430	480	540	615	720	865	1085
26	1620	110	110	115	115	120	120	125	130	130	135	140	145	145	150	155	160	170	175	180	185	195	205	210	220	230	245	255	270	285	305	325	345	375	405	440	485	540	610	695	810	975	1220
27	1420	95	95	100	100	105	105	110	110	115	120	120	125	130	135	135	140	145	150	160	165	170	180	185	195	205	215	225	235	250	265	285	305	330	355	385	425	475	535	610	710	855	1070
28	1845	125	125	130	130	135	140	140	145	150	155	160	165	170	175	180	185	190	200	205	215	220	230	240	250	265	275	290	310	325	345	370	395	425	460	505	555	615	690	790	925	1110	1385
29	1650	110	115	115	120	120	125	125	130	135	140	140	145	150	155	160	165	170	175	185	190	200	205	215	225	235	250	260	275	290	310	330	355	380	415	450	495	550	620	705	825	995	1240
30	1890	125	130	130	135	140	140	145	150	155	160	160	165	170	175	185	190	195	205	210	220	225	235	245	260	270	285	300	315	335	355	380	405	435	475	515	565	630	710	810	945	1140	1420

PROGRESS GRAPH

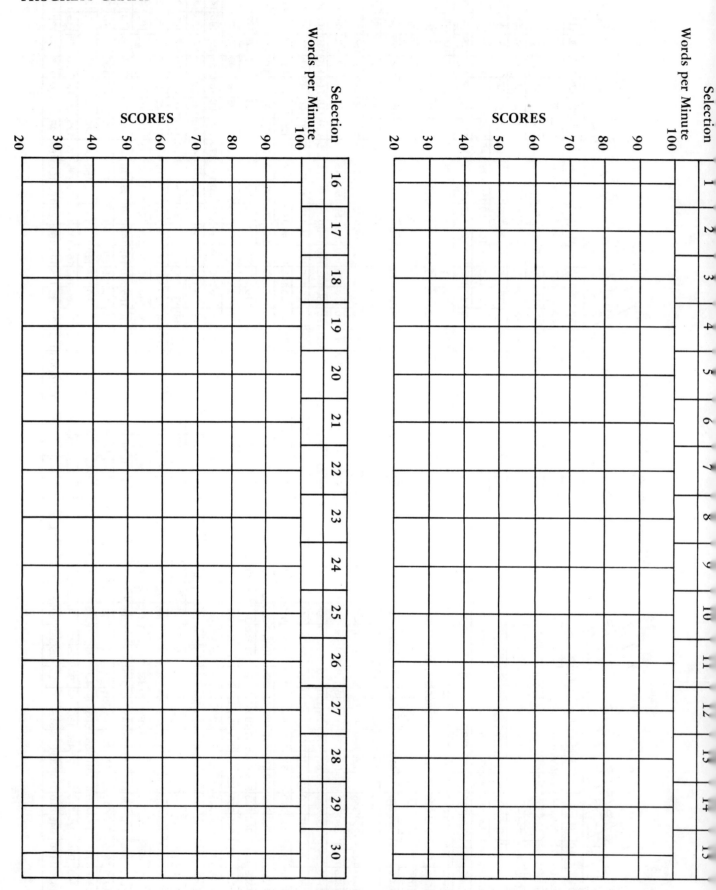

COMPREHENSION SKILLS PROFILE

The graph below is designed to help you see your areas of comprehension weakness. Because all the comprehension questions in this text are coded, it is possible for you to determine which kinds of questions give you the most trouble.

On the graph below, keep a record of questions you have failed. Following each selection, fill in one square on the graph for each question missed.

The columns are labeled to correspond with the letter codes accompanying each question.

When you discover a particular weakness, give greater time and attention to answering questions of that type. Also, confer with your instructor. You may be assigned to work in the Comprehension Skills Booklet from Jamestown Publishers which corresponds to your weakness, or your instructor may recommend some other appropriate remedial material.

COMPREHENSION SKILLS

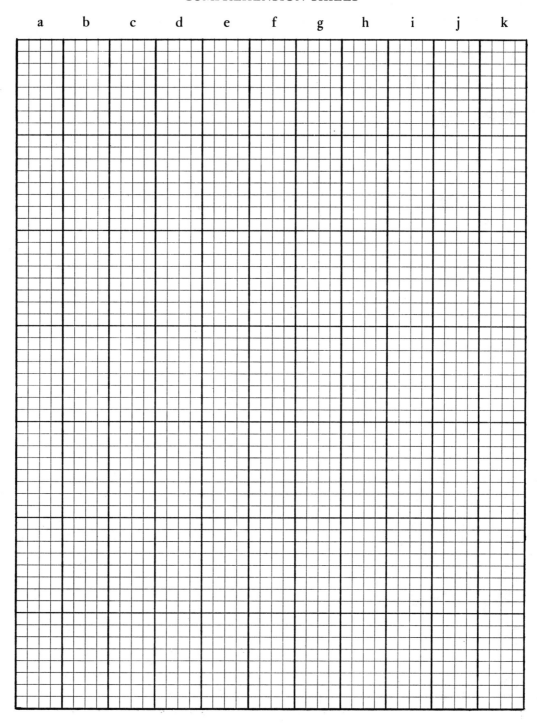